Visual and Performing *Arts* Framework for California Public Schools

Kindergarten Through Grade Twelve

Developed by the
Curriculum Development and Supplemental
Materials Commission

Adopted by the
California State Board of Education

Published by the
California Department of Education

D1534385

Publishing Information

When the *Visual and Performing Arts Framework for California Public Schools, Kindergarten Through Grade Twelve* was adopted by the California State Board of Education on January 7, 2004, the members of the State Board were as follows: Reed Hastings, President; Joe Nuñez, Vice President; Robert Abernethy; Donald G. Fisher; Nancy Ichinaga; and Suzanne Tacheny.

The framework was developed by the Curriculum Development and Supplemental Materials Commission. (See pages vii–ix for the names of the members of the commission and the names of the principal writer and others who made significant contributions to the framework.)

This publication was edited by Edward O'Malley, working in cooperation with Director Thomas Adams, Administrator Don Kairott, and consultants Christopher Dowell, Martha Rowland, and Mary Sprague, Curriculum Frameworks and Instructional Resources Division; and consultants Nancy Carr and Don Doyle, Professional Development and Curriculum Support Division, California Department of Education. The framework was designed and prepared for printing by the staff of CDE Press, with the cover designed by Paul Lee and the interior design created and prepared by Paul Lee and Cheryl McDonald. Typesetting was done by Jeannette Reyes. The framework was published by the Department of Education, 1430 N Street, Sacramento, CA 95814-5901. It was distributed under the provisions of the Library Distribution Act and *Government Code* Section 11096.

ISBN 0-8011-1592-2

Ordering Information

Copies of this publication are available for $19.95 each, plus shipping and handling charges. California residents are charged sales tax. Orders may be sent to the California Department of Education, CDE Press, Sales Office, 1430 N Street, Suite 3207, Sacramento, CA 95814; FAX (916) 323-0823. Prices on all publications are subject to change.

An illustrated *Educational Resources Catalog* describing publications, videos, and other instructional media available from the Department can be obtained without charge by writing to the address given above or by calling the Sales Office at (916) 445-1260 or (800) 995-4099.

Photo Credits

We gratefully acknowledge the use in this publication of the photographs provided by the following persons and organizations: Moreau Catholic High School, pp. xii, 1, 78, 96, 98, 116, 119, 140, 166; Lee Hanson, pp. 2, 33, 107, 122, 123, 145, 190; Carlsbad Unified School District, pp. 6, 7, 151; Glendale Senior High School, p. 13; Helen K. Garber © 1995 (photographs of students from the 1995 California State Summer School for the Arts), pp. 19, 57, 96, 97, 101, 112, 164, 186, 187; Kathi Kent Volzke, courtesy of Orange County Performing Arts Center, pp. 20, 21, 149; Pleasant Valley School District, p. 23; Los Angeles Unified School District, pp. 24, 38, 45, 70, 72, 89, 129, 168, 169; Trish Oakes, pp. 29, 64, 154; Live Oak School District, pp. 40, 54; California State University, Chico, Department of Education, pp. 49, 160, 189; Orange Unified School District, pp. 61, 86, 173, 175; Lake Elsinore Unified School District, p. 124; Stockton Unified School District, pp. 80, 97, 178, 179; Cheryl McDonald, p. 104; Westmont High School, p. 110; AXIS Dance Company, photo by Andy Mogg, p. 135; Emery Unified School District, p. 157; Sacramento City Unified School District, pp. 180; and Craig Schwartz, Music Center Education Division, The Los Angeles Music Center, p. 185.

Cover Art

This 1994 work, titled *Blueprint for a Better Tomorrow,* is a mural conceived, designed, and painted by students in Professor Malaquias Montoya's Mexican and Chicano Mural Workshop. Professor Montoya teaches Chicana/Chicano Studies at the University of California, Davis. The mural, which measures 14 feet by 87 feet, is located at Will C. Wood High School in Vacaville, California. The mural was photographed by Jim Prigoff. The inset on the back cover was photographed by Lezlie Salkowitz-Montoya. Used by permission.

Contents

Page

Foreword v

Acknowledgments vii

Introduction x

Chapter 1. Guiding Principles of the Framework 2

**Chapter 2. Planning, Implementing, and Evaluating Arts Education
Programs** 8

Planning Arts Education Programs 8

Administering Arts Education Programs 9

Conducting Arts Education Programs 12

Partnering with the School Library Staff 14

Promoting Partnerships and Collaborations 14

Evaluating Arts Education Programs 16

Providing Access for All Students 17

Applying New Media and Electronic Technology 18

Chapter 3. Visual and Performing Arts Content Standards 22

Format of the Content Standards 22

Key Content Standards 23

Kindergarten 24

Grade One 32

Grade Two 40

Grade Three 48

Grade Four 56

Grade Five 64

Grade Six 72

Grade Seven 80

Grade Eight 88

Grades Nine Through Twelve 96

Chapter 4. Guidance for Visual and Performing Arts Programs 124

Dance 125

Music 136

Theatre 146

Visual Arts 156

Page

Chapter 5. Assessment in the Arts 170

Purpose of Student Assessment 170

Types of Assessment 171

Considerations in Arts Assessment 172

Chapter 6. Professional Development in the Arts 180

Teacher Preparation in the Arts 180

Organization of Professional Development in the Arts 181

Resources for Professional Development in Arts Education 181

Content of Professional Development in the Arts 182

Chapter 7. Criteria for Evaluating Instructional Materials:
Kindergarten Through Grade Eight 188

Appendixes

A. *Education Code* Sections Governing Arts Education Programs 198

B. Recommendations for Clarification of the New Visual and
Performing Arts Requirement for Freshman Admission to the
University of California and the California State University 204

C. Careers in the Visual and Performing Arts 211

D. Continuum for Implementing Arts Education Programs 218

E. Copyright Law and the Visual and Performing Arts 230

F. Guidelines for the Safe Use of Art and Craft Materials 238

G. Funding for Arts Education Programs 242

Glossary of Selected Terms 243

Selected References and Resources 264

Foreword

Pablo Picasso once observed, "Every child is an artist. The problem is how to remain an artist once he grows up." One of our jobs as educators is to nurture our students' creativity and knowledge. To achieve this goal, the California Department of Education and the California State Board of Education are pleased to present the *Visual and Performing Arts Framework for California Public Schools, Kindergarten Through Grade Twelve (2004)*, which will help educators provide students with a solid foundation in the arts.

This framework is based upon the visual and performing arts content standards adopted in January 2001. The framework incorporates the content standards for dance, music, theater, and visual arts and defines the five strands of an arts program: artistic perception; creative expression; historical and cultural context; aesthetic valuing; and connections, relationships, and applications.

This framework is especially noteworthy for its inclusion of the multifaceted role of media and electronic technology in the arts. California is an international leader in the technology and entertainment industries; providing our students with an education in the arts supports our state's future and our economy.

It should also be recognized that the importance of the arts extends into other areas of schooling. A 1999 study from the Arts Education Partnership indicated that students with higher levels of arts involvement were more likely to be high achievers on tests, were less likely to drop out by grade ten, and were more engaged with learning during the school day.

We ask that all education stakeholders—including families, artists, community groups, and representatives of museums, galleries, colleges, and universities—collaborate with schools to ensure that students have a variety of experiences for imagining, exploring, and creating the visual and performing arts. California leads the nation and the world in the arts, and this framework will ensure that we continue our prominence in arts education.

JACK O'CONNELL
State Superintendent of Public Instruction

RUTH GREEN
President, State Board of Education

Acknowledgments

The *Visual and Performing Arts Framework for California Public Schools, Kindergarten Through Grade Twelve* was adopted by the California State Board of Education in January 2004. Members of the State Board of Education who were serving at the time the framework was approved were:

Reed Hastings, President
Joe Nuñez, Vice President
Robert J. Abernethy
Donald Fisher
Nancy Ichinaga
Suzanne Tacheny

The original draft of the framework was prepared by the Visual and Performing Arts Curriculum Framework and Criteria Committee (CFCC) between February and August 2002. This diverse group included teachers, school administrators, university faculty members, and arts specialists working in public schools. The State Board of Education and the Curriculum Development and Supplemental Materials Commission (Curriculum Commission) commend the following members of the CFCC and extend great appreciation to them:

Roy Anthony, Chair, Grossmont Union High School District
Donna Banning, Orange Unified School District
Linda Bechtel, San Juan Unified School District
Prem Bovie-Ware, Corona-Norco Unified School District
Richard Burrows, Los Angeles Unified School District
Wayne Cook, California Arts Council
Ann Edwards, Chino Valley Unified School District
Carolyn Elder, Elk Grove Unified School District
Denise Faucher-Garcia, Sonora Elementary School District
Patricia Fernández, Fenton Avenue Elementary Charter School
Wendy Huang, ABC Unified School District
Chi Kim, Reed Union Elementary School District
Patty Larrick, Palo Alto Unified School District
Andrea Lee, Berkeley Unified School District

Note: The titles and affiliations of persons named in this section were current at the time the document was developed.

Vicki Lind, University of California, Los Angeles

Margaret Marshall, University of California, Office of the President, Academic Affairs

Suzanne Regan, California State University, Los Angeles

Ann Marie Stanley, St. Helena Unified School District

Ella Steinberg, San Diego Unified School District

Michael Stone, Bakersfield City Elementary School District

Jim Thomas, Orange County Office of Education

Charline Wills, Lake Elsinore Unified School District

Commendation and appreciation are extended also to **Patty Taylor,** Visual and Performing Arts Consultant, California Department of Education, who was the principal writer of the *Visual and Performing Arts Framework.*

Curriculum Commission Chair **Karen Yamamoto** and the members of the Curriculum Commission's Visual and Performing Arts Subject Matter Committee, a subcommittee of the Curriculum Commission, provided outstanding leadership in overseeing the development and editing of the *Visual and Performing Arts Framework:*

Lora Griffin, Chair, (retired), Sacramento City Unified School District

William Brakemeyer, Vice Chair, (retired), Fontana Unified School District

Mary Coronado Calvario, Sacramento City Unified School District

Kerry Hammil, Oakland Unified School District

Julie Maravilla, Los Angeles Unified School District

Other members of the Curriculum Commission who were serving at the time it was recommended for approval to the State Board were:

Edith Crawford, Vice Chair, San Juan Unified School District

Norma Baker, Los Angeles Unified School District

Catherine Banker, Upland, California

Milissa Glen-Lambert, Los Angeles Unified School District

Deborah Keys, Oakland Unified School District

Sandra Mann, San Diego City Unified School District

Michael Matsuda, Anaheim High School District

Stan Metzenberg, California State University, Northridge

Veronica Norris, Tustin, California

Rosa Perez, Canada College, Redwood City

California Department of Education staff who contributed to the development of the *Visual and Performing Arts Framework* included:

Sue Stickel, Deputy Superintendent, Curriculum and Instruction Branch

Thomas Adams, Director, Curriculum Frameworks and Instructional Resources Division

Donald Kairott, Administrator, Curriculum Frameworks Unit

Nancy Carr, Visual and Performing Arts Consultant, Curriculum Leadership Unit

Christopher Dowell, Education Programs Consultant, Curriculum Frameworks Unit

Don Doyle, Visual and Performing Arts Consultant, Curriculum Leadership Unit

Martha Rowland, Education Programs Consultant, Curriculum Frameworks Unit

Stacy Sinclair, (former) Education Programs Consultant, Curriculum Frameworks Unit

Mary Sprague, Education Programs Consultant, Curriculum Frameworks Unit

Tonya Odums, Office Technician, Curriculum Frameworks Unit

Teri Ollis, Analyst, Curriculum Frameworks Unit

Patrice Roseboom, Analyst, Instructional Resources Unit

Tracie Yee, Analyst, Curriculum Frameworks Unit

Introduction

A discussion of the arts focuses on how people communicate their perceptions, responses, and understanding of the world to themselves and to others. Since their first appearance thousands of years ago, the arts have been evolving continually, exhibiting the ability of human beings to intuit, symbolize, think, and express themselves through dance, music, theatre, and the visual arts. Each of the arts contains a distinct body of knowledge and skills that characterize the power of each to expand the perceptual, intellectual, cultural, and spiritual dimensions of human experience.

This capacity of human beings to create and appreciate the arts is just one of many reasons to teach the arts in the schools. Study and practice in the arts refine students' abilities to perceive aesthetically, make connections between works of art and the everyday lives of people, and discuss visual, kinesthetic, and auditory relationships. Students are taught to locate works of art in time and place, make reasoned judgments about them, and investigate how works of art create meaning.

Acknowledging that the arts enhance and balance curriculum, this framework for the twenty-first century implements the visual and performing arts content standards adopted by the California State Board of Education in January 2001. The purpose of those standards, which express in the highest form what students need to learn and be able to accomplish in the arts, is described in the *Visual and Performing Arts Content Standards.*[1]

The standards were developed in response to Senate Bill 1390 (Murray), signed by Governor Gray Davis in September 2000. That bill calls for the adoption of visual and performing arts content standards by the California State Board of Education and states that instruction in the visual and performing arts should be made available to all students. However, as with standards in other curriculum areas, the bill does not require schools to follow the content standards and does not mandate an assessment of pupils in the visual and performing arts. As stated in the bill, "The content standards are intended to provide a framework for programs that a school may offer in the instruction of visual and performing arts."[2]

The *Visual and Performing Arts Framework* is designed to help classroom teachers and other educators develop curriculum and instruction in the arts so

---

[1] *Visual and Performing Arts Content Standards for California Public Schools, Prekindergarten Through Grade Twelve.* Sacramento: California Department of Education, 2001.

[2] Ibid., p.ix.

that all students will meet or exceed the content standards in dance, music, theatre, and the visual arts. Specifically, the framework:

- Presents guiding principles for instruction in dance, music, theatre, and the visual arts (Chapter 1)

- Guides the planning, implementation, and evaluation of comprehensive, standards-based visual and performing arts education programs (Chapter 2)

- Presents the key content standards for kindergarten through grade eight that provide a beginning point for standards-based instruction; the complete content standards in dance, music, theatre, and the visual arts for kindergarten through grade eight; and the content standards for the beginning or proficient level and advanced level for grades nine through twelve (Chapter 3)

- Guides curriculum development for comprehensive, standards-based visual and performing arts education programs (Chapter 4)

- Provides information on the purpose and forms of assessment in the arts (Chapter 5)

- Presents details on teacher preparation and professional development for each arts discipline (Chapter 6)

- Provides criteria for the evaluation of instructional materials in the arts for kindergarten through grade eight (Chapter 7)

- Includes a glossary of terms that appears after the appendixes

- Provides an extensive list of selected references and resources that appears at the back of this publication

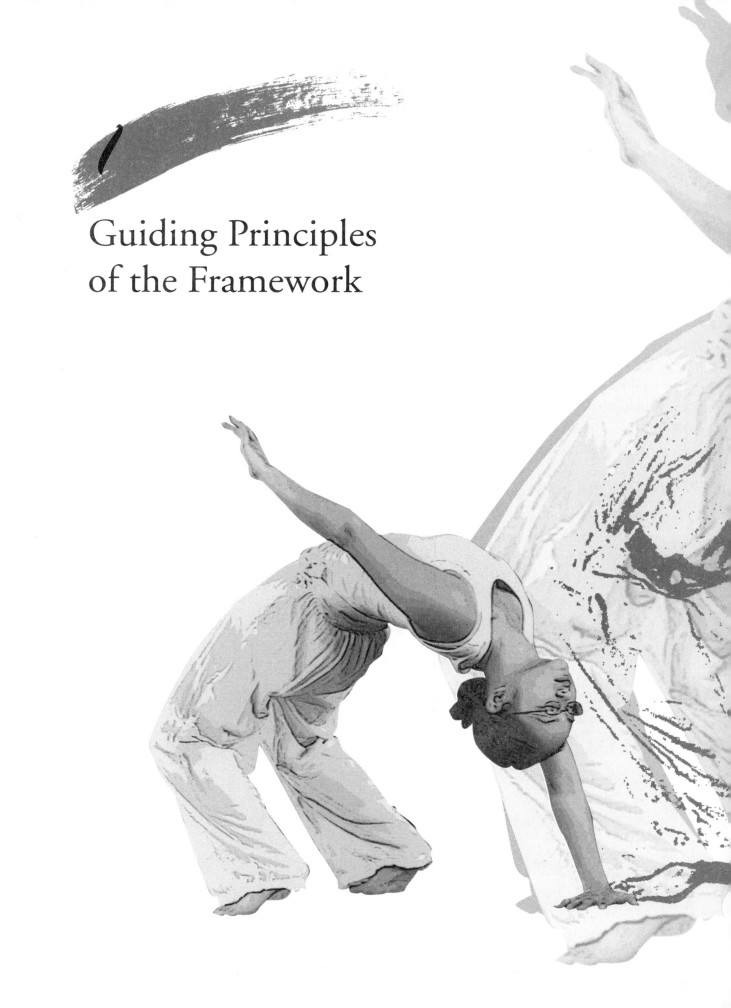

Guiding Principles
of the Framework

Guiding Principles of the Framework

This framework incorporates ten principles to accelerate and sustain proficiency in the visual and performing arts for all learners. These principles are used to guide the framework and address the complexity of the content and delivery of instruction in dance, music, theatre, and the visual arts. They also direct the purpose, design, delivery, and evaluation of instruction. The principles established are as follows:

1. **Support of *Education Code* sections 51210 and 51220 requiring instruction in the arts.**

   Section 51210 specifies that the required adopted course of study used by schools for grades one through six must include the visual and performing arts. Section 51220 specifies the same requirement for grades seven through twelve. As with all other subject areas except physical education, the *Education Code* does not state the number of minutes of instruction required, although it does require schools to provide instruction in the arts for all students. (See Appendix A.)

2. **Use of the visual and performing arts content standards adopted by the State Board of Education as the basis of curriculum.**

   Those standards serve as curriculum guideposts for teachers and provide clear-cut curriculum goals for all learners. (*Note:* The Western Association of Schools and Colleges also looks for standards-based courses during its accreditation process.) Curriculum based on the content standards requires active learning through the study, practice, creation, or performance of works of art. It also requires reading about the arts and artists; researching the arts from the past and present; writing about the arts and artists to reflect on one's own observations, experiences, and ideas about the arts; and participating in arts criticism based on reliable information and clear criteria.

3. **Definition of a balanced, comprehensive arts program as one in which the arts are studied as discrete disciplines related to each other and, when appropriate, to other subject areas in the curriculum.**

   Students in a comprehensive program are expected to master the standards of an arts discipline, which are grouped under the following strands:

   a. *Artistic perception* refers to processing, analyzing, and responding to sensory information through the use of the language and skills unique to dance, music, theatre, and the visual arts.

   b. *Creative expression* involves creating a work, performing, and participating in the arts disciplines. Students apply processes and skills in composing, arranging, and performing a work and use a variety of means to communicate meaning and intent in their own original formal and informal works.

   c. *Historical and cultural context* concerns the work students do toward understanding the historical contributions and cultural dimensions of an arts discipline. Students analyze roles, functions, development in the discipline, and human diversity as it relates to that discipline. They also examine closely musicians, composers, artists, writers, actors, dancers, and choreographers as well as cultures and historical periods.

   d. *Aesthetic valuing* includes analyzing and critiquing works of dance, music, theatre, and the visual arts. Students apply processes and skills to productions or performances. They also critically assess and derive meaning from the work of a discipline, including their own, and from performances and original works based on the elements and principles of an arts discipline, aesthetic qualities, and human responses.

   e. *Connections, relationships, and applications* involve connecting and applying what is learned in one arts discipline and comparing it to learning in the other arts, other subject areas, and careers. Students develop competencies and creative skills in problem solving, communication, and time management that contribute to lifelong learning, including career skills. They also learn about careers in and related to arts disciplines.

4. **Promotion of alignment of standards-based curriculum, assessment, and instruction throughout the grades at the school and school district levels to provide a comprehensive, coherent structure for visual and performing arts teaching and learning.**

   That alignment will prepare students to meet the new visual and performing arts requirement for freshman admission to the University of California and the California State University (see Appendix B). It will also require that teachers be prepared through preservice and in-service professional development programs to teach a standards-based curriculum in the arts.

5. **View of assessment of student work as essential to a standards-based program in the arts.**

The assessment of student work in the arts helps students learn more about what they know and can do, provides teachers with information for improving curriculum and instruction, and gives school districts the data required for ensuring accountability. Performance assessments, such as those involving portfolios, projects, exhibitions, and reflections, are inherent in the arts and in the artistic process.

6. **Expansion of an emphasis on using new media and electronic technology in the arts.**

In the past 200 years, technological processes have provided many new ways of making, recording, and delivering the arts, allowing a variety of systems to document, create, and teach dance, music, theatre, and the visual arts. This framework uses the term *new media and electronic technology* to reach back over the past 200 years to photography and film and includes the most recent developments in computer technology and electronic, audio, and digital media.

7. **Inclusion of all learners in the classroom.**

At each school level arts instruction should provide avenues in which each student can work at a personalized pace to learn and develop self-expression and self-confidence. Curriculum and instruction may need to be modified or adapted to encourage the successful participation of students with a variety of disabilities and those who excel or have a special interest in the arts.

8. **A broad view of culture.**

Students experience the five component strands in the arts content standards from the perspective of American culture and of worldwide ethnic, racial, religious, and cultural groups. Respect for the multiplicity of cultures pervades the framework and the content standards.

9. **Recognition of the role the arts play in preparing students for careers and full participation in society.**

Arts education provides direct training for jobs in the flourishing arts industry in California. (See examples of careers in the visual and performing arts in Appendix C.) According to information on workforce development related to arts education, "Creative industries are key to the economy of California and a source of future employment for up to one in five California students."[1] Further, education in the arts prepares students for work in any field. The National Governors Association (NGA) states that "programs incorporating the arts have proven to be educational, developmentally rich, and cost-effective ways to provide students with the skills they need to be productive participants in today's economy." It also expresses the conviction that the arts are one tool that states can use to enhance workforce readiness for students in both general and at-risk populations.[2]

10. Usefulness to teachers, arts professionals, library media teachers, administrators, parents, and supporters of the arts.

The *Visual and Performing Arts Framework* is a tool for teachers and a guide for publishers and those who develop educational materials. It is also useful to those planning arts programs as well as to staff developers, artists who teach in the schools, principals, district and county leaders of curriculum and instruction, those who provide the arts in the community, college and university arts teachers and educators, parents, community members, and business and industry leaders.

Those involved in teaching the visual and performing arts may include classroom teachers, library media teachers, arts specialist teachers, artists, and community members. All who teach the arts are helping to shape students' abilities to think, observe, create, use imagination, organize thoughts and feelings, assess critically, and respond in predictable and unpredictable ways. They communicate to their students that the arts are about enjoying the rich benefits of life, engaging in multiple opportunities for self-expression, and delighting in the creative efforts of others. As students achieve in the arts, they participate in society by looking at things carefully, hearing things thoughtfully, and feeling things sensitively. When students have access to the arts throughout their school years, they have opportunities to grow as creative, intellectual, and spiritual human beings.

[1] *An Arts Education Research Compendium.* Sacramento: California Arts Council, 2001, p. 6.
[2] "The Impact of Arts Education on Workforce Preparation." Issue brief, National Governors Association for Best Practices, May 1, 2002.

2

Planning, Implementing, and Evaluating Arts Education Programs

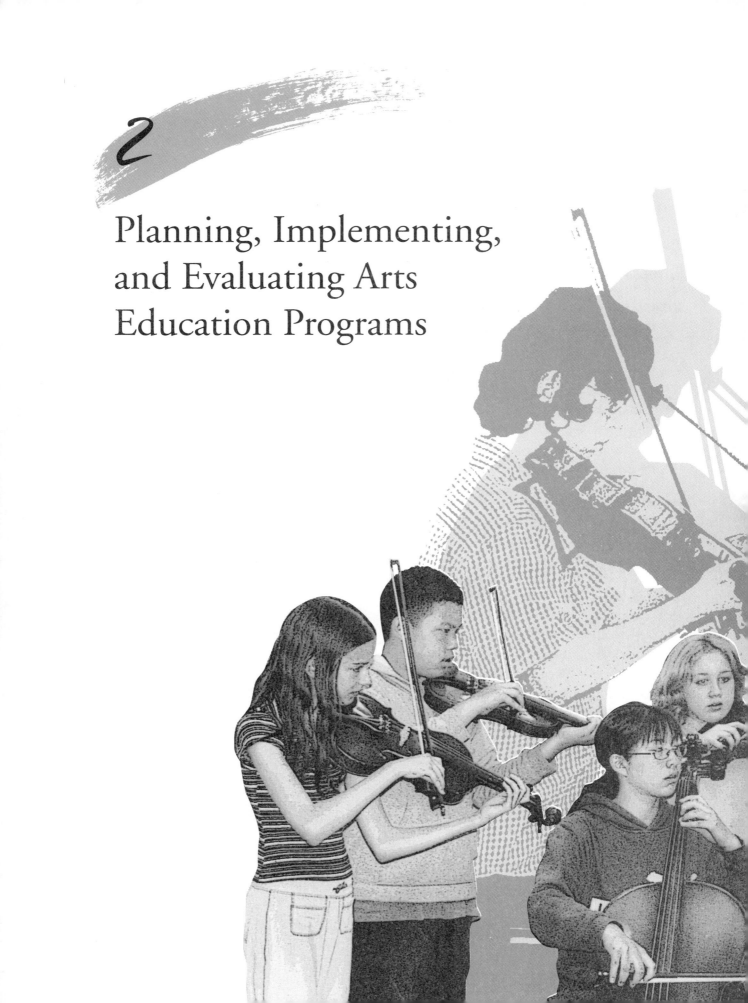

Chapter 2
Planning,
Implementing,
and Evaluating
Arts Education
Programs

Planning, Implementing, and Evaluating Arts Education Programs

The careful planning and implementation of comprehensive, standards-based visual and performing arts education programs are essential to success. (See Chapter 1 for a discussion of the guiding principles for such programs.) Topics discussed in this chapter are as follows:

- Planning and administering comprehensive, standards-based arts education programs
- Conducting arts education programs at three levels of schooling
- Partnering with the school library staff
- Promoting partnerships and collaborations
- Evaluating arts education programs
- Providing access for all students
- Applying new media and electronic technology

Teachers, artists who teach in the schools, and those who plan or develop local arts education programs will benefit from the content of this chapter because it includes all of the arts within the context of comprehensive visual and performing arts education programs. In addition, administrators, superintendents, principals, curriculum developers, and school board members will find the descriptions in this chapter helpful as they plan arts education programs for all students.

Planning Arts Education Programs

Much of the success of educational programs hinges on how well counties, school districts, and schools collaborate, how much the parents are involved, and to what extent colleges, universities, and communities participate in designing and implementing the programs. All students benefit when the school district governing board, district administrators, school staff members, parents, and the community together acknowledge the arts as basic in education, value the arts, and consider each arts discipline in planning for facilities, resources, professional development, and assessment.

Chapter 2
Planning,
Implementing,
and Evaluating
Arts Education
Programs

Establishing arts education programs in a school or school district requires examining existing site or district programs. In doing so, school or district administrators may want to consider using an assessment tool, such as the *Arts Education Program Toolkit*.[1] Developed by the Model Arts Program Network School Districts in collaboration with the California Department of Education, the toolkit provides a way for schools and school districts to determine what they have and what they need in their arts education programs. This self-study helps develop short- and long-term plans for the gradual implementation of a standards-based curriculum articulated through the grade levels.

The toolkit is but one example of many available self-evaluation and planning processes, each following similar steps. By using it, a district or school site can determine the implementation level of an arts program—foundation, building, or best practices—and identify the next steps to be taken. The use of the toolkit's continuum generates conversation, stimulates research, builds consensus, enhances decision making, and supports planning. As each of the ten focus areas and criteria is discussed, issues arise about the elements valued in an arts education program for all students. In examining a school or district program, school or district administrators should consider the following areas (identified in the toolkit):

- Standards-based curriculum
- Instruction and methodology
- Student assessment
- Professional development for those implementing the arts education program
- Qualified teachers, personnel, and program administration
- Partnerships and collaborations
- Budgetary needs
- Facilities, logistics, and necessary resources
- Program evaluation
- Time and timing

Administering Arts Education Programs

District-level administrators and staff, from superintendents to visual and performing arts coordinators and lead teachers, are key participants in implementing district policies for arts education programs. The first steps to be taken are to complete a self-study of the current arts education programs; gain the endorsement of a long-range plan by district, school, and community

---

[1] *Arts Education Program Toolkit: A Visual and Performing Arts Assessment Process.* Sacramento: California Department of Education, 2001.

Chapter 2
Planning,
Implementing,
and Evaluating
Arts Education
Programs

stakeholders; and have the plan adopted by the school district governing board. The long-range plan should include the following elements:

- Allocating personnel and instructional resources, including appropriate materials, equipment, and facilities
- Ensuring that the district has a standards-based arts curriculum for kindergarten through grade eight and high school
- Developing collaboration to support the program with school district, community, state, and national resources
- Securing funding and grants for the arts education program within and outside the district

When educators analyze standards-based instruction, many discover that their classroom instruction already follows a standards-based approach. Students are engaged in meaningful work and the creative process, know what is expected of them, can describe what they are doing and why, demonstrate habits of rehearsal and revision, can discuss work in progress in terms of quality, describe what assistance they need, and see their teachers as advocates and coaches.

Implementing comprehensive arts education programs involves different levels of administration: school district, school site, and classroom levels.

School District Level

In implementing a standards-based visual and performing arts curriculum, district administrators should consider:

- Short- and long-range plans (How well are arts programs being developed in the short term and over time at the school site and school district levels?)
- Teacher capacity (In what areas do teachers need professional development to teach a standards-based visual and performing arts curriculum?)
- Benchmarks for success in the arts for all students (How do we know students are gaining proficiency in the visual and performing arts standards?)
- Distribution of arts instruction across all grades (How do we implement standards-based arts instruction across the grade levels for all students?)
- Allocation of resources (What teachers, materials, equipment, books, electronic media, facilities, and community partnerships do we need?)

For further information see Appendix D, "Continuum for Implementing Arts Education Programs."

School Site Level

The roles of site administrators and school site councils are crucial to the planning and success of visual and performing arts programs at schools.

Chapter 2
Planning,
Implementing,
and Evaluating
Arts Education
Programs

Although site administrators are not required to be arts experts, they must be advocates for the arts. Accordingly, they must know the content standards and understand the connection between the visual and performing arts standards and the five strands that connect instruction and content (see Chapter 1). Site administrators must work with school staff members, parents, and the community to set a plan in motion that includes broad-based representation and participation and ensures that all students receive a standards-based curriculum in the visual and performing arts.

In addition to establishing a collaborative planning and implementation process, site administrators must ensure that the arts are included in the basic education of all students by:

- Allowing enough time to teach the arts to all students and preparation time for those teaching the arts
- Providing appropriate facilities, necessary equipment, equipment repair, and materials
- Ensuring that subject-centered instruction and arts instruction relating art to other subjects are occurring in elementary school classrooms and that student have access to the arts through appropriate scheduling of teachers and students in subject-centered classes at the middle school and high school levels
- Allowing opportunities for teachers to meet across grade levels and subject areas for planning
- Advocating the importance of the arts for all students to parents and members of the community
- Providing opportunities for exhibitions and performances of works in progress and final products in schools and in the community as curricular and cocurricular educational experiences
- Providing opportunities for community artists and performers to collaborate with teachers in delivering a standards-based visual and performing arts curriculum to students in classrooms and in community museums, galleries, and performance venues
- Providing time for periodic evaluation of the arts education program at the school level

Classroom Level

In implementing a comprehensive, standards-based visual and performing arts curriculum, teachers will:

- Design and conduct instructional activities aligned with the standards.
- Evaluate student work and make fair and credible judgments of quality.
- Manage data and plan instruction accordingly.

Chapter 2
Planning,
Implementing,
and Evaluating
Arts Education
Programs

- Communicate specific expectations and provide explicit feedback to students.
- Use student feedback to improve arts instruction.
- Teach students to evaluate their own work.
- Be relentless in pursuit of improved performance.
- Understand the community's expectations for student performance.

Conducting Arts Education Programs

The elements and benefits of high-quality, comprehensive, standards-based visual and performing arts programs implemented at the elementary school, middle school, and high school levels are described as follows. Expectations for teachers and students are included.

Elementary School Level

Arts programs in the early grades provide essential first steps for students as they develop their ability to communicate their thoughts, feelings, and understanding concerning the world around them. Through the arts the students gain the knowledge and skills needed to express their ideas creatively in verbal and nonverbal ways. The programs should include performing and experiencing the arts as well as talking, reading, and writing about them. The delivery of programs to help students achieve the arts content standards may involve the collaboration of credentialed arts specialists, classroom teachers, professional artists, and other community resource persons to support standards-based arts experiences. For example, the classroom teacher, who knows the curriculum, can provide follow-up lessons after a visit by a guest artist or a community performance and can make connections, highlight relationships, and introduce applications as appropriate.

Teachers, knowledgeable about the artistic and aesthetic development of their students, should respect the students' self-expressions. They should include activities in the arts that relate to the interests of the students, such as artwork and performances initiated, designed, and completed by the students, and should balance student-initiated and teacher-directed activities. In addition, by having students read literature about the arts and artists that includes stories, biographies, and histories of dance, music, theatre, and the visual arts, the teacher helps the students understand the connections between the creative work they do and that done by others.

Middle School Level

Exploration, an important part of a middle school arts program, should include all the requisites of the standards-based elementary-level program with essential additions. Courses in the four arts disciplines (dance, music, theatre,

13

Chapter 2
Planning,
Implementing,
and Evaluating
Arts Education
Programs

and the visual arts) are designed to increase and refine students' knowledge and skills beyond those learned at the elementary school level. Students may experience one or all four arts disciplines to expand their knowledge and skill and to make personal connections with the world, the school, and themselves. When students are taught by specialists in each discipline, they should continue their development in the five strands of each of those disciplines. Strategies for implementation may include a rotation or exploratory schedule for all students along with yearlong courses for students interested in more in-depth study in one or more of the arts.

In middle school arts specialist teachers should direct students to achieve the content standards within each discipline. School district and school administrators and faculty should collaborate with visiting artists and community arts resources to provide a comprehensive arts program for all students that is standards-based and relevant. Middle school students should begin to develop a firm foundation in the arts disciplines to be prepared for more focused study in one or more of the arts in high school. Accordingly, articulation needs to occur between the middle school and high school arts teachers.

High School Level

High school arts programs should be based on an overall vision of secondary education. That is, they should engage every student in a rigorous, standards-based curriculum enabling the student to make the transition from high school to higher education and a career. During their high school years, students have the opportunity to continue with in-depth instruction in the arts by selecting standards-based courses in one or more of the four arts disciplines. After a one-year course, a student should reach the beginning or proficient level of achievement described in the arts content standards. And after two or more years in the same discipline, a student should reach the advanced level of achievement (see Chapter 3). Yearlong high school courses in dance, music, theatre, and the visual arts should all be approved to meet the new visual and performing arts requirement for freshman admission to the University of California and the California State University (see Appendix B).

Through careful planning and allocation of resources, problems in scheduling and cooperative curriculum planning of subject-centered and arts-connected instruction can be accommodated. Credentialed arts specialist teachers should provide the instruction, and professional artists and other arts providers can serve as important resources. Student clubs, parent groups, and community resources all enhance the curriculum by helping to create an environment that encourages all students to develop an appreciation of and support for the arts. A later section, titled "Promoting Partnerships and Collaborations," in this chapter provides ideas on working with the arts community to ensure unified support for a successful arts program.

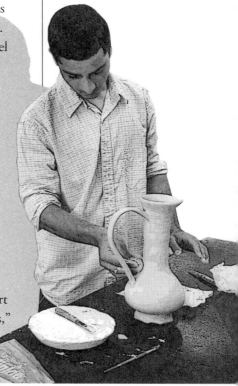

Chapter 2
Planning,
Implementing,
and Evaluating
Arts Education
Programs

Partnering with the School Library Staff

The school library serves as an integral partner in the delivery of the visual and performing arts curriculum. It should house a large shared collection of materials in various formats accessible to all students and staff and should provide assistance and support for the visual and performing arts instructional program.

The school library should provide a variety of resources for all students to help them talk, read, and write about the arts. Suggested examples would include biographies of people in the arts suitable to various reading levels, picture books that illustrate a variety of art genres, and circulating collections of art prints, audio CDs, rhythm instruments, videos that showcase artists in production, and fine art reproductions. Such materials provide students with hands-on experiences and background for artistic development and expression. In addition, plays, monologues, sheet music, art production software, specialized magazines, and online resources help middle and high school students to refine their knowledge and skills in the arts.

Because the school library is used by all students and staff and is often open to parents and the community, it provides an effective location for a variety of activities related to the arts. It can be a prime location for rotating displays of student artwork, often including ceramics, photography, and digital art projects. Further, puppet plays, skits, and storytelling that are a regular part of the school library program can be presented as a natural link to the dramatic arts. As with guest authors, illustrators of children's books can meet with groups of students in the library. In a middle school or high school, the school library can also be a venue for performances by a chamber music group, jazz band, or madrigal group.

The credentialed library media teacher should serve as a partner in instruction, technology applications, and use of resources, collaborating with classroom teachers and visual and performing arts specialists in providing enriching experiences for students in the arts. Research projects related to the arts should be designed and coordinated within this collaborative partnership, thus infusing rich resources and information literacy into the content areas.

Promoting Partnerships and Collaborations

The collaborative nature of the arts should lead to partnerships between schools, school districts, county offices of education, the business community, professional artists, nonprofit and for-profit arts providers, parents with arts expertise, and parent volunteers. Such partnerships expand the capabilities of the school and bring students into direct contact with the arts and artists. Further, they satisfy the responsibility of arts organizations to the community, improve their educational function, and, by involving the participation of the

15

Chapter 2
Planning,
Implementing,
and Evaluating
Arts Education
Programs

next generation, advance their interest in building audiences. Partnerships also allow the pooling of resources and ideas, the sharing of workloads, and the expansion of funding bases; strengthen political advocacy; and provide professional development. All partners should benefit from collaborations. For example, when a school is linked with a community performing arts group, performing artists may be permitted to rehearse in the school arts facilities and present performances in the auditorium. Visual artists may be offered the use of studio space.

Each school district should provide leadership and support for coordinating arts resources. For example, a district arts coordinator might develop community partnerships, write grants to fund special programs, and ensure that arts resources reach every school. A comprehensive, articulated program of arts education should incorporate the unique resources of the whole community. In California these resources may include administrators and teachers who understand the goals of arts education, individual artists in each discipline, arts providers, local arts agencies or councils, architects, public art, museums, special exhibitions, performing arts centers, theatres, performing companies, artist studios and cooperatives, clubs and societies, and businesses and industries that support the arts.

Often, dress-rehearsal performances of professional productions are made available to students at a reduced cost, and in some cities the musicians' union arranges programs for schools. Additionally, some community foundations specialize in providing funding and arts programs for schools. Business and industries with a connection to the arts and local and national foundations may provide guest speakers, job shadowing, professional development for teachers, grants, materials, and equipment. And service learning may provide students with the opportunity to build partnerships within and across the arts community. Implementing a standards-based arts curriculum within the context of filling a real need in the community enhances the meaning of the learning experience for students and fosters civic responsibility.

A school-level arts liaison might communicate with the community through a representative of the local arts council or individuals knowledgeable about arts facilities and performances in the area. Meetings between community representatives, arts chairpersons, and teachers of the arts should become routine so that an effective program of community arts experiences can be planned for the school—a program that is aligned with and supports a standards-based curriculum.

Local arts agencies can provide information about artists and performers available for guest appearances or as artists-in-residence. The agencies know about exhibitions or festivals opening in the region and performances scheduled in theatres and concert halls. Then arts chairpersons and faculties can decide which arts experiences should enhance standards-based student learning most effectively and deepen the impact of instruction.

Chapter 2
Planning,
Implementing,
and Evaluating
Arts Education
Programs

Guest artists and artists-in-residence can be an important part of a school's visual and performing arts program. In addition, community resource persons, administrators, parents, arts chairpersons, and arts teachers can ensure that the program is well defined and efficiently run. For example, transportation should be made available for students to visit arts venues, artists should be scheduled for classroom visits, materials should be well organized, and facilities should be up to date and safe.

Joint planning may include a provision for including guest artists and artists-in-residence with the school's generalist and specialist teachers in professional development programs. Programs of this kind are mutually beneficial. That is, the teachers learn about current developments in art forms, and the guest artists and artists-in-residence learn how to adapt their teaching so that the students will gain standards-based knowledge and skills. Whenever possible, such professional development programs might also include school board members, administrators, other faculty, and parents.

Integrating community artists into a comprehensive, standards-based arts program brings the experiences of practicing artists to the students, who learn that artists struggle continually to solve problems, improve their skills, focus on meaning, and communicate effectively in their art form. Thus, students begin to see themselves as members of a community of artists who inherit long-standing traditions across time and place.

Evaluating Arts Education Programs

Once a school district has adopted a policy on arts education and has begun to implement a long-range plan for arts education, it should consider ongoing program evaluation. The program should be reviewed continually to identify areas needing improvement. After students, parents, teachers, administrators, and community members have submitted their comments on the proposed evaluation, it should be revised and expanded, including providing a new timeline.

A structured, ongoing evaluation of the visual and performing arts education program and implementation plan should provide a general profile of what has been accomplished, what is still needed, and what would revitalize the program. An ongoing arts education committee can be effective in monitoring the implementation process and keeping the school board, the district superintendent, the school staff, and the community updated on progress.

A preliminary self-evaluation instrument may include questions designed to collect baseline data for comparing program results later. Such questions may include asking why the program has been effective and successful, what the contributing factors have been, which resources have been particularly effective, and what has been left undone.

In the revision and expansion of the arts education program and implementation plan, focus should be placed on what financial and human resources are

17

Chapter 2
Planning,
Implementing,
and Evaluating
Arts Education
Programs

available to expand a program, what changes have occurred in the student demographics in the school or district that require program changes, and what kind of professional staff development is needed.

Answers to such questions provide information and data that drive long-term planning efforts. Therefore, because additional program goals and tasks may become evident, the cycle of planning, implementing, and evaluating begins again. As plans and objectives are accomplished, revised, and expanded, the focus should remain on providing a high-quality, standards-based education in the visual and performing arts for all students at each grade level.

Providing Access for All Students

Visual and performing arts education should provide all students with opportunities to advance artistically and cognitively, develop self-expression and self-confidence, and experience accomplishment. Instruction in each of the arts disciplines provides experiences and avenues for student learning and ways to meet the needs of students with diverse learning styles and abilities. Because in the visual arts most production is individualized, different learning styles can be accommodated. And in the performing arts, the use of ensembles provides opportunities for students of varied ages and expertise to succeed and learn from each other. The use of a variety of teaching strategies (for example, separating students individually, in pairs, in small groups, and in large groups) provides opportunities for everyone to succeed. All students should be encouraged to participate in dance, music, theatre, and the visual arts as performers and as members of the audience.

Arts instruction should be modified to encourage the successful participation of students with disabilities. The advent of theatre for the deaf, wheelchair dance, museum tours for the visually impaired, and access by touch to musical sounds makes the arts more accessible. Special education staff can collaborate with teachers to plan, suggest, and recommend modifications.

The following Web sites provide resources for addressing the needs of students with disabilities:

California Special Education Programs: A Composite of Laws Database. *Education Code,* Part 30, "Other Related Laws," and *California Code of Regulations, Title 5. http://www.cde.ca.gov/sp/se/sr/selinks.asp*
Special Education Laws and Regulations Database. *http://eit.otan.dni.us/speced/laws_search/searchlaws.cfm.*

Appropriate accommodations can be made to challenge students who excel in the visual and performing arts. They should be provided with instruction and opportunities to enrich and extend their expertise. And they should have access to such special district offerings as the gifted and talented education and international baccalaureate programs, arts magnet schools, advanced placement classes, and districtwide or communitywide events or performances.

Chapter 2
Planning,
Implementing,
and Evaluating
Arts Education
Programs

Applying New Media and Electronic Technology

The computer is an amplifier. It can only make what you bring to it larger. If you come to new media, electronic arts, without a firm grounding in the foundations of your art, you'll miss art's major lessons that connect you with a long history of human endeavor in that realm. . . . Teach sculpture with clay first, and once students have clay under their fingernails, once they know you have to walk around a sculpture to experience it, they can start on 3D computer modeling, where you stand still and rotate the artwork. The difference may be subtle from the outside, but those who succeed are those who have breadth to go with their depth, who bring a solid knowledge of the traditional to their amazing work mixing technology and art.

—Randy Nelson, Dean, Pixar University, Pixar Animation Studios

New media and electronic technology extend the horizons of the arts in directions not yet imagined. In all disciplines artists have traditionally used and combined technologies to create and express ideas. The use of electronic media (digital video, animation, and photo software) juxtaposed with the use of traditional media (paper, paints, classroom tools) expands the boundaries of space and time. For today's artists new media are altering the direction and escalating the pace of exploration within and between arts disciplines. They have easy access to vast amounts of artistic media, materials, processes, and information about historical and contemporary artists. Through technological advances the means for creating, displaying, duplicating, enhancing, and communicating aesthetic ideas are provided to artists.

The development of a solid foundation in an arts discipline brings depth to the mixing of technology and art so that students can be bold and innovative in discovering themselves and the world around them. As equipment becomes more accessible, students have the opportunity to use technology to enhance their artistic skills and create more professional productions and performances. They can use technology to produce animation, analyze works of art, create graphic designs, design sets, develop choreography, computerize stage lighting and scenery, and compose, edit, mix, practice, and sequence music.

New media and electronic technology can be incorporated into lessons, presentations, and explorations in each of the arts disciplines and utilized to connect the arts with other curriculum areas. For example, videos of significant moments in world history or monologues based on important speeches produced in theatre classes can be shared in history–social science classes. And color theory learned through the use of computer software in the visual arts class can be applied to vocational courses, such as interior decoration, floral design, or fashion design. Creating works through electronic technology

19

Chapter 2
Planning,
Implementing,
and Evaluating
Arts Education
Programs

requires a variety of life skills, such as planning and preparing, managing time, meeting deadlines, collaborating, and resolving conflicts.

When school districts and schools plan for improving and adding new media and electronic technology, the arts teachers should be included in the discussion. Infusing new media and electronic technology into the arts curriculum provides a great opportunity for building partnerships with business and industry, especially in California, the home of numerous computer and software companies, animation studios, and television and motion picture production centers. These companies may be resources for grants, equipment, software, educational materials, staff development, job shadowing, guest speakers, career education, and field trips. When creating partnerships, one must remember that partnering is a two-way process with benefits to all participants.

Examples of Technology in the Arts

In some classrooms across California right now:

- Kindergarten students use electronic media as a tool and a delivery system by taking digital photos of works of art and downloading them into a digital slideshow for an electronic gallery. The slideshow itself may become a work of art.
- Digital photos of a third-grade mural project are uploaded to a school Web site and shared with the community and relatives across the country.
- Fourth graders create individual dance videos with the digital camera and short videos to share with other students.
- Middle school students create three-dimensional figures, using animation software and blueprint design to create clay sculptures.
- As part of their community service, high school students create digital or video film documentaries or docudramas to share an experience in theatre class with eighth-grade students.

- High school jazz ensemble students review the videotape of the past week's clinic with an adjudicator and learn how they can improve their technique and performance.
- Teachers and students visit visual and performing artists and return to the classroom with a videotaped interview and demonstration of a process to share with other students.

Visual and Performing Arts
Content Standards

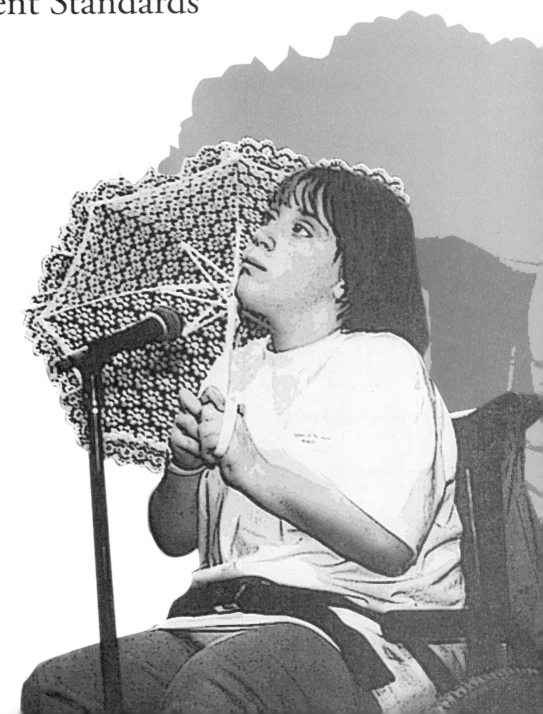

Visual and Performing Arts Content Standards

For the first time in the history of California public schools, the content of the visual and performing arts curriculum for each grade level has been officially adopted by the California State Board of Education (see the *Visual and Performing Arts Content Standards for California Public Schools).*[1] These content standards provide guidance to schools as they determine the curricula and desired outcomes for students, ensuring sequential building and expanding of knowledge and skills as the students advance through the grades. Together, teachers and curriculum developers decide on what will best support attainment of the content standards, what the desired outcomes will be, and how students can demonstrate what they know and can do.

Standards-based instruction in dance, music, theatre, and the visual arts is designed to ensure that students reach the proficient level of achievement in each of the five strands of the content standards: artistic perception; creative expression; historical and cultural context; aesthetic valuing; and connections, relationships, and applications. The content standards establish the basis for curriculum development and professional development for those involved in visual and performing arts programs. Classroom teachers, arts teacher specialists, teaching artists, visiting artists, parents, and community members may be involved in teaching the arts in the schools. Therefore, it is extremely important to have agreed-upon written expectations for student learning at each grade level.

Format of the Content Standards

The content standards are presented in this framework in charts designed for use by administrators, teachers, curriculum planners, and parents. At a glance one can see the standards for each of the arts disciplines at a given grade level according to strand and learn what needs to be accomplished at each level.

For grades nine through twelve, the proficient and advanced levels are shown side by side for each strand in each arts discipline. The term *proficient*

---

[1] *Visual and Performing Arts Content Standards for California Public Schools, Prekindergarten Through Grade Twelve.* Sacramento: California Department of Education, 2001.

refers to what students should know and be able to do on completion of a one-year course in one of the arts disciplines. The expectation is based on the accomplishment of students who participated in an arts education program from kindergarten through grade eight.

Many students elect to take additional high school arts courses to achieve the advanced level of achievement. The term *advanced* means that students have completed more than one course in a given arts discipline. That level can be attained at the end of a second year of high school study in an arts discipline after the proficient or beginning-level course has been completed. What is taught at the proficient level and how the advanced-level content builds on that knowledge and skill become evident on the charts.

When reading the standards at a particular grade level, one must know which standards were accomplished in all the previous grade levels to understand how expectations are based on prior learning. In addition, an examination of the standards for any of the art forms at a given grade level reveals overlaps and points of connection across the strands because the strands and the visual and performing arts content standards are intrinsically related.

Key Content Standards

Each arts discipline and artistic process has many entry points throughout the grades. Because particular ideas, concepts, and experiences are critical to student achievement at certain times in their artistic and cognitive development, the standards provide students with a picture of what is essential to know and be able to do, kindergarten through grade eight, in each of the four arts disciplines. The key content standards provide a beginning point for standards-based instruction in each of the elementary school and middle school grades, focusing on fundamental content that students with any level of prior knowledge need to move to the next level of understanding and expression. Like the complete standards, the key standards build up content in each successive grade level and spiral throughout the curriculum for kindergarten through grade eight. They are essential in preparing students for beginning-level high school arts courses in which they engage in more focused and independent work.

Kindergarten

Kindergarten students dance, sing, act, and paint, exploring their world through their senses and improving their perceptual skills, so important to learning and performing in the arts. They can act like cats; move to music, rhythm, and sounds; and turn everyday movements such as walking and jumping into dance. Listening to music, they repeat the tempo with rhythm sticks and pretend and act out the stories they hear and the pictures they see by performing group pantomimes and improvisations. They like to talk about what they see in pictures and use glue and scissors with enthusiasm while learning about line, color, shape, texture, value, and space in the world around them and in works of art. While learning vocabulary in each of the arts disciplines, they see, listen, and respond to dance, music, theatre, and the visual arts from various cultures and time periods. For kindergarten students the arts are among their first exciting adventures in learning. They are beginning to develop the vocabulary and skills unique to the arts.

Dance

Students learn many ways to move through space and respond to their teacher's instructions to hop, turn, wiggle, or be still. They use this ability to control their movements, express ideas, and respond to different types of music. By learning folk and traditional dances, they can talk about how the dances are the same or different by using such terms as *costume, speed,* and *force.* They also learn to distinguish between everyday movements and dance movements.

Music

In music students sing and play instruments, become aware of music in their daily experience, and learn about music from various cultures. Creating movements in response to music helps them connect to dance and discern variations in rhythm, tempo, and dynamics.

Theatre

In theatre students learn the difference between an actor portraying an imaginary character and a real person. Like actors, they begin to use their senses to observe the world and people and re-create in their minds a feeling or situation to help with character development. They learn that sense memory, which involves sight, smell, touch, taste, or hearing, is an important skill for actors to develop. With their newly acquired skills, they can retell a familiar story, myth, or fable and enjoy adding costumes and props to their performance. By portraying firefighters, teachers, and clerks, they learn acting skills. And by developing important skills through working together in dramatizations, they begin to understand what it means to be a member of the audience.

Visual Arts

In the visual arts students may walk together and observe the repeated patterns made by the leaves on a tree or the bricks on the side of a building. They also may identify lines, colors, shapes and forms, and textures and observe changes in the shadows and in sunlight. And they may begin to talk about perspective, noticing how objects appear to be larger when close and smaller when far away. Students use this visual information to create works of art on paper and in three-dimensional constructions, using geometric shapes and lines that express feelings. Then they advance into analysis as they discover meaning and stories in works of art and see how other artists use the same lines, colors, shapes, and textures as the students did in their own work. Now they have a vocabulary to use as they tell why they like a work of art they made and learn about a variety of artwork in the world around them.

Kindergarten

Key Content Standards
Kindergarten

Dance	Music	Theatre	Visual Arts

Dance

1.2 *(Artistic Perception)* Perform basic locomotor skills (e.g., walk, run, gallop, jump, hop, and balance).

1.3 *(Artistic Perception)* Understand and respond to a wide range of opposites (e.g., high/low, forward/backward, wiggle/freeze).

2.1 *(Creative Expression)* Create movements that reflect a variety of personal experiences (e.g., recall feeling happy, sad, angry, excited).

4.1 *(Aesthetic Valuing)* Explain basic features that distinguish one kind of dance from another (e.g., speed, force/energy use, costume, setting, music).

Music

1.2 *(Artistic Perception)* Identify and describe basic elements in music (e.g., high/low, fast/slow, loud/soft, beat).

2.2 *(Creative Expression)* Sing age-appropriate songs from memory.

2.3 *(Creative Expression)* Play instruments and move or verbalize to demonstrate awareness of beat, tempo, dynamics, and melodic direction.

Theatre

1.1 *(Artistic Perception)* Use the vocabulary of theatre, such as actor, character, cooperation, setting, the five senses, and audience to describe theatrical experiences.

2.2 *(Creative Expression)* Perform group pantomimes and improvisations to retell familiar stories.

3.1 *(Historical and Cultural Context)* Retell or dramatize stories, myths, fables, and fairy tales from various cultures and times.

Visual Arts

1.3 *(Artistic Perception)* Identify the elements of art (line, color, shape/form, texture, value, space) in the environment and in works of art, emphasizing line, color, and shape/form.

4.2 *(Aesthetic Valuing)* Describe what is seen (including both literal and expressive content) in selected works of art.

Kindergarten Content Standards

Component Strand: *1.0 Artistic Perception*

Dance Processing, Analyzing, and Responding to Sensory Information Through the Language and Skills Unique to Dance	**Music** Processing, Analyzing, and Responding to Sensory Information Through the Language and Skills Unique to Music	**Theatre** Processing, Analyzing, and Responding to Sensory Information Through the Language and Skills Unique to Theatre	**Visual Arts** Processing, Analyzing, and Responding to Sensory Information Through the Language and Skills Unique to the Visual Arts
Students perceive and respond, using the elements of dance. They demonstrate movement skills, process sensory information, and describe movement, using the vocabulary of dance. *Development of Motor Skills and Technical Expertise* 1.1 Build the range and capacity to move in a variety of ways. **1.2 Perform basic locomotor skills (e.g., walk, run, gallop, jump, hop, and balance).** *Comprehension and Analysis of Dance Elements* **1.3 Understand and respond to a wide range of opposites (e.g., high/low, forward/backward, wiggle/freeze).** *Development of Dance Vocabulary* 1.4 Perform simple movements in response to oral instructions (e.g., walk, turn, reach).	Students read, notate, listen to, analyze, and describe music and other aural information, using the terminology of music. *Read and Notate Music* 1.1 Use icons or invented symbols to represent beat. *Listen to, Analyze, and Describe Music* 1.2 Identify and describe basic elements in music (e.g., high/low, fast/slow, loud/soft, beat).	Students observe their environment and respond, using the elements of theatre. They also observe formal and informal works of theatre, film/video, and electronic media and respond, using the vocabulary of theatre. *Development of the Vocabulary of Theatre* **1.1 Use the vocabulary of theatre, such as actor, character, cooperation, setting, the five senses, and audience, to describe theatrical experiences.** *Comprehension and Analysis of the Elements of Theatre* 1.2 Identify differences between real people and imaginary characters.	Students perceive and respond to works of art, objects in nature, events, and the environment. They also use the vocabulary of the visual arts to express their observations. *Develop Perceptual Skills and Visual Arts Vocabulary* 1.1 Recognize and describe simple patterns found in the environment and works of art. 1.2 Name art materials (e.g., clay, paint, and crayons) introduced in lessons. *Analyze Art Elements and Principles of Design* **1.3 Identify the elements of art (line, color, shape/form, texture, value, space) in the environment and in works of art, emphasizing line, color, and shape/form.**

Indicates a key content standard for the grade level. See page 23 for information on key content standards.

Kindergarten Content Standards

Component Strand: 2.0 Creative Expression

Dance Creating, Performing, and Participating in Dance	**Music** Creating, Performing, and Participating in Music	**Theatre** Creating, Performing, and Participating in Theatre	**Visual Arts** Creating, Performing, and Participating in the Visual Arts
Students apply choreographic principles, processes, and skills to create and communicate meaning through the improvisation, composition, and performance of dance. *Creation/Invention of Dance Movements* **2.1 Create movements that reflect a variety of personal experiences (e.g., recall feeling happy, sad, angry, excited).** 2.2 Respond to a variety of stimuli (e.g., sounds, words, songs, props, and images) with original movements. 2.3 Respond spontaneously to different types of music, rhythms, and sounds.	Students apply vocal and instrumental musical skills in performing a varied repertoire of music. They compose and arrange music and improvise melodies, variations, and accompaniments, using digital/electronic technology when appropriate. *Apply Vocal and Instrumental Skills* 2.1 Use the singing voice to echo short, melodic patterns. **2.2 Sing age-appropriate songs from memory.** **2.3 Play instruments and move or verbalize to demonstrate awareness of beat, tempo, dynamics, and melodic direction.** *Compose, Arrange, and Improvise* 2.4 Create accompaniments, using the voice or a variety of classroom instruments.	Students apply processes and skills in acting, directing, designing, and scriptwriting to create formal and informal theatre, film/videos, and electronic media productions and to perform in them. *Development of Theatrical Skills* 2.1 Perform imitative movements, rhythmical activities, and theatre games (freeze, statues, and mirrors). *Creation/Invention in Theatre* **2.2 Perform group pantomimes and improvisations to retell familiar stories.** 2.3 Use costumes and props in role playing.	Students apply artistic processes and skills, using a variety of media to communicate meaning and intent in original works of art. *Skills, Processes, Materials, and Tools* 2.1 Use lines, shapes/forms, and colors to make patterns. 2.2 Demonstrate beginning skill in the use of tools and processes, such as the use of scissors, glue, and paper in creating a three-dimensional construction. 2.3 Make a collage with cut or torn paper shapes/forms. *Communication and Expression Through Original Works of Art* 2.4 Paint pictures expressing ideas about family and neighborhood. 2.5 Use lines in drawings and paintings to express feelings. 2.6 Use geometric shapes/forms (circle, triangle, square) in a work of art. 2.7 Create a three-dimensional form, such as a real or imaginary animal.

Indicates a key content standard for the grade level. See page 23 for information on key content standards.

Kindergarten Content Standards

Component Strand: *3.0 Historical and Cultural Context*

Dance	Music	Theatre	Visual Arts
Understanding the Historical Contributions and Cultural Dimensions of Dance	Understanding the Historical Contributions and Cultural Dimensions of Music	Understanding the Historical Contributions and Cultural Dimensions of Theatre	Understanding the Historical Contributions and Cultural Dimensions of the Visual Arts

Dance

Students analyze the function and development of dance in past and present cultures throughout the world, noting human diversity as it relates to dance and dancers.

Development of Dance

3.1 Name and perform folk/traditional dances from the United States and other countries.

Music

Students analyze the role of music in past and present cultures throughout the world, noting cultural diversity as it relates to music, musicians, and composers.

Role of Music

3.1 Identify the various uses of music in daily experiences.

Diversity of Music

3.2 Sing and play simple singing games from various cultures.

3.3 Use a personal vocabulary to describe voices and instruments from diverse cultures.

3.4 Use developmentally appropriate movements in responding to music from various genres and styles (rhythm, melody).

Theatre

Students analyze the role and development of theatre, film/video, and electronic media in past and present cultures throughout the world, noting diversity as it relates to theatre.

Role and Cultural Significance of Theatre

3.1 Retell or dramatize stories, myths, fables, and fairy tales from various cultures and times.

3.2 Portray different community members, such as firefighters, family, teachers, and clerks, through role-playing activities.

Visual Arts

Students analyze the role and development of the visual arts in past and present cultures throughout the world, noting human diversity as it relates to the visual arts and artists.

Role and Development of the Visual Arts

3.1 Describe functional and nonutilitarian art seen in daily life; that is, works of art that are used versus those that are only viewed.

3.2 Identify and describe works of art that show people doing things together.

Diversity of the Visual Arts

3.3 Look at and discuss works of art from a variety of times and places.

Indicates a key content standard for the grade level. See page 23 for information on key content standards.

Kindergarten Content Standards

Component Strand: *4.0 Aesthetic Valuing*

Dance Responding to, Analyzing, and Making Judgments About Works of Dance	**Music** Responding to, Analyzing, and Making Judgments About Works of Music	**Theatre** Responding to, Analyzing, and Critiquing Theatrical Experiences	**Visual Arts** Responding to, Analyzing, and Making Judgments About Works in the Visual Arts
Students critically assess and derive meaning from works of dance, performance of dancers, and original works based on the elements of dance and aesthetic qualities.	Students critically assess and derive meaning from works of music and the performance of musicians according to the elements of music, aesthetic qualities, and human responses.	Students critique and derive meaning from works of theatre, film/video, electronic media, and theatrical artists on the basis of aesthetic qualities.	Students analyze, assess, and derive meaning from works of art, including their own, according to the elements of art, the principles of design, and aesthetic qualities.
Description, Analysis, and Criticism of Dance	*Derive Meaning*	*Critical Assessment of Theatre*	*Derive Meaning*
4.1 **Explain basic features that distinguish one kind of dance from another (e.g., speed, force/energy use, costume, setting, music).**	4.1 Create movements that correspond to specific music. 4.2 Identify, talk about, sing, or play music written for specific purposes (e.g., work song, lullaby).	4.1 Respond appropriately to a theatrical experience as an audience member. *Derivation of Meaning from Works of Theatre* 4.2 Compare a real story with a fantasy story.	4.1 Discuss their own works of art, using appropriate art vocabulary (e.g., color, shape/form, texture). 4.2 **Describe what is seen (including both literal and expressive content) in selected works of art.** *Make Informed Judgments* 4.3 Discuss how and why they made a specific work of art. 4.4 Give reasons why they like a particular work of art they made, using appropriate art vocabulary.

Indicates a key content standard for the grade level. See page 23 for information on key content standards.

Kindergarten Content Standards

Component Strand: 5.0 Connections, Relationships, Applications

Dance	Music	Theatre	Visual Arts
Connecting and Applying What Is Learned in Dance to Learning in Other Art Forms and Subject Areas and to Careers	Connecting and Applying What Is Learned in Music to Learning in Other Art Forms and Subject Areas and to Careers	Connecting and Applying What Is Learned in Theatre, Film/Video, and Electronic Media to Other Art Forms and Subject Areas and to Careers	Connecting and Applying What Is Learned in the Visual Arts to Other Art Forms and Subject Areas and to Careers

Dance

Students apply what they learn in dance to learning across subject areas. They develop competencies and creative skills in problem solving, communication, and management of time and resources that contribute to lifelong learning and career skills. They also learn about careers in and related to dance.

Connections and Applications Across Disciplines

5.1 Give examples of the relationship between everyday movement in school and dance movement.

Music

Students apply what they learn in music across subject areas. They develop competencies and creative skills in problem solving, communication, and management of time and resources that contribute to lifelong learning and career skills. They also learn about careers in and related to music.

Connections and Applications

5.1 Use music, together with dance, theatre, and the visual arts, for storytelling.

Careers and Career-Related Skills

5.2 Identify and talk about the reasons artists have for creating dances, music, theatre pieces, and works of visual art.

Theatre

Students apply what they learn in theatre, film/video, and electronic media across subject areas. They develop competencies and creative skills in problem solving, communication, and time management that contribute to lifelong learning and career skills. They also learn about careers in and related to theatre.

Connections and Applications

5.1 Dramatize information from other content areas. Use movement and voice, for example, to reinforce vocabulary, such as *fast, slow, in, on, through, over, under.*

Careers and Career-Related Skills

5.2 Demonstrate the ability to participate cooperatively in performing a pantomime or dramatizing a story.

Visual Arts

Students apply what they learn in the visual arts across subject areas. They develop competencies and creative skills in problem solving, communication, and management of time and resources that contribute to lifelong learning and career skills. They also learn about careers in and related to the visual arts.

Connections and Applications

5.1 Draw geometric shapes/forms (e.g., circles, squares, triangles) and repeat them in dance/movement sequences.

5.2 Look at and draw something used every day (e.g., scissors, toothbrush, fork) and describe how the object is used.

Visual Literacy

5.3 Point out images (e.g., photographs, paintings, murals, ceramics, sculptures) and symbols found at home, in school, and in the community, including national and state symbols and icons.

Careers and Career-Related Skills

5.4 Discuss the various works of art (e.g., ceramics, paintings, sculpture) that artists create and the type of media used.

Indicates a key content standard for the grade level. See page 23 for information on key content standards.

Grade One

F irst-grade students learn to work with others, know where they live, and recognize that other people live far away. They also learn to listen when others speak, and they begin to understand the role of school in their lives.

Students have much to learn in art classes. They are expected to begin to develop the focus needed to succeed in creating and performing art. As they sing, play music, do dramatics, draw, and paint, their purpose and intent become apparent. They learn how artists in the past performed the same activities that contemporary artists continue today. By connecting the arts with other content areas, students build their vocabulary and prereading skills, such as defining the plot, predicting, summarizing, and recognizing the sequence of events in a story.

Dance

Students use locomotor movements that carry them across the room as well as axial movements of different parts of their bodies while staying in place. As they learn to vary their movements by using different degrees of force or energy, the movements become dynamic. By joining the movements, students can perform brief dance sequences with a beginning, middle, and end as in a story. They incorporate variety and patterns and find that they can express emotions in the way they move. And through folk and traditional dances, students learn more about why, when, and where people dance and how dances are similar or different.

Music

Singing and playing classroom instruments improve students' listening skills, accuracy and technique, and understanding of musical forms. By improvising simple rhythmic accompaniments and learning singing games from various cultures, students begin their creative work in music. And they focus their listening and relate to music and dance by creating and performing movements.

Theatre

Acting through facial expression, gestures, and movements alone helps students develop characters. Without prior rehearsing or scripting to improve their ability to improvise, students can create scenes. For example, they can create tableaux, which are enjoyable and provide a useful learning experience. In that activity they perform a silent, motionless depiction of a scene from, for example, a story, a famous painting, or a moment in history. In the process they identify the cultural and geographic origins of stories.

Visual Arts

Students, working in flat, two-dimensional formats, create three-dimensional works of art, using texture and color. Along with learning the elements of art, such as line, color, shape, and texture, students describe a variety of subject matter in works of art. For example, they can examine landscapes portrayed in early morning light or at night; seascapes on a calm or stormy day; portraits of men and women, boys and girls; and still-life compositions of objects large to small, bright to dull, and rough to smooth.

Key Content Standards
Grade One

Dance	Music	Theatre	Visual Arts

Dance

1.2 *(Artistic Perception)* Perform short movement problems, emphasizing the element of space (e.g., shapes/lines, big/small, high/low).

2.3 *(Creative Expression)* Create a short movement sequence with a beginning, a middle, and an end.

2.8 *(Creative Expression)* Work with others in a group to solve a specific dance problem (e.g., design three shapes—high, medium and low; create slow and fast movements).

4.2 *(Aesthetic Valuing)* Describe the experience of dancing two different dances (e.g., Seven Jumps, La Raspa).

Music

2.1 *(Creative Expression)* Sing with accuracy in a developmentally appropriate range.

2.4 *(Creative Expression)* Improvise simple rhythmic accompaniments, using body percussion or classroom instruments.

4.1 *(Aesthetic Valuing)* Create movements to music that reflect focused listening.

Theatre

1.1 *(Artistic Perception)* Use the vocabulary of the theatre, such as *play, plot (beginning, middle* and *end), improvisation, pantomime, stage, character,* and *audience,* to describe theatrical experiences.

2.1 *(Creative Expression)* Demonstrate skills in pantomime, tableau, and improvisation.

3.1 *(Historical and Cultural Context)* Identify the cultural and geographic origins of stories.

Visual Arts

2.1 *(Creative Expression)* Use texture in two-dimensional and three-dimensional works of art.

3.2 *(Historical and Cultural Context)* Identify and describe various subject matter in art (e.g., landscapes, seascapes, portraits, still life).

Grade One Content Standards

Component Strand: *1.0 Artistic Perception*

Dance Processing, Analyzing, and Responding to Sensory Information Through the Language and Skills Unique to Dance	**Music** Processing, Analyzing, and Responding to Sensory Information Through the Language and Skills Unique to Music	**Theatre** Processing, Analyzing, and Responding to Sensory Information Through the Language and Skills Unique to Theatre	**Visual Arts** Processing, Analyzing, and Responding to Sensory Information Through the Language and Skills Unique to the Visual Arts
Students perceive and respond, using the elements of dance. They demonstrate movement skills, process sensory information, and describe movement, using the vocabulary of dance.	Students read, notate, listen to, analyze, and describe music and other aural information, using the terminology of music.	Students observe their environment and respond, using the elements of theatre. They also observe formal and informal works of theatre, film/video, and electronic media and respond, using the vocabulary of theatre.	Students perceive and respond to works of art, objects in nature, events, and the environment. They also use the vocabulary of the visual arts to express their observations.
Development of Motor Skills and Technical Expertise	*Read and Notate Music*	*Development of the Vocabulary of Theatre*	*Develop Perceptual Skills and Visual Arts Vocabulary*
1.1 Demonstrate the ability to vary control and direct force/energy used in basic locomotor and axial movements (e.g., skip lightly, turn strongly, fall heavily).	1.1 Read, write, and perform simple patterns of rhythm and pitch, using beat, rest, and divided beat (two sounds on one beat).	**1.1 Use the vocabulary ☛ of the theatre, such as *play, plot (beginning, middle,* and *end), improvisation, panto- mime, stage, character,* and *audience,* to describe theatrical experiences.**	1.1 Describe and replicate repeated patterns in nature, in the environment, and in works of art.
Comprehension and Analysis of Dance Elements	*Listen to, Analyze, and Describe Music*	*Comprehension and Analysis of the Elements of Theatre*	1.2 Distinguish among various media when looking at works of art (e.g., clay, paints, drawing materials).
1.2 Perform short ☛ movement problems, emphasizing the element of space (e.g., shapes/lines, big/small, high/low).	1.2 Identify simple musical forms (e.g., phrase, AB, echo).	1.2 Observe and describe the traits of a character.	*Analyze Art Elements and Principles of Design*
Development of Dance Vocabulary	1.3 Identify common instruments visually and aurally in a variety of music.		1.3 Identify the elements of art in objects in nature, in the environ- ment, and in works of art, emphasizing line, color, shape/form, and texture.
1.3 Name basic locomotor and axial movements (e.g., skip, slide, stretch, roll).			

☛ Indicates a key content standard for the grade level. See page 23 for information on key content standards.

Grade One Content Standards

Component Strand: 2.0 Creative Expression

Dance Creating, Performing, and Participating in Dance	**Music** Creating, Performing, and Participating in Music	**Theatre** Creating, Performing, and Participating in Theatre	**Visual Arts** Creating, Performing, and Participating in the Visual Arts
Students apply choreographic principles, processes, and skills to create and communicate meaning through the improvisation, composition, and performance of dance.	Students apply vocal and instrumental musical skills in performing a varied repertoire of music. They compose and arrange music and improvise melodies, variations, and accompaniments, using digital/electronic technology when appropriate.	Students apply processes and skills in acting, directing, designing, and scriptwriting to create formal and informal theatre, film/videos, and electronic media productions and to perform in them.	Students apply artistic processes and skills, using a variety of media to communicate meaning and intent in original works of art.
Creation/Invention of Dance Movements 2.1 Use improvisation to discover movements in response to a specific movement problem (e.g., find a variety of ways to walk; create five types of circular movement). 2.2 Respond in movement to a wide range of stimuli (e.g., music, books, pictures, rhymes, fabrics, props). *Application of Choreographic Principles and Processes to Creating Dance* **2.3 Create a short movement sequence with a beginning, a middle, and an end.** 2.4 Create shapes and movements at low, middle, and high levels. 2.5 Imitate simple movement patterns. *Communication of Meaning in Dance* 2.6 Express basic emotional qualities (e.g., angry, sad, excited, happy) through movement. 2.7 Perform improvised movement ideas for peers. *Development of Partner and Group Skills* **2.8 Work with others in a group to solve a specific dance problem (e.g., design three shapes—high, medium, and low; create slow and fast movements).**	*Apply Vocal and Instrumental Skills* **2.1 Sing with accuracy in a developmentally appropriate range.** 2.2 Sing age-appropriate songs from memory. 2.3 Play simple accompaniments on classroom instruments. *Compose, Arrange, and Improvise* **2.4 Improvise simple rhythmic accompaniments, using body percussion or classroom instruments.**	*Development of Theatrical Skills* **2.1 Demonstrate skills in pantomime, tableau, and improvisation.** *Creation/Invention in Theatre* 2.2 Dramatize or improvise familiar simple stories from classroom literature or life experiences, incorporating plot (beginning, middle, and end) and using a tableau or a pantomime.	*Skills, Processes, Materials, and Tools* **2.1 Use texture in two-dimensional and three-dimensional works of art.** 2.2 Mix secondary colors from primary colors and describe the process. 2.3 Demonstrate beginning skill in the manipulation and use of sculptural materials (clay, paper, and papier maché) to create form and texture in works of art. *Communication and Expression Through Original Works of Art* 2.4 Plan and use variations in line, shape/form, color, and texture to communicate ideas or feelings in works of art. 2.5 Create a representational sculpture based on people, animals, or buildings. 2.6 Draw or paint a still life, using secondary colors. 2.7 Use visual and actual texture in original works of art. 2.8 Create artwork based on observations of actual objects and everyday scenes.

Indicates a key content standard for the grade level. See page 23 for information on key content standards.

Grade One Content Standards
Component Strand: *3.0 Historical and Cultural Context*

Dance Understanding the Historical Contributions and Cultural Dimensions of Dance	**Music** Understanding the Historical Contributions and Cultural Dimensions of Music	**Theatre** Understanding the Historical Contributions and Cultural Dimensions of Theatre	**Visual Arts** Understanding the Historical Contributions and Cultural Dimensions of the Visual Arts
Students analyze the function and development of dance in past and present cultures throughout the world, noting human diversity as it relates to dance and dancers.	Students analyze the role of music in past and present cultures throughout the world, noting cultural diversity as it relates to music, musicians, and composers.	Students analyze the role and development of theatre, film/video, and electronic media in past and present cultures throughout the world, noting diversity as it relates to theatre.	Students analyze the role and development of the visual arts in past and present cultures throughout the world, noting human diversity as it relates to the visual arts and artists.

Development of Dance

3.1 Name and perform folk/traditional dances from other countries.

3.2 Describe aspects of the style, costumes, and music of a dance.

3.3 List commonalities among basic locomotor movements in dances from various countries.

History and Function of Dance

3.4 Identify where and when people dance.

Role of Music

3.1 Recognize and talk about music and celebrations of the cultures represented in the school population.

Diversity of Music

3.2 Sing and play simple singing games from various cultures.

3.3 Use a personal vocabulary to describe voices, instruments, and music from diverse cultures.

3.4 Use developmentally appropriate movements in responding to music from various genres, periods, and styles (rhythm, melody, form).

Role and Cultural Significance of Theatre

3.1 Identify the cultural and geographic origins of stories.

History of Theatre

3.2 Identify theatrical conventions, such as props, costumes, masks, and sets.

3.3 Describe the roles and responsibilities of audience and actor.

Role and Development of the Visual Arts

3.1 Recognize and discuss the design of everyday objects from various time periods and cultures.

3.2 Identify and describe various subject matter in art (e.g., landscapes, seascapes, portraits, still life).

Diversity of the Visual Arts

3.3 View and then describe art from various cultures.

3.4 Identify art objects from various cultures (e.g., Japanese screen painting, Mexican tin art, African masks) and describe what they have in common and how they differ.

Indicates a key content standard for the grade level. See page 23 for information on key content standards.

Grade One Content Standards

Component Strand: 4.0 Aesthetic Valuing

Dance Responding to, Analyzing, and Making Judgments About Works of Dance	**Music** Responding to, Analyzing, and Making Judgments About Works of Music	**Theatre** Responding to, Analyzing, and Critiquing Theatrical Experiences	**Visual Arts** Responding to, Analyzing, and Making Judgments About Works in the Visual Arts

Students critically assess and derive meaning from works of dance, performance of dancers, and original works based on the elements of dance and aesthetic qualities.

Students critically assess and derive meaning from works of music and the performance of musicians according to the elements of music, aesthetic qualities, and human responses.

Students critique and derive meaning from works of theatre, film/video, electronic media, and theatrical artists on the basis of aesthetic qualities.

Students analyze, assess, and derive meaning from works of art, including their own, according to the elements of art, the principles of design, and aesthetic qualities.

Description, Analysis, and Criticism of Dance

4.1 Use basic dance vocabulary to identify and describe a dance observed or performed (e.g., shapes, levels, directions, tempo/fast-slow).

Meaning and Impact of Dance

4.2 Describe the experi-🔑 **ence of dancing two different dances (e.g., Seven Jumps, La Raspa).**

4.3 Describe how they communicate an idea or a mood in a dance (e.g., with exaggerated everyday gesture or emotional energies).

Derive Meaning

4.1 Create movements🔑 **to music that reflect focused listening.**

4.2 Describe how ideas or moods are communicated through music.

Critical Assessment of Theatre

4.1 Describe what was liked about a theatrical work or a story.

Derivation of Meaning from Works of Theatre

4.2 Identify and discuss emotional reactions to a theatrical experience.

Derive Meaning

4.1 Discuss works of art created in the classroom, focusing on selected elements of art (e.g., shape/form, texture, line, color).

4.2 Identify and describe various reasons for making art.

Make Informed Judgments

4.3 Describe how and why they made a selected work of art, focusing on the media and technique.

4.4 Select something they like about their work of art and something they would change.

🔑 Indicates a key content standard for the grade level. See page 23 for information on key content standards.

Grade One Content Standards

Component Strand: *5.0 Connections, Relationships, Applications*

Dance	Music	Theatre	Visual Arts
Connecting and Applying What Is Learned in Dance to Learning in Other Art Forms and Subject Areas and to Careers	Connecting and Applying What Is Learned in Music to Learning in Other Art Forms and Subject Areas and to Careers	Connecting and Applying What Is Learned in Theatre, Film/Video, and Electronic Media to Other Art Forms and Subject Areas and to Careers	Connecting and Applying What Is Learned in the Visual Arts to Other Art Forms and Subject Areas and to Careers

Dance

Students apply what they learn in dance to learning across subject areas. They develop competencies and creative skills in problem solving, communication, and management of time and resources that contribute to lifelong learning and career skills. They also learn about careers in and related to dance.

Connections and Applications Across Disciplines

5.1 Demonstrate curricular concepts through dance (e.g., growth cycle, animal movement).

5.2 Give examples of how dance relates to other subjects (e.g., mathematics—shape, counting; language arts—beginning, middle, and end).

Music

Students apply what they learn in music across subject areas. They develop competencies and creative skills in problem solving, communication, and management of time and resources that contribute to lifelong learning and career skills. They also learn about careers in and related to music.

Connections and Applications

5.1 Recognize and explain how people respond to their world through music.

Careers and Career-Related Skills

5.2 Describe how the performance of songs and dances improves after practice and rehearsal.

Theatre

Students apply what they learn in theatre, film/video, and electronic media across subject areas. They develop competencies and creative skills in problem solving, communication, and time management that contribute to lifelong learning and career skills. They also learn about careers in and related to theatre.

Connections and Applications

5.1 Apply the theatrical concept of beginning, middle, and end to other content areas. For example, act out the life cycle of a butterfly.

Careers and Career-Related Skills

5.2 Demonstrate the ability to work cooperatively in presenting a tableau, an improvisation, or a pantomime.

Visual Arts

Students apply what they learn in the visual arts across subject areas. They develop competencies and creative skills in problem solving, communication, and management of time and resources that contribute to lifelong learning and career skills. They also learn about careers in and related to the visual arts.

Connections and Applications

5.1 Clap out rhythmic patterns found in the lyrics of music and use symbols to create visual representations of the patterns.

5.2 Compare and contrast objects of folk art from various time periods and cultures.

Visual Literacy

5.3 Identify and sort pictures into categories according to the elements of art emphasized in the works (e.g., color, line, shape/form, texture).

Careers and Career-Related Skills

5.4 Describe objects designed by artists (e.g., furniture, appliances, cars) that are used at home and at school.

Indicates a key content standard for the grade level. See page 23 for information on key content standards.

Grade Two

Second-grade students have learned a lot. They become excited when they can connect their previous learning with something new or when they can demonstrate their expanding skills. On their own and in small groups, they are working to experiment and solve problems. Among their accomplishments may appear brightly colored bits of modeling clay fashioned into tree frogs representing a "new species" from a study of the diversity of life in the rainforest; use of chants and clapping to mathematical rhythms and use of rap music to memorize mathematical facts; a journal entry about a child's picture that includes the following sentence: "The diagonal lines show my legs are moving." Clearly, students are demonstrating acquired knowledge through artistic self-expression.

Dance

Students begin to combine dance movements into short sequences by using varied tempos and rhythms. They move fast and then very slowly, first in an $\overline{AB}$ sequence and then in an $\overline{ABA}$ sequence. Their sequences have movements that reach high and bend down low. Naming locomotor and axial movements used in dance, they identify them in dances from various countries that they learn to perform. When they describe how movements in dance communicate ideas or moods and are alike and different, they use the dance vocabulary they are learning, such as *tempo, rhythm,* and *levels.* And they learn (1) that dance can benefit overall health and well being; and (2) that working with partners and groups is an important part of dance.

Music

Students learn verbal syllables, such as *sol* and *fa,* for the degrees of the musical scale, called *solfège.* In doing so, they learn to read, write, and perform simple patterns of pitch, a process that leads to a whole world of listening to, playing, singing, and composing music.

Theatre

Students perform in group improvisations and learn theatrical games to improve their skills. In the process they develop cooperative skills and concentration and learn the vocabulary of the theatre, such as *plot, scene, sets, conflict,* and *script.* As students retell familiar stories and those from other cultures, they identify universal character types.

Visual Arts

Students continue to expand their understanding of the elements of art and apply them as they learn to use basic tools and art-making processes, such as printmaking and collage. They describe art objects from various cultures and time periods brought into the classroom for analysis. The objects are also analyzed by a docent from a local museum. Now students are beginning to evaluate their own work as they analyze what they intended to paint and how well they succeeded.

Key Content Standards
Grade Two

Dance	Music	Theatre	Visual Arts

Dance

1.3 *(Artistic Perception)* Perform short movement problems, emphasizing the element of time (e.g., varied tempos, rhythmic patterns, counting).

3.1 *(Historical and Cultural Context)* Name and perform social and traditional dances from various cultures.

4.2 *(Aesthetic Valuing)* Describe how the movement in dances of peers communicates ideas or moods to the viewer (e.g., ocean environment or a sad or joyous dance).

5.2 *(Connections, Relationships, Applications)* Demonstrate language arts concepts through dance (e.g., show different punctuation marks through movement).

Music

1.2 *(Artistic Perception)* Read, write, and perform simple patterns of pitch, using solfège.

2.4 *(Creative Expression)* Improvise simple rhythmic and melodic accompaniments, using voice and a variety of classroom instruments.

4.2 *(Aesthetic Valuing)* Create developmentally appropriate movements to express pitch, tempo, form, and dynamics in music.

Theatre

1.1 *(Artistic Perception)* Use the vocabulary of theatre, such as *plot (beginning, middle, and end)*, *scene*, *sets*, *conflict*, *script*, and *audience*, to describe theatrical experiences.

2.1 *(Creative Expression)* Perform in group improvisational theatrical games that develop cooperative skills and concentration.

4.1 *(Aesthetic Valuing)* Critique an actor's performance as to the use of voice, gesture, facial expression, and movement to create character.

Visual Arts

1.3 *(Artistic Perception)* Identify the elements of art objects in nature, the environment, and works of art, emphasizing line, color, shape/form, texture, and space.

2.1 *(Creative Expression)* Demonstrate beginning skill in the use of basic tools and art-making processes, such as printing, crayon rubbings, collage, and stencils.

3.2 *(Historical and Cultural Context)* Recognize and use the vocabulary of art to describe art objects from various cultures and time periods.

4.3 *(Aesthetic Valuing)* Use the vocabulary of art to talk about what they wanted to do in their own works of art and how they succeeded.

Grade Two Content Standards

Component Strand: *1.0 Artistic Perception*

Dance	Music	Theatre	Visual Arts
Processing, Analyzing, and Responding to Sensory Information Through the Language and Skills Unique to Dance	Processing, Analyzing, and Responding to Sensory Information Through the Language and Skills Unique to Music	Processing, Analyzing, and Responding to Sensory Information Through the Language and Skills Unique to Theatre	Processing, Analyzing, and Responding to Sensory Information Through the Language and Skills Unique to the Visual Arts

Dance

Students perceive and respond, using the elements of dance. They demonstrate movement skills, process sensory information, and describe movement, using the vocabulary of dance.

Development of Motor Skills and Technical Expertise

1.1 Show a variety of combinations of basic locomotor skills (e.g., walk and run, gallop and jump, hop and skip, slide and roll).

1.2 Show a variety of combinations of axial movements (e.g., swing and balanced shapes, turn and stretch, bend and twist).

Comprehension and Analysis of Dance Elements

1.3 Perform short movement problems, emphasizing the element of time (e.g., varied tempos, rhythmic patterns, counting).

1.4 Expand the ability to incorporate spatial concepts with movement problems.

Development of Dance Vocabulary

1.5 Name a large number of locomotor and axial movements used in dance.

Music

Students read, notate, listen to, analyze, and describe music and other aural information, using the terminology of music.

Read and Notate Music

1.1 Read, write, and perform simple rhythmic patterns, using eighth notes, quarter notes, half notes, and rests.

1.2 Read, write, and perform simple patterns of pitch, using solfège.

Listen to, Analyze, and Describe Music

1.3 Identify ascending/descending melody and even/uneven rhythm patterns in selected pieces of music.

1.4 Identify simple musical forms, emphasizing verse/refrain, AB, ABA.

1.5 Identify visually and aurally individual wind, string, brass, and percussion instruments used in a variety of music.

Theatre

Students observe their environment and respond, using the elements of theatre. They also observe formal and informal works of theatre, film/video, and electronic media and respond, using the vocabulary of theatre.

Development of the Vocabulary of Theatre

1.1 Use the vocabulary of theatre, such as plot (beginning, middle, and end), scene, sets, conflict, script, and audience, to describe theatrical experiences.

Comprehension and Analysis of the Elements of Theatre

1.2 Use body and voice to improvise alternative endings to a story.

Visual Arts

Students perceive and respond to works of art, objects in nature, events, and the environment. They also use the vocabulary of the visual arts to express their observations.

Develop Perceptual Skills and Visual Arts Vocabulary

1.1 Perceive and describe repetition and balance in nature, in the environment, and in works of art.

1.2 Perceive and discuss differences in mood created by warm and cool colors.

Analyze Art Elements and Principles of Design

1.3 Identify the elements of art in objects in nature, the environment, and works of art, emphasizing line, color, shape/form, texture, and space.

Indicates a key content standard for the grade level. See page 23 for information on key content standards.

Grade Two Content Standards

Component Strand: 2.0 Creative Expression

Dance Creating, Performing, and Participating in Dance	Music Creating, Performing, and Participating in Music	Theatre Creating, Performing, and Participating in Theatre	Visual Arts Creating, Performing, and Participating in the Visual Arts
Students apply choreographic principles, processes, and skills to create and communicate meaning through improvisation, composition, and performance of dance.	Students apply vocal and instrumental musical skills in performing a varied repertoire of music. They compose and arrange music and improvise melodies, variations, and accompaniments, using digital/electronic technology when appropriate.	Students apply processes and skills in acting, directing, designing, and scriptwriting to create formal and informal theatre, film/videos, and electronic media productions and to perform in them.	Students apply artistic processes and skills, using a variety of media to communicate meaning and intent in original works of art.

Creation/Invention of Dance Movements

2.1 Create and improvise movement patterns and sequences.

2.2 Demonstrate multiple solutions in response to a given movement problem (e.g., In how many ways can you travel from point A to point B?).

Application of Choreographic Principles and Processes to Creating Dance

2.3 Create a simple sequence of movement with a beginning, a middle, and an end, incorporating level and directional changes.

2.4 Create shapes and movements, using fast and slow tempos.

2.5 Develop a dance phrase that has a sense of unity.

Communication of Meaning in Dance

2.6 Create, memorize, and perform original expressive movements for peers.

Development of Partner and Group Skills

2.7 Work cooperatively in small and large groups.

2.8 Demonstrate partner skills (e.g., imitating and leading/following).

Apply Vocal and Instrumental Skills

2.1 Sing with accuracy in a developmentally appropriate range.

2.2 Sing age-appropriate songs from memory.

2.3 Play rhythmic ostinatos on classroom instruments.

Compose, Arrange, and Improvise

2.4 Improvise simple rhythmic and melodic accompaniments, using voice and a variety of classroom instruments.

Development of Theatrical Skills

2.1 Perform in group improvisational theatrical games that develop cooperative skills and concentration.

Creation/Invention in Theatre

2.2 Retell familiar stories, sequencing story points and identifying character, setting, and conflict.

2.3 Use improvisation to portray such concepts as friendship, hunger, or seasons.

2.4 Create costume pieces, props, or sets for a theatrical experience.

Skills, Processes, Materials, and Tools

2.1 Demonstrate beginning skill in the use of basic tools and art-making processes, such as printing, crayon rubbings, collage, and stencils.

2.2 Demonstrate beginning skill in the use of art media, such as oil pastels, watercolors, and tempera.

Communication and Expression Through Original Works of Art

2.3 Depict the illusion of depth (space) in a work of art, using overlapping shapes, relative size, and placement within the picture.

2.4 Create a painting or drawing, using warm or cool colors expressively.

2.5 Use bilateral or radial symmetry to create visual balance.

Indicates a key content standard for the grade level. See page 23 for information on key content standards.

Grade Two Content Standards

Component Strand: *3.0 Historical and Cultural Context*

Dance	**Music**	**Theatre**	**Visual Arts**
Understanding the Historical Contributions and Cultural Dimensions of Dance	Understanding the Historical Contributions and Cultural Dimensions of Music	Understanding the Historical Contributions and Cultural Dimensions of Theatre	Understanding the Historical Contributions and Cultural Dimensions of the Visual Arts

Students analyze the function and development of dance in past and present cultures throughout the world, noting human diversity as it relates to dance and dancers.

Development of Dance

3.1 Name and perform ☞ social and traditional dances from various cultures.

3.2 Explain commonalities among basic locomotor and axial movements in dances from various countries.

3.3 Name and perform rhythms from different cultures (e.g., through clapping, stamping, using whole body movement).

History and Function of Dance

3.4 Describe dances seen in celebrations and community events.

Students analyze the role of music in past and present cultures throughout the world, noting cultural diversity as it relates to music, musicians, and composers.

Role of Music

3.1 Identify the uses of specific music in daily or special events.

Diversity of Music

3.2 Sing simple songs and play singing games from various cultures.

3.3 Describe music from various cultures.

Students analyze the role and development of theatre, film/video, and electronic media in past and present cultures throughout the world, noting diversity as it relates to theatre.

Role and Cultural Significance of Theatre

3.1 Identify theatre and storytelling forms from different cultures.

History of Theatre

3.2 Identify universal characters in stories and plays from different periods and places.

Students analyze the role and development of the visual arts in past and present cultures throughout the world, noting human diversity as it relates to the visual arts and artists.

Role and Development of the Visual Arts

3.1 Explain how artists use their work to share experiences or communicate ideas.

3.2 Recognize and use the ☞ vocabulary of art to describe art objects from various cultures and time periods.

Diversity of the Visual Arts

3.3 Identify and discuss how art is used in events and celebrations in various cultures, past and present, including the use in their own lives.

☞ Indicates a key content standard for the grade level. See page 23 for information on key content standards.

Grade Two Content Standards

Component Strand: 4.0 Aesthetic Valuing

Dance Responding to, Analyzing, and Making Judgments About Works of Dance	**Music** Responding to, Analyzing, and Making Judgments About Works of Music	**Theatre** Responding to, Analyzing, and Critiquing Theatrical Experiences	**Visual Arts** Responding to, Analyzing, and Making Judgments About Works in the Visual Arts
Students critically assess and derive meaning from works of dance, performance of dancers, and original works based on the elements of dance and aesthetic qualities.	Students critically assess and derive meaning from works of music and the performance of musicians according to the elements of music, aesthetic qualities, and human responses.	Students critique and derive meaning from works of theatre, film/video, electronic media, and theatrical artists on the basis of aesthetic qualities.	Students analyze, assess, and derive meaning from works of art, including their own, according to the elements of art, the principles of design, and aesthetic qualities.

Dance

Description, Analysis, and Criticism of Dance

4.1 Use basic dance vocabulary to name and describe a dance observed or performed (e.g., levels, rhythm patterns, type of energy).

4.2 Describe how the movement in dances of peers communicates ideas or moods to the viewer (e.g., ocean environment or a sad or joyous dance).

Meaning and Impact of Dance

4.3 Describe the similarities and differences in performing various dances (e.g., direction changes, steps, type of energy and tempo).

Music

Analyze and Critically Assess

4.1 Use the terminology of music in discussing individual preferences for specific music.

Derive Meaning

4.2 Create developmentally appropriate movements to express pitch, tempo, form, and dynamics in music.

4.3 Identify how musical elements communicate ideas or moods.

4.4 Respond to a live performance with appropriate audience behavior.

Theatre

Critical Assessment of Theatre

4.1 Critique an actor's performance as to the use of voice, gesture, facial expression, and movement to create character.

4.2 Respond to a live performance with appropriate audience behavior.

Derivation of Meaning from Works of Theatre

4.3 Identify the message or moral of a work of theatre.

Visual Arts

Derive Meaning

4.1 Compare ideas expressed through their own works of art with ideas expressed in the work of others.

4.2 Compare different responses to the same work of art.

Make Informed Judgments

4.3 Use the vocabulary of art to talk about what they wanted to do in their own works of art and how they succeeded.

4.4 Use appropriate vocabulary of art to describe the successful use of an element of art in a work of art.

Indicates a key content standard for the grade level. See page 23 for information on key content standards.

Grade Two Content Standards

Component Strand: *5.0 Connections, Relationships, Applications*

Dance	Music	Theatre	Visual Arts
Connecting and Applying What Is Learned in Dance to Learning in Other Art Forms and Subject Areas and to Careers	Connecting and Applying What Is Learned in Music to Learning in Other Art Forms and Subject Areas and to Careers	Connecting and Applying What Is Learned in Theatre, Film/Video, and Electronic Media to Other Art Forms and Subject Areas and to Careers	Connecting and Applying What Is Learned in the Visual Arts to Other Art Forms and Subject Areas and to Careers

Dance

Students apply what they learn in dance to learning across subject areas. They develop competencies and creative skills in problem solving, communication, and management of time and resources that contribute to lifelong learning and career skills. They also learn about careers in and related to dance.

Connections and Applications Across Disciplines

5.1 Use literature to inspire dance ideas (e.g., poem, cartoon, nursery rhyme).

5.2 Demonstrate
🔑 **language arts concepts through dance (e.g., show different punctuation marks through movement).**

Development of Life Skills and Career Competencies

5.3 Describe how choreographers create dances.

5.4 Describe how dancing requires good health-related habits (e.g., adequate nutrition, water, and rest; proper preparation for physical activity).

Music

Students apply what they learn in music across subject areas. They develop competencies and creative skills in problem solving, communication, and management of time and resources that contribute to lifelong learning and career skills. They also learn about careers in and related to music.

Connections and Applications

5.1 Identify similar themes in stories, songs, and art forms (e.g., patterns, texture).

Careers and Career-Related Skills

5.2 Identify and discuss who composes and performs music.

Theatre

Students apply what they learn in theatre, film/video, and electronic media across subject areas. They develop competencies and creative skills in problem solving, communication, and time management that contribute to lifelong learning and career skills. They also learn about careers in and related to theatre.

Connections and Applications

5.1 Use problem-solving and cooperative skills in dramatizing a story, a current event, or a concept from another subject area.

Careers and Career-Related Skills

5.2 Demonstrate the ability to participate cooperatively in the different jobs required to create a theatrical production.

Visual Arts

Students apply what they learn in the visual arts across subject areas. They develop competencies and creative skills in problem solving, communication, and management of time and resources that contribute to lifelong learning and career skills. They also learn about careers in and related to the visual arts.

Connections and Applications

5.1 Use placement, overlapping, and size differences to show opposites (e.g., up/down, in/out, over/under, together/apart, fast/slow, stop/go).

5.2 Select and use expressive colors to create mood and show personality within a portrait of a hero from long ago or the recent past.

Visual Literacy

5.3 Identify pictures and sort them into categories according to expressive qualities (e.g., theme and mood).

Careers and Career-Related Skills

5.4 Discuss artists in the community who create different kinds of art (e.g., prints, ceramics, paintings, sculpture).

🔑 Indicates a key content standard for the grade level. See page 23 for information on key content standards.

Grade Three

The doors of knowledge open wide for third-grade students, offering them new possibilities through the arts. As they start thinking abstractly and their levels of perception become more sophisticated, they can describe their thoughts orally and in writing. And their increased fine motor skills help them learn all kinds of things, from cursive writing to classroom instruments. As they begin to learn about their community, they become more curious about themselves and about others. Their study of the arts leads them to gain knowledge about many different subjects. For example, excited by a walking trip through the community, they draw pictures representing landmark buildings. They also learn to dance and sing to music from their community's many cultural heritages and use their theatrical skills to explore what they imagine and to portray a character.

Dance

Students combine movement in place, movement across the room, and a sense of space and time as they sequence the movements to different tempos. By practicing to combine the various movements and the elements of dance, they create and perform original dance sequences that exhibit variety and kinesthetic and visual rhythm. For example, they learn to perform increasingly complex improvisations and movement sequences more expressively by emphasizing the dance element of force or energy. When they create dance sequences, they can identify a clear beginning, middle, and end and include a variety of shapes, movements, and levels in space. As they work to improve their own proficiency, they also create, memorize, and perform original movement sequences with a partner or a small group.

Learning to compare and contrast dances from various countries enriches students' repertoires or movements and their understanding of how dance functions in many cultures. When students evaluate the dance performance of their peers, they can use specific criteria, such as how focused the dancer was during the performance. And they can comment on how dance skills help communicate the idea and mood of the dance. As they gain experience in creating dance in collaboration with others, they learn more about the time-management, problem-solving, and self-discipline skills required for dance and determine how those skills apply to other areas of study and to careers.

Music

Students focus on rhythmic patterns, musical forms, melody, harmony, and timbre as they read, write, and perform music. Their increased listening skills help them identify those qualities in music selections, in the four families of orchestral instruments, and in male and female adult voices. By singing from memory, they improve their accuracy and create rhythmic and

49

Chapter 3
Visual and
Performing Arts
Content
Standards

Grade Three

melodic phrases. As students sing and play songs from diverse cultures, they can compare and contrast music from throughout the world. When they play and sing music, they are honing their ability to select and use specific criteria to judge the quality of a musical performance. Focusing on the use of the musical elements for their criteria, they can describe how the elements help the composer or performer to communicate an idea or mood in the music and can identify the use of similar elements, such as pattern and rhythm, in other art forms.

Theatre

Students identify and describe important elements of theatre, such as *character, setting, conflict, motivation, props, stage areas,* and *blocking.* They do cooperative scriptwriting and improvisations, including determining basic blocking and stage areas, by applying their knowledge of the five Ws (who, what, where, when, and why). By dramatizing different cultural versions of similar stories from around the world, they increase their repertoire and can identify universal themes. When evaluating scripts and staging performances, they learn which criteria are appropriate. And if they like a scene in a play they are reading, they can explain how the playwright succeeded. By participating in theatrical experiences, they gain many opportunities to demonstrate their problem-solving and cooperative skills.

Visual Arts

Students increase their understanding of how to create the illusion of space and apply those techniques in their own work, allowing them to recognize near and far distances in a painting. They also compare works of art made with different media, such as watercolor or oil paint, and different art objects, such as a woodcut or computer-generated prints. Creating works of visual art based on their observations of objects and scenes, they include drawing, painting, sculpture, printmaking, and other forms of expression in their efforts. Students also become familiar with local artists and their works as well as artists throughout the state and from various parts of the world.

Students progress into analyzing how diverse works may communicate similar themes, ideas, or moods and can distinguish among representational, abstract, and nonrepresentational works of art, including developing and applying appropriate criteria for evaluation. For example, they might consider how effectively the artist used elements of art, such as line, shape, and color, to communicate a mood. In addition, students apply criteria to their own artwork and explain how it might be improved. Another activity allows students to apply their understanding of the communicative quality of the visual arts as they describe, for example, how costumes contribute to the meaning of a dance, how an artist tells a story in a figurative painting, how a work of art can be the inspiration for a poem, or how artists have affected people's lives.

Key Content Standards
Grade Three

Dance	Music	Theatre	Visual Arts

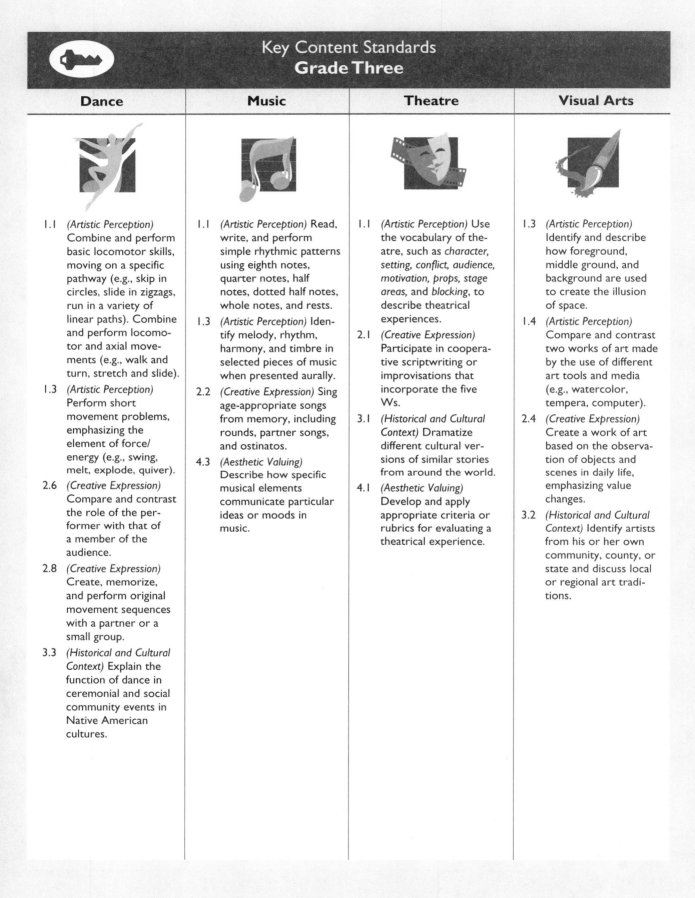

Dance

1.1 *(Artistic Perception)* Combine and perform basic locomotor skills, moving on a specific pathway (e.g., skip in circles, slide in zigzags, run in a variety of linear paths). Combine and perform locomotor and axial movements (e.g., walk and turn, stretch and slide).

1.3 *(Artistic Perception)* Perform short movement problems, emphasizing the element of force/energy (e.g., swing, melt, explode, quiver).

2.6 *(Creative Expression)* Compare and contrast the role of the performer with that of a member of the audience.

2.8 *(Creative Expression)* Create, memorize, and perform original movement sequences with a partner or a small group.

3.3 *(Historical and Cultural Context)* Explain the function of dance in ceremonial and social community events in Native American cultures.

Music

1.1 *(Artistic Perception)* Read, write, and perform simple rhythmic patterns using eighth notes, quarter notes, half notes, dotted half notes, whole notes, and rests.

1.3 *(Artistic Perception)* Identify melody, rhythm, harmony, and timbre in selected pieces of music when presented aurally.

2.2 *(Creative Expression)* Sing age-appropriate songs from memory, including rounds, partner songs, and ostinatos.

4.3 *(Aesthetic Valuing)* Describe how specific musical elements communicate particular ideas or moods in music.

Theatre

1.1 *(Artistic Perception)* Use the vocabulary of theatre, such as *character, setting, conflict, audience, motivation, props, stage areas,* and *blocking,* to describe theatrical experiences.

2.1 *(Creative Expression)* Participate in cooperative scriptwriting or improvisations that incorporate the five Ws.

3.1 *(Historical and Cultural Context)* Dramatize different cultural versions of similar stories from around the world.

4.1 *(Aesthetic Valuing)* Develop and apply appropriate criteria or rubrics for evaluating a theatrical experience.

Visual Arts

1.3 *(Artistic Perception)* Identify and describe how foreground, middle ground, and background are used to create the illusion of space.

1.4 *(Artistic Perception)* Compare and contrast two works of art made by the use of different art tools and media (e.g., watercolor, tempera, computer).

2.4 *(Creative Expression)* Create a work of art based on the observation of objects and scenes in daily life, emphasizing value changes.

3.2 *(Historical and Cultural Context)* Identify artists from his or her own community, county, or state and discuss local or regional art traditions.

Grade Three Content Standards

Component Strand: 1.0 Artistic Perception

Dance	Music	Theatre	Visual Arts
Processing, Analyzing, and Responding to Sensory Information Through the Language and Skills Unique to Dance	Processing, Analyzing, and Responding to Sensory Information Through the Language and Skills Unique to Music	Processing, Analyzing, and Responding to Sensory Information Through the Language and Skills Unique to Theatre	Processing, Analyzing, and Responding to Sensory Information Through the Language and Skills Unique to the Visual Arts

Dance

Students perceive and respond, using the elements of dance. They demonstrate movement skills, process sensory information, and describe movement, using the vocabulary of dance.

Development of Motor Skills and Technical Expertise

1.1 Combine and perform basic locomotor skills, moving on a specific pathway (e.g., skip in circles, slide in zigzags, run in a variety of linear paths). Combine and perform locomotor and axial movements (e.g., walk and turn, stretch and slide).

1.2 Demonstrate the ability to start, change, and stop movement.

Comprehension and Analysis of Dance Elements

1.3 Perform short movement problems, emphasizing the element of force/energy (e.g., swing, melt, explode, quiver).

1.4 Expand the ability to incorporate spatial and time concepts in movement problems (e.g., select and combine three locomotor movements traveling in three different pathways and using three different tempos).

Development of Dance Vocabulary

1.5 Describe dance elements used in personal work and that of others.

Music

Students read, notate, listen to, analyze, and describe music and other aural information, using the terminology of music.

Read and Notate Music

1.1 Read, write, and perform simple rhythmic patterns using eighth notes, quarter notes, half notes, dotted half notes, whole notes, and rests.

1.2 Read, write, and perform pentatonic patterns, using solfège.

Listen to, Analyze, and Describe Music

1.3 Identify melody, rhythm, harmony, and timbre in selected pieces of music when presented aurally.

1.4 Identify visually and aurally the four families of orchestral instruments and male and female adult voices.

1.5 Describe the way in which sound is produced on various instruments.

1.6 Identify simple musical forms (e.g., AABA, AABB, round).

Theatre

Students observe their environment and respond, using the elements of theatre. They also observe formal and informal works of theatre, film/video, and electronic media and respond, using the vocabulary of theatre.

Development of the Vocabulary of Theatre

1.1 Use the vocabulary of theatre, such as *character, setting, conflict, audience, motivation, props, stage areas,* and *blocking,* to describe theatrical experiences.

Comprehension and Analysis of the Elements of Theatre

1.2 Identify who, what, where, when, and why (the five Ws) in a theatrical experience.

Visual Arts

Students perceive and respond to works of art, objects in nature, events, and the environment. They also use the vocabulary of the visual arts to express their observations.

Develop Perceptual Skills and Visual Arts Vocabulary

1.1 Perceive and describe rhythm and movement in works of art and in the environment.

1.2 Describe how artists use tints and shades in painting.

1.3 Identify and describe how foreground, middle ground, and background are used to create the illusion of space.

1.4 Compare and contrast two works of art made by the use of different art tools and media (e.g., watercolor, tempera, computer).

Analyze Art Elements and Principles of Design

1.5 Identify and describe elements of art in works of art, emphasizing line, color, shape/form, texture, space, and value.

Indicates a key content standard for the grade level. See page 23 for information on key content standards.

Grade Three Content Standards

Component Strand: *2.0 Creative Expression*

Dance Creating, Performing, and Participating in Dance	**Music** Creating, Performing, and Participating in Music	**Theatre** Creating, Performing, and Participating in Theatre	**Visual Arts** Creating, Performing, and Participating in the Visual Arts
Students apply choreographic principles, processes, and skills to create and communicate meaning through the improvisation, composition, and performance of dance.	Students apply vocal and instrumental musical skills in performing a varied repertoire of music. They compose and arrange music and improvise melodies, variations, and accompaniments, using digital/electronic technology when appropriate.	Students apply processes and skills in acting, directing, designing, and scriptwriting to create formal and informal theatre, film/videos, and electronic media productions and to perform in them.	Students apply artistic processes and skills, using a variety of media to communicate meaning and intent in original works of art.

Dance

Creation/Invention of Dance Movements

2.1 Create and perform complex improvised movement patterns, dance sequences, and studies.

2.2 Improvise and select multiple possibilities to solve a given movement problem (e.g., find four different ways to combine a turn, stretch, and jump).

Application of Choreographic Principles and Processes to Creating Dance

2.3 Create a sequence that has a beginning, a middle, and an end. Name and refine the parts of the sequence.

2.4 Create a wide variety of shapes and movements, using different levels in space.

Communication of Meaning in Dance

2.5 Perform dances to communicate personal meaning, using focus and expression.

2.6 Compare and contrast
🔑 **the role of the performer with that of a member of the audience.**

Development of Partner and Group Skills

2.7 Demonstrate a variety of partner skills (e.g., imitation, leading/following, mirroring).

2.8 Create, memorize,
🔑 **and perform original movement sequences with a partner or a small group.**

Music

Apply Vocal and Instrumental Skills

2.1 Sing with accuracy in a developmentally appropriate range.

2.2 Sing age-appropri-
🔑 **ate songs from memory, including rounds, partner songs, and ostinatos.**

2.3 Play rhythmic and melodic ostinatos on classroom instruments.

Compose, Arrange, and Improvise

2.4 Create short rhythmic and melodic phrases in question-and-answer form.

Theatre

Development of Theatrical Skills

2.1 Participate in coop-
🔑 **erative scriptwriting or improvisations that incorporate the five Ws.**

Creation/Invention in Theatre

2.2 Create for classmates simple scripts that demonstrate knowledge of basic blocking and stage areas.

Visual Arts

Skills, Processes, Materials, and Tools

2.1 Explore ideas for art in a personal sketchbook.

2.2 Mix and apply tempera paints to create tints, shades, and neutral colors.

Communication and Expression Through Original Works of Art

2.3 Paint or draw a landscape, seascape, or cityscape that shows the illusion of space.

2.4 Create a work of
🔑 **art based on the observation of objects and scenes in daily life, emphasizing value changes.**

2.5 Create an imaginative clay sculpture based on an organic form.

2.6 Create an original work of art emphasizing rhythm and movement, using a selected printing process.

🔑 Indicates a key content standard for the grade level. See page 23 for information on key content standards.

Grade Three Content Standards

Component Strand: *3.0 Historical and Cultural Context*

Dance Understanding the Historical Contributions and Cultural Dimensions of Dance	**Music** Understanding the Historical Contributions and Cultural Dimensions of Music	**Theatre** Understanding the Historical Contributions and Cultural Dimensions of Theatre	**Visual Arts** Understanding the Historical Contributions and Cultural Dimensions of the Visual Arts
Students analyze the function and development of dance in past and present cultures throughout the world, noting human diversity as it relates to dance and dancers.	Students analyze the role of music in past and present cultures throughout the world, noting cultural diversity as it relates to music, musicians, and composers.	Students analyze the role and development of theatre, film/video, and electronic media in past and present cultures throughout the world, noting diversity as it relates to theatre.	Students analyze the role and development of the visual arts in past and present cultures throughout the world, noting human diversity as it relates to the visual arts and artists.
Development of Dance	*Role of Music*	*Role and Cultural Significance of Theatre*	*Role and Development of the Visual Arts*
3.1 Describe commonalities among and differences between dances from various countries.	3.1 Identify the uses of music in various cultures and time periods.	**3.1 Dramatize different cultural versions of similar stories from around the world.**	3.1 Compare and describe various works of art that have a similar theme and were created at different time periods.
3.2 Describe and demonstrate ceremonial and folk/traditional dances that show work activities (e.g., harvesting, fishing, weaving).	*Diversity of Music* 3.2 Sing memorized songs from diverse cultures. 3.3 Play memorized songs from diverse cultures.	*History of Theatre* 3.2 Identify universal themes in stories and plays from different periods and places.	**3.2 Identify artists from his or her own community, county, or state and discuss local or regional art traditions.**
History and Function of Dance	3.4 Identify differences and commonalities in music from various cultures.		3.3 Distinguish and describe representational, abstract, and nonrepresentational works of art.
3.3 Explain the function of dance in ceremonial and social community events in Native American cultures.			*Diversity of the Visual Arts*
3.4 Describe how costumes and shoes influence dance movement.			3.4 Identify and describe objects of art from different parts of the world observed in visits to a museum or gallery (e.g., puppets, masks, containers).
Diversity of Dance			3.5 Write about a work of art that reflects a student's own cultural background.
3.5 Name and demonstrate dances of Native Americans.			

Indicates a key content standard for the grade level. See page 23 for information on key content standards.

Grade Three Content Standards

Component Strand: *4.0 Aesthetic Valuing*

Dance Responding to, Analyzing, and Making Judgments About Works of Dance	**Music** Responding to, Analyzing, and Making Judgments About Works of Music	**Theatre** Responding to, Analyzing, and Critiquing Theatrical Experiences	**Visual Arts** Responding to, Analyzing, and Making Judgments About Works in the Visual Arts
Students critically assess and derive meaning from works of dance, performance of dancers, and original works based on the elements of dance and aesthetic qualities. *Description, Analysis, and Criticism of Dance* 4.1 Name specific criteria to assess the quality of a dance performance of peers (e.g., focus, level of personal involvement, physical control). 4.2 Explain and demonstrate what it means to be a good audience member. *Meaning and Impact of Dance* 4.3 Explain how a performer's dance skills contribute to communication of ideas and moods when performing a dance (e.g., focus, strength, coordination).	Students critically assess and derive meaning from works of music and the performance of musicians according to the elements of music, aesthetic qualities, and human responses. *Analyze and Critically Assess* 4.1 Select and use specific criteria in making judgments about the quality of a musical performance. *Derive Meaning* 4.2 Create developmentally appropriate movements to express pitch, tempo, form, and dynamics. **4.3 Describe how specific musical elements communicate particular ideas or moods in music.**	Students critique and derive meaning from works of theatre, film/video, electronic media, and theatrical artists on the basis of aesthetic qualities. *Critical Assessment of Theatre* **4.1 Develop and apply appropriate criteria or rubrics for evaluating a theatrical experience.** *Derivation of Meaning from Works of Theatre* 4.2 Compare the content or message in two different works of theatre.	Students analyze, assess, and derive meaning from works of art, including their own, according to the elements of art, the principles of design, and aesthetic qualities. *Derive Meaning* 4.1 Compare and contrast selected works of art and describe them, using appropriate vocabulary of art. *Make Informed Judgments* 4.2 Identify successful and less successful compositional and expressive qualities of their own works of art and describe what might be done to improve them. 4.3 Select an artist's work and, using appropriate vocabulary of art, explain its successful compositional and communicative qualities.

Grade Three Content Standards

Component Strand: 5.0 Connections, Relationships, Applications

Dance	Music	Theatre	Visual Arts
Connecting and Applying What Is Learned in Dance to Learning in Other Art Forms and Subject Areas and to Careers	Connecting and Applying What Is Learned in Music to Learning in Other Art Forms and Subject Areas and to Careers	Connecting and Applying What Is Learned in Theatre, Film/Video, and Electronic Media to Other Art Forms and Subject Areas and to Careers	Connecting and Applying What Is Learned in the Visual Arts to Other Art Forms and Subject Areas and to Careers

Dance

Students apply what they learn in dance to learning across subject areas. They develop competencies and creative skills in problem solving, communication, and management of time and resources that contribute to lifelong learning and career skills. They also learn about careers in and related to dance.

Connections and Applications Across Disciplines

5.1 Explain relationships between dance elements and other subjects (e.g., spatial pathways—maps and grids; geometric shapes—body shapes).

5.2 Describe how dancing develops physical and mental well-being (e.g., control, flexibility, posture, strength, risk taking).

Development of Life Skills and Career Competencies

5.3 Explain how the time management, problem solving, and self-discipline skills required for composing a dance apply to other school activities.

5.4 Give examples of ways in which the activities of professionals in the performing arts are similar to each other (e.g., observing discipline, practicing skills, rehearsing performances).

Music

Students apply what they learn in music across subject areas. They develop competencies and creative skills in problem solving, communication, and management of time and resources that contribute to lifelong learning and career skills. They also learn about careers in and related to music.

Connections and Applications

5.1 Identify the use of similar elements in music and other art forms (e.g., form, pattern, rhythm).

Careers and Career-Related Skills

5.2 Identify what musicians and composers do to create music.

Theatre

Students apply what they learn in theatre, film/video, and electronic media across subject areas. They develop competencies and creative skills in problem solving, communication, and time management that contribute to lifelong learning and career skills. They also learn about careers in and related to theatre.

Connections and Applications

5.1 Use problem-solving and cooperative skills to dramatize a story or a current event from another content area, with emphasis on the five Ws.

Careers and Career-Related Skills

5.2 Develop problem-solving and communication skills by participating collaboratively in theatrical experiences.

Visual Arts

Students apply what they learn in the visual arts across subject areas. They develop competencies and creative skills in problem solving, communication, and management of time and resources that contribute to lifelong learning and career skills. They also learn about careers in and related to the visual arts.

Connections and Applications

5.1 Describe how costumes contribute to the meaning of a dance.

5.2 Write a poem or story inspired by their own works of art.

Visual Literacy

5.3 Look at images in figurative works of art and predict what might happen next, telling what clues in the work support their ideas.

Careers and Career-Related Skills

5.4 Describe how artists (e.g., architects, book illustrators, muralists, industrial designers) have affected people's lives.

Indicates a key content standard for the grade level. See page 23 for information on key content standards.

Grade Four

Excitement rises when fourth-grade students recognize the artist within them and the importance of the arts in learning. In their study of California history, they learn that the arts can help them discover the rich cultural heritage of their state as reflected in dance, music, theatre, and the visual arts. Building on previous experiences, they discover their own ability to communicate through the arts and can use music notation, knowledge of structure and style, and advanced technical skill to create works of art. At this age they understand that the arts are more than lines, spaces, colors, movements, or notes on a page. Rather, these elements can be combined to create meaning.

Dance

Students demonstrate concentration and physical control, improvising longer and more technical movement phrases as they learn the foundation of choreography. They describe music and dance from various countries and the relationship of the dance forms to their geographic location, thereby increasing their perceptual and aesthetic valuing skills. In their descriptions and discussions, they use dance vocabulary and apply specific criteria in their evaluations. By experiencing the choreographic process, they can talk about how it is related to the creative writing process.

Music

Students not only sing and play melodies and accompaniments in various forms and from many cultures but also compose melodic patterns, a precursor to writing music. They also employ their expanding vocabulary of music and classify a variety of instruments by how they produce sound. By learning more about music from around the world, they can recognize the influence of various cultures on music. They also evaluate how practice and rehearsal improve their performance.

Theatre

Students increase their theatre vocabulary as they improve their acting skills by exploring how voice affects meaning and how costumes and makeup communicate information about character. They also describe how an audience is affected differently by live theatre, movies, television, and radio. In designing costumes, props, makeup, or masks,

57

Chapter 3
Visual and
Performing Arts
Content
Standards

Grade Four

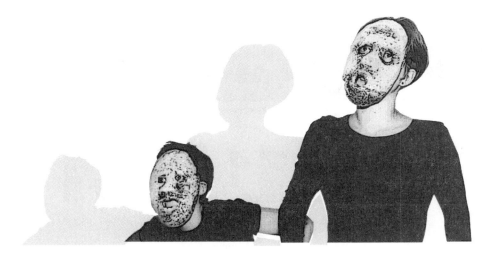

students learn how to apply color, perspective, composition, and other visual art elements and principles. They also learn that storytelling and theatrical traditions from many cultures are a part of the history of California and that the entertainment industry has an important role in the state.

Visual Arts

Students use their knowledge of proportion and measurement learned in mathematics when they create a portrait. Measuring from the top of the head to under the chin, they find that the eyes are halfway between. Another thing learned is that blank space in a painting (negative space) is just as important to what is being expressed as are the objects in the painting (positive space). And by learning the concept of point of view, students can describe how a person's own cultural point of view may influence that person's responses to a work of art. Connecting the visual arts and California history, they can discuss the content of artworks created by artists from various cultures.

Key Content Standards
Grade Four

Dance	Music	Theatre	Visual Arts

Dance

1.1 *(Artistic Perception)* Demonstrate mental concentration and physical control in performing dance skills.

2.2 *(Creative Expression)* Improvise extended movement phrases.

3.2 *(Historical and Cultural Context)* Name the musical accompaniment and explain how it relates to the dances they have studied.

5.4 *(Connections, Relationships, Applications)* Analyze the choreographic process and its relation to the writing process (e.g., brainstorming, exploring and developing ideas, putting ideas into a form, sequencing).

Music

1.1 *(Artistic Perception)* Read, write, and perform melodic notation for simple songs in major keys, using solfège.

2.1 *(Creative Expression)* Sing a varied repertoire of music from diverse cultures, including rounds, descants, and songs with ostinatos, alone and with others.

2.2 *(Creative Expression)* Use classroom instruments to play melodies and accompaniments from a varied repertoire of music from diverse cultures, including rounds, descants, and ostinatos, by oneself and with others.

2.3 *(Creative Expression)* Compose and improvise simple rhythmic and melodic patterns on classroom instruments.

Theatre

2.3 *(Creative Expression)* Design or create costumes, props, makeup, or masks to communicate a character in formal or informal performances.

3.1 *(Historical and Cultural Context)* Identify theatrical or storytelling traditions in the cultures of ethnic groups throughout the history of California.

4.2 *(Aesthetic Valuing)* Compare and contrast the impact on the audience of theatre, film, television, radio, and other media.

Visual Arts

2.5 *(Creative Expression)* Use accurate proportions to create an expressive portrait or a figure drawing or painting.

2.6 *(Creative Expression)* Use the interaction between positive and negative space expressively in a work of art.

3.2 *(Historical and Cultural Context)* Identify and discuss the content of works of art in the past and present, focusing on the different cultures that have contributed to California's history and art heritage.

4.2 *(Aesthetic Valuing)* Identify and describe how a person's own cultural context influences individual responses to works of art.

Grade Four Content Standards

Component Strand: *1.0 Artistic Perception*

Dance Processing, Analyzing, and Responding to Sensory Information Through the Language and Skills Unique to Dance	**Music** Processing, Analyzing, and Responding to Sensory Information Through the Language and Skills Unique to Music	**Theatre** Processing, Analyzing, and Responding to Sensory Information Through the Language and Skills Unique to Theatre	**Visual Arts** Processing, Analyzing, and Responding to Sensory Information Through the Language and Skills Unique to the Visual Arts

Dance

Students perceive and respond, using the elements of dance. They demonstrate movement skills, process sensory information, and describe movement, using the vocabulary of dance.

Development of Motor Skills and Technical Expertise

1.1 **Demonstrate mental concentration and physical control in performing dance skills.**

1.2 Demonstrate the ability to use smoother transitions when connecting one movement phrase to another.

Comprehension and Analysis of Dance Elements

1.3 Demonstrate increased range and use of space, time, and force/energy concepts (e.g., pulse/accents, melt/collapse, weak/strong).

1.4 Explain the principles of variety, contrast, and unity and apply to a dance sequence.

Development of Dance Vocabulary

1.5 Describe a specific movement, using appropriate dance vocabulary.

1.6 Identify, define, and use *phrasing* in dances learned or observed.

Music

Students read, notate, listen to, analyze, and describe music and other aural information, using the terminology of music.

Read and Notate Music

1.1 **Read, write, and perform melodic notation for simple songs in major keys, using solfège.**

1.2 Read, write, and perform diatonic scales.

1.3 Read, write, and perform rhythmic notation, including sixteenth notes, dotted notes, and syncopation (e.g., eighth/quarter/eighth note and eighth-rest/quarter/eighth note).

Listen to, Analyze, and Describe Music

1.4 Describe music according to its elements, using the terminology of music.

1.5 Classify how a variety of instruments from diverse cultures produce sound (e.g., idiophone, aerophone, chordaphone, membranophone).

1.6 Recognize and describe aural examples of musical forms, including rondo.

Theatre

Students observe their environment and respond, using the elements of theatre. They also observe formal and informal works of theatre, film/video, and electronic media and respond, using the vocabulary of theatre.

Development of the Vocabulary of Theatre

1.1 Use the vocabulary of theatre, such as *plot, conflict, climax, resolution, tone, objectives, motivation,* and *stock characters*, to describe theatrical experiences.

Comprehension and Analysis of the Elements of Theatre

1.2 Identify a character's objectives and motivations to explain that character's behavior.

1.3 Demonstrate how voice (diction, pace, and volume) may be used to explore multiple possibilities for a live reading. *Examples:* "*I* want you to go." "I want *you* to go." "I want you to *go.*"

Visual Arts

Students perceive and respond to works of art, objects in nature, events, and the environment. They also use the vocabulary of the visual arts to express their observations.

Develop Visual Arts Vocabulary

1.1 Perceive and describe contrast and emphasis in works of art and in the environment.

1.2 Describe how negative shapes/forms and positive shapes/forms are used in a chosen work of art.

1.3 Identify pairs of complementary colors (yellow/violet; red/green; orange/blue) and discuss how artists use them to communicate an idea or mood.

1.4 Describe the concept of proportion (in face, figure) as used in works of art.

Analyze Art Elements and Principles of Design

1.5 Describe and analyze the elements of art (color, shape/form, line, texture, space, value), emphasizing form, as they are used in works of art and found in the environment.

Grade Four Content Standards

Component Strand: 2.0 *Creative Expression*

Dance Creating, Performing, and Participating in Dance	**Music** Creating, Performing, and Participating in Music	**Theatre** Creating, Performing, and Participating in Theatre	**Visual Arts** Creating, Performing, and Participating in the Visual Arts
Students apply choreographic principles, processes, and skills to create and communicate meaning through the improvisation, composition, and performance of dance. *Creation/Invention of Dance Movements* 2.1 Create, develop, and memorize set movement patterns and sequences. **2.2 Improvise extended movement phrases.** *Application of Choreographic Principles and Processes to Creating Dance* 2.3 Describe, discuss, and analyze the process used by choreographers to create a dance. 2.4 Create a dance study that has a beginning, a middle, and an end. Review, revise, and refine. *Communication of Meaning in Dance* 2.5 Convey a range of feelings through shape/postures and movements when performing for peers. 2.6 Perform improvised movement and dance studies with focus and expression. *Development of Partner and Group Skills* 2.7 Demonstrate additional partner and group skills (e.g., imitating, leading/following, mirroring, calling/responding, echoing).	Students apply vocal and instrumental musical skills in performing a varied repertoire of music. They compose and arrange music and improvise melodies, variations, and accompaniments, using digital/electronic technology when appropriate. *Apply Vocal and Instrumental Skills* **2.1 Sing a varied repertoire of music from diverse cultures, including rounds, descants, and songs with ostinatos, alone and with others.** **2.2 Use classroom instruments to play melodies and accompaniments from a varied repertoire of music from diverse cultures, including rounds, descants, and ostinatos, by oneself and with others.** *Compose, Arrange, and Improvise* **2.3 Compose and improvise simple rhythmic and melodic patterns on classroom instruments.**	Students apply processes and skills in acting, directing, designing, and scriptwriting to create formal and informal theatre, film/videos, and electronic media productions and to perform in them. *Development of Theatrical Skills* 2.1 Demonstrate the emotional traits of a character through gesture and action. *Creation/Invention in Theatre* 2.2 Retell or improvise stories from classroom literature in a variety of tones (gossipy, sorrowful, comic, frightened, joyful, sarcastic). **2.3 Design or create costumes, props, makeup, or masks to communicate a character in formal or informal performances.**	Students apply artistic processes and skills, using a variety of media to communicate meaning and intent in original works of art. *Skills, Processes, Materials, and Tools* 2.1 Use shading (value) to transform a two-dimensional shape into what appears to be a three-dimensional form (e.g., circle to sphere). 2.2 Use the conventions of facial and figure proportions in a figure study. 2.3 Use additive and subtractive processes in making simple sculptural forms. 2.4 Use fibers or other materials to create a simple weaving. *Communication and Expression Through Original Works of Art* **2.5 Use accurate proportions to create an expressive portrait or a figure drawing or painting.** **2.6 Use the interaction between positive and negative space expressively in a work of art.** 2.7 Use contrast (light and dark) expressively in an original work of art. 2.8 Use complementary colors in an original composition to show contrast and emphasis.

🔑 Indicates a key content standard for the grade level. See page 23 for information on key content standards.

Grade Four Content Standards
Component Strand: *3.0 Historical and Cultural Context*

Dance Understanding the Historical Contributions and Cultural Dimensions of Dance	**Music** Understanding the Historical Contributions and Cultural Dimensions of Music	**Theatre** Understanding the Historical Contributions and Cultural Dimensions of Theatre	**Visual Arts** Understanding the Historical Contributions and Cultural Dimensions of the Visual Arts
Students analyze the function and development of dance in past and present cultures throughout the world, noting human diversity as it relates to dance and dancers.	Students analyze the role of music in past and present cultures throughout the world, noting cultural diversity as it relates to music, musicians, and composers.	Students analyze the role and development of theatre, film/video, and electronic media in past and present cultures throughout the world, noting diversity as it relates to theatre.	Students analyze the role and development of the visual arts in past and present cultures throughout the world, noting human diversity as it relates to the visual arts and artists.

Dance

Development of Dance

3.1 Perform and identify dances from various countries with different arrangements of dancers (e.g., lines, circles, couples).

3.2 Name the musical accompaniment and explain how it relates to the dances they have studied.

History and Function of Dance

3.3 Perform and describe dances that reflect the geographical place in which the dances are performed (e.g., deserts, rain forests, islands).

Diversity of Dance

3.4 Perform and identify folk/traditional and social dances from California history.

Music

Role of Music

3.1 Explain the relationship between music and events in history.

Diversity of Music

3.2 Identify music from diverse cultures and time periods.

3.3 Sing and play music from diverse cultures and time periods.

3.4 Compare musical styles from two or more cultures.

3.5 Recognize the influence of various cultures on music in California.

Theatre

Role and Cultural Significance of Theatre

3.1 Identify theatrical or storytelling traditions in the cultures of ethnic groups throughout the history of California.

History of Theatre

3.2 Recognize key developments in the entertainment industry in California, such as the introduction of silent movies, animation, radio and television broadcasting, and interactive video.

Visual Arts

Role and Development of the Visual Arts

3.1 Describe how art plays a role in reflecting life (e.g., in photography, quilts, architecture).

Diversity of the Visual Arts

3.2 Identify and discuss the content of works of art in the past and present, focusing on the different cultures that have contributed to California's history and art heritage.

3.3 Research and describe the influence of religious groups on art and architecture, focusing primarily on buildings in California both past and present.

Indicates a key content standard for the grade level. See page 23 for information on key content standards.

Grade Four Content Standards

Component Strand: *4.0 Aesthetic Valuing*

Dance Responding to, Analyzing, and Making Judgments About Works of Dance	**Music** Responding to, Analyzing, and Making Judgments About Works of Music	**Theatre** Responding to, Analyzing, and Critiquing Theatrical Experiences	**Visual Arts** Responding to, Analyzing, and Making Judgments About Works in the Visual Arts
Students critically assess and derive meaning from works of dance, performance of dancers, and original works based on the elements of dance and aesthetic qualities.	Students critically assess and derive meaning from works of music and the performance of musicians according to the elements of music, aesthetic qualities, and human responses.	Students critique and derive meaning from works of theatre, film/video, electronic media, and theatrical artists on the basis of aesthetic qualities.	Students analyze, assess, and derive meaning from works of art, including their own, according to the elements of art, the principles of design, and aesthetic qualities.

Dance

Description, Analysis, and Criticism of Dance

4.1 Use dance vocabulary to describe unique characteristics of dances they have watched or performed from countries studied in the history—social science curriculum (e.g., rhythms, spatial patterns, gestures, intent).

4.2 Name and use specific criteria in assessing personal and professional dance choreography (e.g., contrast, phrasing, unity).

Meaning and Impact of Dance

4.3 Describe ways in which a dancer effectively communicates ideas and moods (strong technique, projection, and expression).

4.4 List the expectations the audience has for a performer and vice versa.

Music

Analyze and Critically Assess

4.1 Use specific criteria when judging the relative quality of musical performances.

Derive Meaning

4.2 Describe the characteristics that make a performance a work of art.

Theatre

Critical Assessment of Theatre

4.1 Develop and apply appropriate criteria or rubrics for critiquing performances as to characterization, diction, pacing, gesture, and movement.

4.2 Compare and contrast the impact on the audience of theatre, film, television, radio, and other media.

Derivation of Meaning from Works of Theatre

4.3 Describe students' responses to a work of theatre and explain what the scriptwriter did to elicit those responses.

Visual Arts

Derive Meaning

4.1 Describe how using the language of the visual arts helps to clarify personal responses to works of art.

4.2 Identify and describe how a person's own cultural context influences individual responses to works of art.

4.3 Discuss how the subject and selection of media relate to the meaning or purpose of a work of art.

Make Informed Judgments

4.4 Identify and describe how various cultures define and value art differently.

4.5 Describe how the individual experiences of an artist may influence the development of specific works of art.

Indicates a key content standard for the grade level. See page 23 for information on key content standards.

Grade Four Content Standards

Component Strand: 5.0 Connections, Relationships, Applications

Dance	Music	Theatre	Visual Arts
Connecting and Applying What Is Learned in Dance to Learning in Other Art Forms and Subject Areas and to Careers	Connecting and Applying What Is Learned in Music to Learning in Other Art Forms and Subject Areas and to Careers	Connecting and Applying What Is Learned in Theatre, Film/Video, and Electronic Media to Other Art Forms and Subject Areas and to Careers	Connecting and Applying What Is Learned in the Visual Arts to Other Art Forms and Subject Areas and to Careers

Students apply what they learn in dance to learning across subject areas. They develop competencies and creative skills in problem solving, communication, and management of time and resources that contribute to lifelong learning and career skills. They also learn about careers in and related to dance.

Connections and Applications Across Disciplines

5.1 Explain how dance practice relates to and uses the vocabulary of other art subjects (e.g., positive and negative space, shape, line, rhythm, character).

5.2 Describe how dancing develops strength, flexibility, and endurance in accordance with physical education standards.

5.3 Demonstrate a recognition of personal space and respect for the personal space of others.

Development of Life Skills and Career Competencies

5.4 Analyze the choreographic process and its relation to the writing process (e.g., brainstorming, exploring and developing ideas, putting ideas into a form, sequencing).

Students apply what they learn in music across subject areas. They develop competencies and creative skills in problem solving, communication, and management of time and resources that contribute to lifelong learning and career skills. They also learn about careers in and related to music.

Connections and Applications

5.1 Identify and interpret expressive characteristics in works of art and music.

5.2 Integrate several art disciplines (dance, music, theatre, or the visual arts) into a well-organized presentation or performance.

5.3 Relate dance movements to express musical elements or represent musical intent in specific music.

Careers and Career-Related Skills

5.4 Evaluate improvement in personal musical performances after practice or rehearsal.

Students apply what they learn in theatre, film/video, and electronic media across subject areas. They develop competencies and creative skills in problem solving, communication, and time management that contribute to lifelong learning and career skills. They also learn about careers in and related to theatre.

Connections and Applications

5.1 Dramatize events in California history.

5.2 Use improvisation and dramatization to explore concepts in other content areas.

Careers and Career-Related Skills

5.3 Exhibit team identity and commitment to purpose when participating in theatrical experiences.

Students apply what they learn in the visual arts across subject areas. They develop competencies and creative skills in problem solving, communication, and management of time and resources that contribute to lifelong learning and career skills. They also learn about careers in and related to the visual arts.

Connections and Applications

5.1 Select a nonobjective painting, work in small groups to interpret it through dance/movement, and then write a paragraph reporting on the arts experience.

5.2 Identify through research twentieth-century artists who have incorporated symmetry as part of their work and then create a work of art, using bilateral or radial symmetry.

Visual Literacy

5.3 Construct diagrams, maps, graphs, timelines, and illustrations to communicate ideas or tell a story about a historical event.

Careers and Career-Related Skills

5.4 Read biographies and stories about artists and summarize the readings in short reports, telling how the artists mirrored or affected their time period or culture.

Indicates a key content standard for the grade level. See page 23 for information on key content standards.

Grade Five

Fifth-grade students bring to the classroom a strong sense of what they like and dislike and can tell why they hold their opinions. At this age they are growing in ability to talk about, describe, and evaluate the arts, using specific criteria, and understand and work with complex concepts in the arts. Inventing new possibilities for dance sequences, composing music, developing plots in theatre, and using perspective in the visual arts are all within their grasp.

With this new level of sophistication, students can explore the rich history of the arts in this country, working to gain a deep understanding of the vast array of artists and works of art this nation has to offer. Having dance, music, theatre, and the visual arts in the classroom can provide students with a broad background in the arts and with experiences to support learning throughout the curriculum. Using their increased knowledge and skills, students can now improvise, create, and perform in all the arts.

Dance

Students use variety, contrast, and unity as they create, learn, and perform dances, applying their knowledge of dance and performance skills to analyze possible solutions and strategies for specific problems with movement. In their study of United States history, they learn to perform traditional, social, and theatrical dances from the eighteenth and nineteenth centuries. They also develop and apply specific criteria for critiquing dance performances that show more in-depth analysis and assessment of technical skill, musicality, dynamics, and mood.

Chapter 3
Visual and
Performing Arts
Content
Standards

Grade Five

Music

Students analyze how different elements are used in music of various styles and from many cultures as they increase their musical skills by singing and playing instruments. They also learn to create simple melodies and read and write those melodies on the treble clef. And because of their increased knowledge of musical elements and vocabulary, they develop and apply appropriate criteria to support their opinions about specific musical selections.

Theatre

Students describe theatrical experiences with an increased vocabulary, using such terms as *protagonist* and *antagonist*. They identify more complex structural elements of plot in a script, discover universal themes in the theatrical literature they are studying, and recognize more fully how theatre, television, and films play a part in their daily lives. Using appropriate criteria for critiquing theatrical performances, they can judge what they see and hear.

Visual Arts

Principles of design, such as composition, emphasis, unity, and the depiction of space, become part of the visual arts vocabulary and are applied as students create original works of art with traditional and new media. Students refine their artistic skills, such as perspective, and use those skills in drawings, sculpture, mixed media, and digital media (e.g., computer-generated art, digital photography, and videography). Using a defined set of criteria to describe how they would change or improve their work, they become more proficient in assessing their artwork.

Key Content Standards
Grade Five

Dance	Music	Theatre	Visual Arts

Dance

1.4 *(Artistic Perception)* Incorporate the principles of variety, contrast, and unity with dance studies.

2.2 *(Creative Expression)* Invent multiple possibilities to solve a given movement problem and analyze problem-solving strategies and solutions.

3.2 *(Historical and Cultural Context)* Identify and perform folk/traditional, social, and theatrical dances done by Americans in the eighteenth and nineteenth centuries.

4.2 *(Aesthetic Valuing)* Apply specific criteria to analyze and assess the quality of a dance performance by well-known dancers or dance companies (e.g., technical skill, musicality, dynamics, mood).

5.1 *(Connections, Relationships, Applications)* Describe how historical events relate to dance forms (e.g., the rebellion of the 1960s was represented in popular social dances with a move from partners to individual expression).

Music

1.1 *(Artistic Perception)* Read, write, and perform simple melodic notation in treble clef in major and minor keys.

1.4 *(Artistic Perception)* Analyze the use of music elements in aural examples from various genres and cultures.

2.3 *(Creative Expression)* Compose, improvise, and perform basic rhythmic, melodic, and chordal patterns independently on classroom instruments.

4.2 *(Aesthetic Valuing)* Develop and apply appropriate criteria to support personal preferences for specific musical works.

Theatre

1.1 *(Artistic Perception)* Use the vocabulary of theatre, such as *sense memory, script, cue, monologue, dialogue, protagonist,* and *antagonist,* to describe theatrical experiences.

2.1 *(Creative Expression)* Participate in improvisational activities to explore complex ideas and universal themes in literature and life.

3.3 *(Historical and Cultural Context)* Analyze ways in which theatre, television, and film play a part in our daily lives.

4.1 *(Aesthetic Valuing)* Develop and apply appropriate criteria for critiquing the work of actors, directors, writers, and technical artists in theatre, film, and video.

Visual Arts

1.1 *(Artistic Perception)* Identify and describe the principles of design in visual compositions, emphasizing unity and harmony.

2.3 *(Creative Expression)* Demonstrate beginning skill in the manipulation of digital imagery (e.g., computer-generated art, digital photography, or videography).

2.6 *(Creative Expression)* Use perspective in an original work of art to create a real or imaginary scene.

3.3 *(Historical and Cultural Context)* Identify and compare works of art from various regions of the United States.

4.4 *(Aesthetic Valuing)* Assess their own works of art, using specific criteria, and describe what changes they would make for improvement.

Grade Five Content Standards

Component Strand: *1.0 Artistic Perception*

Dance Processing, Analyzing, and Responding to Sensory Information Through the Language and Skills Unique to Dance	**Music** Processing, Analyzing, and Responding to Sensory Information Through the Language and Skills Unique to Music	**Theatre** Processing, Analyzing, and Responding to Sensory Information Through the Language and Skills Unique to Theatre	**Visual Arts** Processing, Analyzing, and Responding to Sensory Information Through the Language and Skills Unique to the Visual Arts

Dance

Students perceive and respond, using the elements of dance. They demonstrate movement skills, process sensory information, and describe movement, using the vocabulary of dance.

Development of Motor Skills and Technical Expertise

1.1 Demonstrate focus, physical control (e.g., proper alignment, balance), and coordination in performing locomotor and axial movement.

1.2 Name and use a wide variety of movements (e.g., isolations/whole body).

Comprehension and Analysis of Dance Elements

1.3 Demonstrate a greater dynamic range in movement utilizing space, time, and force/energy concepts.

1.4 **Incorporate the principles of variety, contrast, and unity with dance studies.**

Development of Dance Vocabulary

1.5 Use appropriate dance vocabulary to describe dances.

Music

Students read, notate, listen to, analyze, and describe music and other aural information, using the terminology of music.

Read and Notate Music

1.1 **Read, write, and perform simple melodic notation in treble clef in major and minor keys.**

1.2 Read, write, and perform major and minor scales.

1.3 Read, write, and perform rhythmic notation, including quarter note triplets and tied syncopation.

Listen to, Analyze, and Describe Music

1.4 **Analyze the use of music elements in aural examples from various genres and cultures.**

1.5 Identify vocal and instrumental ensembles from a variety of genres and cultures.

1.6 Identify and describe music forms, including theme and variations and twelve-bar blues.

Theatre

Students observe their environment and respond, using the elements of theatre. They also observe formal and informal works of theatre, film/video, and electronic media and respond, using the vocabulary of theatre.

Development of the Vocabulary of Theatre

1.1 **Use the vocabulary of theatre, such as *sense memory, script, cue, monologue, dialogue, protagonist,* and *antagonist,* to describe theatrical experiences.**

Comprehension and Analysis of the Elements of Theatre

1.2 Identify the structural elements of plot (exposition, complication, crisis, climax, and resolution) in a script or theatrical experience.

Visual Arts

Students perceive and respond to works of art, objects in nature, events, and the environment. They also use the vocabulary of the visual arts to express their observations.

Develop Perceptual Skills and Visual Arts Vocabulary

1.1 **Identify and describe the principles of design in visual compositions, emphasizing unity and harmony.**

1.2 Identify and describe characteristics of representational, abstract, and nonrepresentational works of art.

Analyze Art Elements and Principles of Design

1.3 Use their knowledge of all the elements of art to describe similarities and differences in works of art and in the environment.

Indicates a key content standard for the grade level. See page 23 for information on key content standards.

Grade Five Content Standards

Component Strand: 2.0 Creative Expression

Dance Creating, Performing, and Participating in Dance	Music Creating, Performing, and Participating in Music	Theatre Creating, Performing, and Participating in Theatre	Visual Arts Creating, Performing, and Participating in the Visual Arts
Students apply choreographic principles, processes, and skills to create and communicate meaning through the improvisation, composition, and performance of dance. *Creation/Invention of Dance Movement* 2.1 Create, memorize, and perform complex sequences of movement with greater focus, force/energy, and intent. **2.2 Invent multiple possibilities to solve a given movement problem and analyze problem-solving strategies and solutions.** *Application of Choreographic Principles and Processes to Creating Dance* 2.3 Describe and incorporate simple dance forms in dance studies (e.g., AB form, canon). 2.4 Demonstrate principles of opposing weight and force/energy, balance and counterbalance, or cantilever. *Communication of Meaning in Dance* 2.5 Convey a wide range of feeling and expression through gestures, posture, and movement. *Development of Partner and Group Skills* 2.6 Demonstrate cooperation, collaboration, and empathy in working with partners and in groups (e.g., leading/ following, mirroring, calling/responding, echoing, opposing).	Students apply vocal and instrumental musical skills in performing a varied repertoire of music. They compose and arrange music and improvise melodies, variations, and accompaniments, using digital/ electronic technology when appropriate. *Apply Vocal and Instrumental Skills* 2.1 Sing a varied repertoire of music, including rounds, descants, and songs with ostinatos and songs in two-part harmony, by oneself and with others. 2.2 Use classroom instruments to play melodies and accompaniments from a varied repertoire of music from diverse cultures, including rounds, descants, and ostinatos and two-part harmony, by oneself and with others. *Compose, Arrange, and Improvise* **2.3 Compose, improvise, and perform basic rhythmic, melodic, and chordal patterns independently on classroom instruments.**	Students apply processes and skills in acting, directing, designing, and scriptwriting to create formal and informal theatre, film/videos, and electronic media productions and to perform in them. *Development of Theatrical Skills* **2.1 Participate in improvisational activities to explore complex ideas and universal themes in literature and life.** 2.2 Demonstrate the use of blocking (stage areas, levels, and actor's position, such as full front, quarter, profile, and full back) in dramatizations. *Creation/Invention in Theatre* 2.3 Collaborate as an actor, director, scriptwriter, or technical artist in creating formal or informal theatrical performances.	Students apply artistic processes and skills, using a variety of media to communicate meaning and intent in original works of art. *Skills, Processes, Materials, and Tools* 2.1 Use one-point perspective to create the illusion of space. 2.2 Create gesture and contour observational drawings. **2.3 Demonstrate beginning skill in the manipulation of digital imagery (e.g., computer-generated art, digital photography, or videography).** *Communication and Expression Through Original Works of Art* 2.4 Create an expressive abstract composition based on real objects. 2.5 Assemble a found object sculpture (as assemblage) or a mixed media two-dimensional composition that reflects unity and harmony and communicates a theme. **2.6 Use perspective in an original work of art to create a real or imaginary scene.** 2.7 Communicate values, opinions, or personal insights through an original work of art.

Indicates a key content standard for the grade level. See page 23 for information on key content standards.

Grade Five Content Standards

Component Strand: *3.0 Historical and Cultural Context*

Dance Understanding the Historical Contributions and Cultural Dimensions of Dance	Music Understanding the Historical Contributions and Cultural Dimensions of Music	Theatre Understanding the Historical Contributions and Cultural Dimensions of Theatre	Visual Arts Understanding the Historical Contributions and Cultural Dimensions of the Visual Arts
Students analyze the function and development of dance in past and present cultures throughout the world, noting human diversity as it relates to dance and dancers.	Students analyze the role of music in past and present cultures throughout the world, noting cultural diversity as it relates to music, musicians, and composers.	Students analyze the role and development of theatre, film/video, and electronic media in past and present cultures throughout the world, noting diversity as it relates to theatre.	Students analyze the role and development of the visual arts in past and present cultures throughout the world, noting human diversity as it relates to the visual arts and artists.
Development of Dance 3.1 Describe how and why a traditional dance may be changed when performed on stage for an audience. *History and Function of Dance* **3.2 Identify and perform folk/traditional, social, and theatrical dances done by Americans in the eighteenth and nineteenth centuries.** *Diversity of Dance* 3.3 Select traditional dances that men, women, or children perform and explain the purpose(s) of the dances.	*Role of Music* 3.1 Describe the social functions of a variety of musical forms from various cultures and time periods (e.g., folk songs, dances). *Diversity of Music* 3.2 Identify different or similar uses of musical elements in music from diverse cultures. 3.3 Sing and play music from diverse cultures and time periods. 3.4 Describe the influence of various cultures and historical events on musical forms and styles. 3.5 Describe the influences of various cultures on the music of the United States.	*Role and Cultural Significance of Theatre* 3.1 Select or create appropriate props, sets, and costumes for a cultural celebration or pageant. 3.2 Interpret how theatre and storytelling forms (past and present) of various cultural groups may reflect their beliefs and traditions. *History of Theatre* **3.3 Analyze ways in which theatre, television, and film play a part in our daily lives.** 3.4 Identify types of early American theatre, such as melodrama and musical theatre.	*Role and Development of the Visual Arts* 3.1 Describe how local and national art galleries and museums contribute to the conservation of art. 3.2 Identify and describe various fine, traditional, and folk arts from historical periods worldwide. *Diversity of the Visual Arts* **3.3 Identify and compare works of art from various regions of the United States.** 3.4 View selected works of art from a major culture and observe changes in materials and styles over a period of time.

Indicates a key content standard for the grade level. See page 23 for information on key content standards.

Grade Five Content Standards

Component Strand: *4.0 Aesthetic Valuing*

Dance Responding to, Analyzing, and Making Judgments About Works of Dance	**Music** Responding to, Analyzing, and Making Judgments About Works of Music	**Theatre** Responding to, Analyzing, and Critiquing Theatrical Experiences	**Visual Arts** Responding to, Analyzing, and Making Judgments About Works in the Visual Arts
Students critically assess and derive meaning from works of dance, performance of dancers, and original works according to the elements of dance and aesthetic qualities.	Students critically assess and derive meaning from works of music and the performance of musicians according to the elements of music, aesthetic qualities, and human responses.	Students critique and derive meaning from works of theatre, film/video, electronic media, and theatrical artists on the basis of aesthetic qualities.	Students analyze, assess, and derive meaning from works of art, including their own, according to the elements of art, the principles of design, and aesthetic qualities.

Dance

Description, Analysis, and Criticism of Dance

4.1 Use dance vocabulary to identify and support personal preferences for dances observed or performed.

4.2 Apply specific criteria 👈 to analyze and assess the quality of a dance performance by well-known dancers or dance companies (e.g., technical skill, musicality, dynamics, mood).

Meaning and Impact of Dance

4.3 Identify the special and challenging characteristics of the experience of dancing for an audience.

4.4 Explain how outstanding dancers affect audience members emotionally or intellectually.

Music

Analyze and Critically Assess

4.1 Identify and analyze differences in tempo and dynamics in contrasting music selections.

Derive Meaning

4.2 Develop and apply 👈 appropriate criteria to support personal preferences for specific musical works.

Theatre

Critical Assessment of Theatre

4.1 Develop and apply 👈 appropriate criteria for critiquing the work of actors, directors, writers, and technical artists in theatre, film, and video.

Derivation of Meaning from Works of Theatre

4.2 Describe devices actors use to convey meaning or intent in commercials on television.

Visual Arts

Derive Meaning

4.1 Identify how selected principles of design are used in a work of art and how they affect personal responses to and evaluation of the work of art.

4.2 Compare the different purposes of a specific culture for creating art.

Make Informed Judgments

4.3 Develop and use specific criteria as individuals and in groups to assess works of art.

4.4 Assess their own 👈 works of art, using specific criteria, and describe what changes they would make for improvement.

👈 Indicates a key content standard for the grade level. See page 23 for information on key content standards.

Grade Five Content Standards

Component Strand: *5.0 Connections, Relationships, Applications*

Dance	Music	Theatre	Visual Arts
Connecting and Applying What Is Learned in Dance to Learning in Other Art Forms and Subject Areas and to Careers	Connecting and Applying What Is Learned in Music to Learning in Other Art Forms and Subject Areas and to Careers	Connecting and Applying What Is Learned in Theatre, Film/Video, and Electronic Media to Other Art Forms and Subject Areas and to Careers	Connecting and Applying What Is Learned in the Visual Arts to Other Art Forms and Subject Areas and to Careers

Dance

Students apply what they learn in dance to learning across subject areas. They develop competencies and creative skills in problem solving, communication, and management of time and resources that contribute to lifelong learning and career skills. They also learn about careers in and related to dance.

Connections and Applications Across Disciplines

5.1 Describe how histori-cal events relate to dance forms (e.g., the rebellion of the 1960s was represented in popular social dances with a move from partners to individual expression).

5.2 Describe how dancing requires good health-related habits (e.g., individual and group goals for flexibility, strength, endurance, stress management, nutrition).

5.3 Cite examples of the use of technology in the performing arts.

Development of Life Skills and Career Competencies

5.4 Demonstrate social skills that enable students to become leaders/teachers and followers/learners.

Music

Students apply what they learn in music across subject areas. They develop competencies and creative skills in problem solving, communication, and management of time and resources that contribute to lifelong learning and career skills. They also learn about careers in and related to music.

Connections and Applications

5.1 Explain the role of music in community events.

Careers and Career-Related Skills

5.2 Identify ways in which the music professions are similar to or different from one another.

Theatre

Students apply what they learn in theatre, film/video, and electronic media across subject areas. They develop competencies and creative skills in problem solving, communication, and time management that contribute to lifelong learning and career skills. They also learn about careers in and related to theatre.

Connections and Applications

5.1 Use theatrical skills to dramatize events and concepts from other curriculum areas, such as reenacting the signing of the Declaration of Independence in history—social science.

Careers and Career-Related Skills

5.2 Identify the roles and responsibilities of performing and technical artists in theatre, film, television, and electronic media.

Visual Arts

Students apply what they learn in the visual arts across subject areas. They develop competencies and creative skills in problem solving, communication, and management of time and resources that contribute to lifelong learning and career skills. They also learn about careers in and related to the visual arts.

Connections and Applications

5.1 Use linear perspective to depict geometric objects in space.

Visual Literacy

5.2 Identify and design icons, logos, and other graphic devices as symbols for ideas and information.

Careers and Career-Related Skills

5.3 Research and report on what various types of artists (e.g., architects, designers, graphic artists, animators) produce and how their works play a role in our everyday environment

---

Indicates a key content standard for the grade level. See page 23 for information on key content standards.

Grade Six

Sixth-grade students are beginning to find their way in a wider setting. Starting the process of defining their point of view through the arts, they are also bringing together basic concepts they have learned throughout elementary school, learning more rigorous skills and determining how to apply those skills. Further, they are learning to link particular art forms to the communication of meaning. Becoming more responsible for their aesthetic choices, they want to learn the skills needed to express their individuality effectively because they are constantly comparing themselves to others. They continue to acquire skills that improve their self-confidence and increase their arts vocabulary and begin to understand how culture and the arts interact. And they are learning to be responsible to themselves and their classmates through participation in creative groups and ensembles. Through the arts students achieve a balance leading to a healthy, creative transition to the increasingly complex academic life to come.

Students are enjoying a wealth of arts experiences as their focus shifts from self-contained elementary school classes. Some are instructed by arts specialists, such as the instrumental and vocal directors, who help students increase their ability to read, write, and perform music. In the interactive setting of a theatre class, students study, create, and perform literary works, thereby gaining additional connections with the language arts curriculum. In turn, dance instruction provides students with opportunities for increased expression through movement and spatial awareness, and in the visual arts students might create a project in the tradition of the civilizations they are studying in ancient history. Through all of these rich, interrelated arts studies, students discover a greater sense of self-confidence and a deeper knowledge of their place in history and society. And focused practice in applying the elements of the arts and thoughtful descriptions of their use in artwork help students in both creative expression and artistic valuing.

In all of the arts, students are developing ideas, moods, and themes in increasingly complex dance studies, musical performances, scenes and plays, and original works of visual art. Through their studies in history–social science and their performance and research in the arts, they are learning more about the role the arts have played in varied cultures and time periods. Across the curriculum in each of the arts, students are increasing their ability to apply appropriate criteria to evaluate artwork. Doing so helps them improve their own work and become more discriminating members of the audience and viewers of the arts.

Dance

Students apply variations of force and energy in their dance movements, demonstrating physical control and coordination as they perform different types of movement. Their dances show a variety of movements that use the principles of contrast and unity. At the same time students' movements and dances reveal deeper expressive intent and integrate the elements of dance in more complex ways.

Music

Students use standard music symbols for pitch, meter, and rhythm. They can improvise short, simple melodies and arrange favorite musical examples for different groups of voices or instruments. They are also able to relate why specific musical works of the past are considered exemplary and can explain how music can convey mental images, feelings, and emotions. As they perform, they are able to move beyond rote performances of musical selections and employ deeper emotional subtleties.

Theatre

Students use such terms as *vocal projection* and *subtext* as they describe their theatrical experiences. As they perform, they show effective vocal and facial expressions, gestures, and timing. In writing plays and short theatrical scenes, they include monologues and dialogues showing a range of character types from a variety of cultures. Now students can use and evaluate with more confidence the makeup, lighting, props, and costumes employed in theatre.

Visual Arts

Students analyze how balance is used in two- and three-dimensional works of art. Using artwork to express a mood, a feeling, or an idea, they demonstrate more complexity and technical skill in their drawings, paintings, and sculpture. Through the use of a variety of resources, they can research and discuss the visual arts throughout history. They are also able to recognize and use art as a metaphor for abstract ideas expressed in a variety of cultures and historical periods.

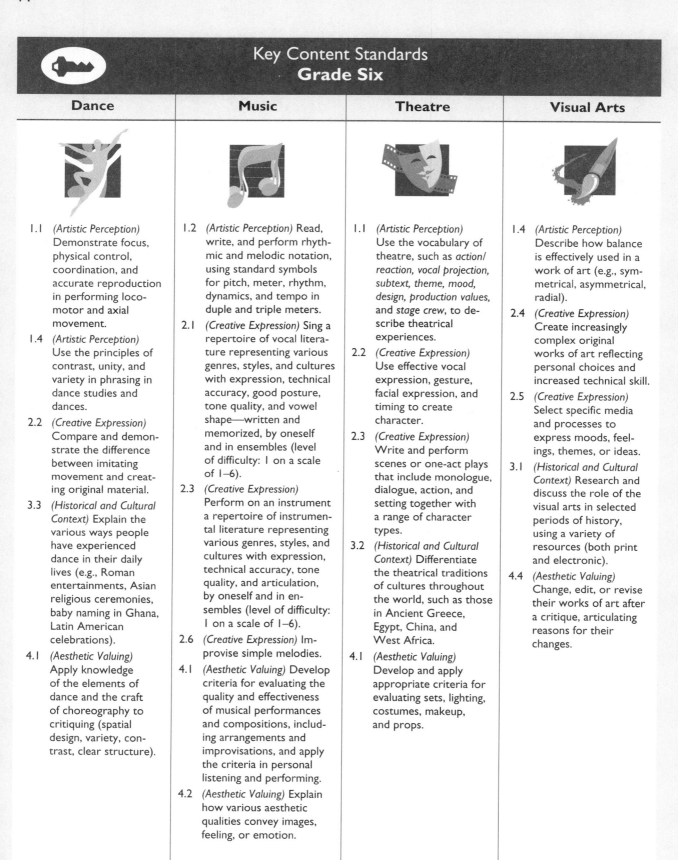

Key Content Standards
Grade Six

Dance	Music	Theatre	Visual Arts

Dance

1.1 *(Artistic Perception)* Demonstrate focus, physical control, coordination, and accurate reproduction in performing locomotor and axial movement.

1.4 *(Artistic Perception)* Use the principles of contrast, unity, and variety in phrasing in dance studies and dances.

2.2 *(Creative Expression)* Compare and demonstrate the difference between imitating movement and creating original material.

3.3 *(Historical and Cultural Context)* Explain the various ways people have experienced dance in their daily lives (e.g., Roman entertainments, Asian religious ceremonies, baby naming in Ghana, Latin American celebrations).

4.1 *(Aesthetic Valuing)* Apply knowledge of the elements of dance and the craft of choreography to critiquing (spatial design, variety, contrast, clear structure).

Music

1.2 *(Artistic Perception)* Read, write, and perform rhythmic and melodic notation, using standard symbols for pitch, meter, rhythm, dynamics, and tempo in duple and triple meters.

2.1 *(Creative Expression)* Sing a repertoire of vocal literature representing various genres, styles, and cultures with expression, technical accuracy, good posture, tone quality, and vowel shape—written and memorized, by oneself and in ensembles (level of difficulty: 1 on a scale of 1–6).

2.3 *(Creative Expression)* Perform on an instrument a repertoire of instrumental literature representing various genres, styles, and cultures with expression, technical accuracy, tone quality, and articulation, by oneself and in ensembles (level of difficulty: 1 on a scale of 1–6).

2.6 *(Creative Expression)* Improvise simple melodies.

4.1 *(Aesthetic Valuing)* Develop criteria for evaluating the quality and effectiveness of musical performances and compositions, including arrangements and improvisations, and apply the criteria in personal listening and performing.

4.2 *(Aesthetic Valuing)* Explain how various aesthetic qualities convey images, feeling, or emotion.

Theatre

1.1 *(Artistic Perception)* Use the vocabulary of theatre, such as *action/reaction, vocal projection, subtext, theme, mood, design, production values,* and *stage crew,* to describe theatrical experiences.

2.2 *(Creative Expression)* Use effective vocal expression, gesture, facial expression, and timing to create character.

2.3 *(Creative Expression)* Write and perform scenes or one-act plays that include monologue, dialogue, action, and setting together with a range of character types.

3.2 *(Historical and Cultural Context)* Differentiate the theatrical traditions of cultures throughout the world, such as those in Ancient Greece, Egypt, China, and West Africa.

4.1 *(Aesthetic Valuing)* Develop and apply appropriate criteria for evaluating sets, lighting, costumes, makeup, and props.

Visual Arts

1.4 *(Artistic Perception)* Describe how balance is effectively used in a work of art (e.g., symmetrical, asymmetrical, radial).

2.4 *(Creative Expression)* Create increasingly complex original works of art reflecting personal choices and increased technical skill.

2.5 *(Creative Expression)* Select specific media and processes to express moods, feelings, themes, or ideas.

3.1 *(Historical and Cultural Context)* Research and discuss the role of the visual arts in selected periods of history, using a variety of resources (both print and electronic).

4.4 *(Aesthetic Valuing)* Change, edit, or revise their works of art after a critique, articulating reasons for their changes.

Grade Six Content Standards

Component Strand: *1.0 Artistic Perception*

Dance Processing, Analyzing, and Responding to Sensory Information Through the Language and Skills Unique to Dance	**Music** Processing, Analyzing, and Responding to Sensory Information Through the Language and Skills Unique to Music	**Theatre** Processing, Analyzing, and Responding to Sensory Information Through the Language and Skills Unique to Theatre	**Visual Arts** Processing, Analyzing, and Responding to Sensory Information Through the Language and Skills Unique to the Visual Arts
Students perceive and respond, using the elements of dance. They demonstrate movement skills, process sensory information, and describe movement, using the vocabulary of dance.	Students read, notate, listen to, analyze, and describe music and other aural information, using the terminology of music.	Students observe their environment and respond, using the elements of theatre. They also observe formal and informal works of theatre, film/video, and electronic media and respond, using the vocabulary of theatre.	Students perceive and respond to works of art, objects in nature, events, and the environment. They also use the vocabulary of the visual arts to express their observations.
Development of Motor Skills and Technical Expertise 1.1 **Demonstrate focus, physical control, coordination, and accurate reproduction in performing locomotor and axial movement.** 1.2 Incorporate a variety of force/energy qualities into executing a full range of movements. *Comprehension and Analysis of Dance Elements* 1.3 Identify and use force/energy variations when executing gesture and locomotor and axial movements. 1.4 **Use the principles of contrast, unity, and variety in phrasing in dance studies and dances.** *Development of Dance Vocabulary* 1.5 Describe and analyze movements observed and performed, using appropriate dance vocabulary	*Read and Notate Music* 1.1 Read, write, and perform intervals and triads. 1.2 **Read, write, and perform rhythmic and melodic notation, using standard symbols for pitch, meter, rhythm, dynamics, and tempo in duple and triple meters.** 1.3 Transcribe simple aural examples into rhythmic notation. 1.4 Sight-read simple melodies in the treble clef or bass clef. *Listen to, Analyze, and Describe Music* 1.5 Analyze and compare the use of musical elements representing various genres and cultures, emphasizing meter and rhythm. 1.6 Describe larger music forms (sonata-allegro form, concerto, theme and variations).	Development of the Vocabulary of Theatre 1.1 **Use the vocabulary of theatre, such as action/reaction, vocal projection, subtext, theme, mood, design, production values, and stage crew, to describe theatrical experiences.** *Comprehension and Analysis of the Elements of Theatre* 1.2 Identify how production values can manipulate mood to persuade and disseminate propaganda.	*Develop Visual Arts Knowledge and Vocabulary* 1.1 Identify and describe *all* the elements of art found in selected works of art (color, shape/form, line, texture, space, value). 1.2 Discuss works of art as to theme, genre, style, idea, and differences in media. 1.3 Describe how artists can show the same theme by using different media and styles. *Analyze Art Elements and Principles of Design* 1.4 **Describe how balance is effectively used in a work of art (e.g., symmetrical, asymmetrical, radial).**

Indicates a key content standard for the grade level. See page 23 for information on key content standards.

Grade Six Content Standards

Component Strand: 2.0 Creative Expression

Dance Creating, Performing, and Participating in Dance	**Music** Creating, Performing, and Participating in Music	**Theatre** Creating, Performing, and Participating in Theatre	**Visual Arts** Creating, Performing, and Participating in the Visual Arts
Students apply choreographic principles, processes, and skills to create and communicate meaning through the improvisation, composition, and performance of dance.	Students apply vocal and instrumental musical skills in performing a varied repertoire of music. They compose and arrange music and improvise melodies, variations, and accompaniments, using digital/electronic technology when appropriate.	Students apply processes and skills in acting, directing, designing, and scriptwriting to create formal and informal theatre, film/videos, and electronic media productions and to perform in them.	Students apply artistic processes and skills, using a variety of media to communicate meaning and intent in original works of art.

Dance — continued

Creation/Invention of Dance Movements

2.1 Invent multiple possibilities to solve a given movement problem and develop the material into a short study.

2.2 Compare and demonstrate ☞ the difference between imitating movement and creating original material.

Application of Choreographic Principles and Processes to Creating Dance

2.3 Describe and incorporate dance forms in dance studies.

2.4 Demonstrate the ability to coordinate movement with different musical rhythms and styles (e.g., ABA form, canon).

2.5 Use the elements of dance to create short studies that demonstrate the development of ideas and thematic material.

Communication of Meaning in Dance Through Dance Performance

2.6 Demonstrate an awareness of the body as an instrument of expression when rehearsing and performing.

2.7 Revise, memorize, and rehearse dance studies for the purpose of performing for others.

Development of Partner and Group Skills

2.8 Demonstrate an ability to cooperate and collaborate with a wide range of partners and groups (e.g., imitating, leading/following, mirroring, calling/responding, echoing, sequence building).

Music — continued

Apply Vocal and Instrumental Skills

2.1 Sing a repertoire ☞ of vocal literature representing various genres, styles, and cultures with expression, technical accuracy, good posture, tone quality, and vowel shape—written and memorized, by oneself and in ensembles (level of difficulty: 1 on a scale of 1–6).

2.2 Sing music written in two parts.

2.3 Perform on an instru-☞ ment a repertoire of instrumental literature representing various genres, styles, and cultures with expression, technical accuracy, tone quality, and articulation, by oneself and in ensembles (level of difficulty: 1 on a scale of 1–6).

Compose, Arrange, and Improvise

2.4 Compose short pieces in duple and triple meters.

2.5 Arrange simple pieces for voices or instruments, using traditional sources of sound.

2.6 Improvise simple ☞ melodies.

Theatre — continued

Development of Theatrical Skills

2.1 Participate in improvisational activities, demonstrating an understanding of text, subtext, and context.

Creation/Invention in Theatre

2.2 Use effective ☞ vocal expression, gesture, facial expression, and timing to create character.

2.3 Write and ☞ perform scenes or one-act plays that include monologue, dialogue, action, and setting together with a range of character types.

Visual Arts — continued

Skills, Processes, Materials, and Tools

2.1 Use various observational drawing skills to depict a variety of subject matter.

2.2 Apply the rules of two-point perspective in creating a thematic work of art.

2.3 Create a drawing, using varying tints, shades, and intensities.

Communication and Expression Through Original Works of Art

2.4 Create increasingly ☞ complex original works of art reflecting personal choices and increased technical skill.

2.5 Select specific ☞ media and processes to express moods, feelings, themes, or ideas.

2.6 Use technology to create original works of art.

☞ Indicates a key content standard for the grade level. See page 23 for information on key content standards.

Grade Six Content Standards

Component Strand: 3.0 Historical and Cultural Context

Dance	Music	Theatre	Visual Arts
Understanding the Historical Contributions and Cultural Dimensions of Dance	Understanding the Historical Contributions and Cultural Dimensions of Music	Understanding the Historical Contributions and Cultural Dimensions of Theatre	Understanding the Historical Contributions and Cultural Dimensions of the Visual Arts

Students analyze the function and development of dance in past and present cultures throughout the world, noting human diversity as it relates to dance and dancers.

Development of Dance

3.1 Compare and contrast features of dances already performed from different countries.

History and Function of Dance

3.2 Explain the importance and function of dance in students' lives.

Diversity of Dance

3.3 Explain the various ways people have experienced dance in their daily lives (e.g., Roman entertainments, Asian religious ceremonies, baby naming in Ghana, Latin American celebrations).

Students analyze the role of music in past and present cultures throughout the world, noting cultural diversity as it relates to music, musicians, and composers.

Role of Music

3.1 Compare music from two or more cultures of the world as to the functions the music serves and the roles of musicians.

3.2 Listen to and describe the role of music in ancient civilizations (e.g., Chinese, Egyptian, Greek, Indian, Roman).

Diversity of Music

3.3 Describe distinguishing characteristics of representative musical genres and styles from two or more cultures.

3.4 Listen to, describe, and perform music of various styles from a variety of cultures.

3.5 Classify by style and genre a number of exemplary musical works and explain the characteristics that make each work exemplary.

Students analyze the role and development of theatre, film/ video, and electronic media in past and present cultures throughout the world, noting diversity as it relates to theatre.

Role and Cultural Significance of Theatre

3.1 Create scripts that reflect particular historical periods or cultures.

History of Theatre

3.2 Differentiate the theatrical traditions of cultures throughout the world, such as those in Ancient Greece, Egypt, China, and West Africa.

Students analyze the role and development of the visual arts in past and present cultures throughout the world, noting human diversity as it relates to the visual arts and artists.

Role and Development of the Visual Arts

3.1 Research and discuss the role of the visual arts in selected periods of history, using a variety of resources (both print and electronic).

3.2 View selected works of art from a culture and describe how they have changed or not changed in theme and content over a period of time.

Diversity of the Visual Arts

3.3 Compare, in oral or written form, representative images or designs from at least two selected cultures.

Indicates a key content standard for the grade level. See page 23 for information on key content standards.

Grade Six Content Standards

Component Strand: 4.0 Aesthetic Valuing

Dance Responding to, Analyzing, and Making Judgments About Works of Dance	**Music** Responding to, Analyzing, and Making Judgments About Works of Music	**Theatre** Responding to, Analyzing, and Critiquing Theatrical Experiences	**Visual Arts** Responding to, Analyzing, and Making Judgments About Works in the Visual Arts
Students critically assess and derive meaning from works of dance, performance of dancers, and original works based on the elements of dance and aesthetic qualities.	Students critically assess and derive meaning from works of music and the performance of musicians in a cultural context according to the elements of music, aesthetic qualities, and human responses.	Students critique and derive meaning from works of theatre, film/video, electronic media, and theatrical artists on the basis of aesthetic qualities.	Students analyze, assess, and derive meaning from works of art, including their own, according to the elements of art, the principles of design, and aesthetic qualities.
Description, Analysis, and Criticism of Dance	*Analyze and Critically Assess*	*Critical Assessment of Theatre*	*Derive Meaning*
4.1 Apply knowledge ⚷ **of the elements of dance and the craft of choreography to critiquing (spatial design, variety, contrast, clear structure).**	**4.1 Develop criteria for** ⚷ **evaluating the quality and effectiveness of musical performances and compositions, including arrangements and improvisations, and apply the criteria in personal listening and performing.**	**4.1 Develop and apply** ⚷ **appropriate criteria for evaluating sets, lighting, costumes, makeup, and props.**	4.1 Construct and describe plausible interpretations of what they perceive in works of art.
4.2 Propose ways to revise choreography according to established assessment criteria.		*Derivation of Meaning from Works of Theatre*	4.2 Identify and describe ways in which their culture is being reflected in current works of art.
Meaning and Impact of Dance	*Derive Meaning*	4.2 Identify examples of how theatre, television, and film can influence or be influenced by politics and culture.	*Make Informed Judgments*
4.3 Discuss the experience of performing personal work for others.	**4.2 Explain how various** ⚷ **aesthetic qualities convey images, feeling, or emotion.**		4.3 Develop specific criteria as individuals or in groups to assess and critique works of art.
4.4 Distinguish the differences between viewing live and recorded dance performances.	4.3 Identify aesthetic qualities in a specific musical work.		**4.4 Change, edit, or** ⚷ **revise their works of art after a critique, articulating reasons for their changes.**

Grade Six Content Standards

Component Strand: 5.0 Connections, Relationships, Applications

Dance	Music	Theatre	Visual Arts
Connecting and Applying What Is Learned in Dance to Learning in Other Art Forms and Subject Areas and to Careers	Connecting and Applying What Is Learned in Music to Learning in Other Art Forms and Subject Areas and to Careers	Connecting and Applying What Is Learned in Theatre, Film/Video, and Electronic Media to Other Art Forms and Subject Areas and to Careers	Connecting and Applying What Is Learned in the Visual Arts to Other Art Forms and Subject Areas and to Careers

Dance

Students apply what they learn in dance to learning across subject areas. They develop competencies and creative skills in problem solving, communication, and management of time and resources that contribute to lifelong learning and career skills. They also learn about careers in and related to dance.

Connections and Applications Across Disciplines

5.1 Describe how other arts disciplines are integrated into dance performances (e.g., music, lighting, set design).

5.2 Describe the responsibilities a dancer has in maintaining health-related habits (e.g., balanced nutrition, regular exercise, adequate sleep).

Development of Life Skills and Career Competencies

5.3 Identify careers in dance and dance-related fields (e.g., teacher, therapist, videographer, dance critic, choreographer, notator).

Music

Students apply what they learn in music across subject areas. They develop competencies and creative skills in problem solving, communication, and management of time and resources that contribute to lifelong learning and career skills. They also learn about careers in and related to music.

Connections and Applications

5.1 Describe how knowledge of music connects to learning in other subject areas.

Careers and Career-Related Skills

5.2 Identify career pathways in music.

Theatre

Students apply what they learn in theatre, film/video, and electronic media across subject areas. They develop competencies and creative skills in problem solving, communication, and time management that contribute to lifelong learning and career skills. They also learn about careers in and related to theatre.

Connections and Applications

5.1 Use theatrical skills to communicate concepts or ideas from other curriculum areas, such as a demonstration in history–social science of how persuasion and propaganda are used in advertising.

Careers and Career-Related Skills

5.2 Research career opportunities in media, advertising, marketing, and interactive Web design.

Visual Arts

Students apply what they learn in the visual arts across subject areas. They develop competencies and creative skills in problem solving, communication, and management of time and resources that contribute to lifelong learning and career skills. They also learn about careers in and related to the visual arts.

Connections and Applications

5.1 Research how art was used in theatrical productions in the past and in the present.

5.2 Research how traditional characters (such as the trickster) found in a variety of cultures past and present are represented in illustrations.

5.3 Create artwork containing visual metaphors that express the traditions and myths of selected cultures.

Visual Literacy

5.4 Describe tactics employed in advertising to sway the viewer's thinking and provide examples.

Careers and Career-Related Skills

5.5 Establish criteria to use in selecting works of art for a specific type of art exhibition.

Indicates a key content standard for the grade level. See page 23 for information on key content standards.

Grade Seven

Seventh-grade students have attained basic knowledge and skills in the four arts disciplines that prepare them for in-depth exploration of the arts. In dance, music, theatre, and the visual arts, they expand their ability to express their vision and opinions with differing perspectives. And by refining the foundational skills they have been developing since kindergarten, they can apply them in meaningful, creative ways. During this transitional time of change for students, they should be provided with a curriculum that honors and values them as individuals.

Students reflect on their own creative works and those of others as they begin to convey meaning and develop their own criteria. They continue to learn what is required of them individually as they work cooperatively in groups and ensembles and become part of a creative team. By deepening their knowledge of content and practicing their skills, they learn to express themselves as individuals and within the group. They need not only opportunities to explore but also increased structure and technique as well as practice in self-assessment and reflection on their work. By learning how to render positive and thoughtful feedback to themselves and their peers, they gain a skill that will benefit them throughout their lives.

Engaged in more in-depth research and analysis, students examine many different dance styles and elements of music used in works from various styles and cultures. They also analyze the dramatic elements in a script and discuss how the principles of design in the visual arts, such as line, color, and space, contribute to the expressive quality of their own work.

Dance

Students demonstrate their increased originality and performance skills in choreography and performance. By creating longer and more complex movement sequences, they come to realize how expressive those movements can be. They verbalize those expressive qualities as they describe movements observed in the dancing of others and in their everyday lives and incorporate music into their movement sequences and choreography. They also discuss the function of dance as observed in different countries and among different age groups.

Music

Students sing and perform various styles of music from different cultures to improve their technical accuracy. They learn to discern how musical elements, such as tonality and intervals, vary according to culture and style and study larger and more complex operatic and fugue forms. By applying their vocal or instrumental skills, they can perform a repertoire of music; and their study of music from many styles and cultures helps them compose and arrange original works. Further, by comparing and contrasting two works performed by different musicians or performing groups, they can apply their skills in aesthetic valuing and artistic perception.

Theatre

Students learn and practice directing skills and work to improve their acting techniques. As they analyze the dramatic elements used by scriptwriters, they learn the vocabulary of the theatre and the elements of scriptwriting. Keeping a rehearsal script notebook, they write down directions and blocking notes as a play is being produced. As they compare and contrast various theatre styles used in different countries and time periods, they learn the value of theatre in communicating, enabling them to explain how theatre is influenced by culture.

Visual Arts

Students focus on developing a series of related works to express a personal statement. As they develop their works, they describe how their application of the elements of art and principles of design contribute to what they want to express. Aware that art is not created in isolation, they compare and contrast works from different time periods and cultures and reflect on the artists' styles in relation to time and place. In the process they are identifying what they believe to be important to look for in works of art and what criteria they want to apply as they critique those works.

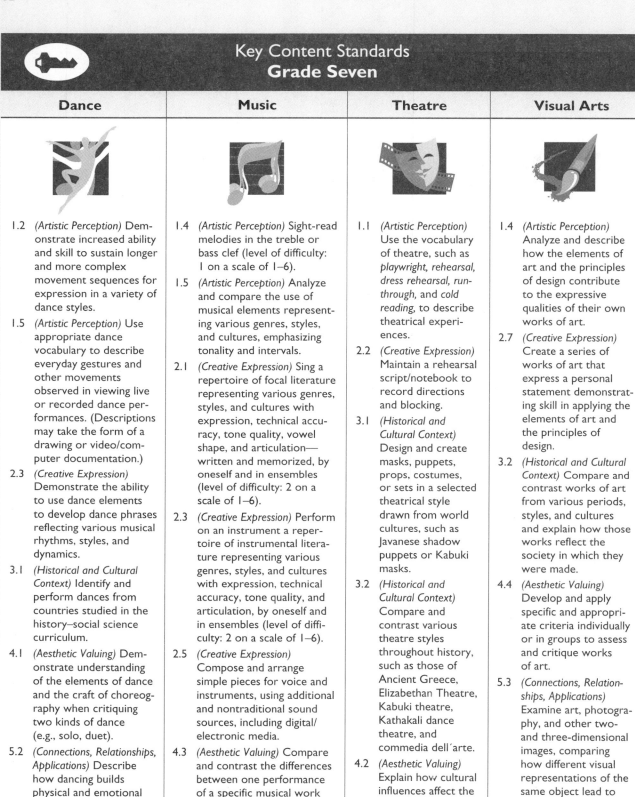

Key Content Standards
Grade Seven

Dance	Music	Theatre	Visual Arts

Dance

1.2 *(Artistic Perception)* Demonstrate increased ability and skill to sustain longer and more complex movement sequences for expression in a variety of dance styles.

1.5 *(Artistic Perception)* Use appropriate dance vocabulary to describe everyday gestures and other movements observed in viewing live or recorded dance performances. (Descriptions may take the form of a drawing or video/computer documentation.)

2.3 *(Creative Expression)* Demonstrate the ability to use dance elements to develop dance phrases reflecting various musical rhythms, styles, and dynamics.

3.1 *(Historical and Cultural Context)* Identify and perform dances from countries studied in the history–social science curriculum.

4.1 *(Aesthetic Valuing)* Demonstrate understanding of the elements of dance and the craft of choreography when critiquing two kinds of dance (e.g., solo, duet).

5.2 *(Connections, Relationships, Applications)* Describe how dancing builds physical and emotional well-being (e.g., positive body imaging, physical goals, creative goals, focus/concentration).

Music

1.4 *(Artistic Perception)* Sight-read melodies in the treble or bass clef (level of difficulty: 1 on a scale of 1–6).

1.5 *(Artistic Perception)* Analyze and compare the use of musical elements representing various genres, styles, and cultures, emphasizing tonality and intervals.

2.1 *(Creative Expression)* Sing a repertoire of focal literature representing various genres, styles, and cultures with expression, technical accuracy, tone quality, vowel shape, and articulation— written and memorized, by oneself and in ensembles (level of difficulty: 2 on a scale of 1–6).

2.3 *(Creative Expression)* Perform on an instrument a repertoire of instrumental literature representing various genres, styles, and cultures with expression, technical accuracy, tone quality, and articulation, by oneself and in ensembles (level of difficulty: 2 on a scale of 1–6).

2.5 *(Creative Expression)* Compose and arrange simple pieces for voice and instruments, using additional and nontraditional sound sources, including digital/ electronic media.

4.3 *(Aesthetic Valuing)* Compare and contrast the differences between one performance of a specific musical work and another performance of the same work.

Theatre

1.1 *(Artistic Perception)* Use the vocabulary of theatre, such as *playwright, rehearsal, dress rehearsal, run-through,* and *cold reading,* to describe theatrical experiences.

2.2 *(Creative Expression)* Maintain a rehearsal script/notebook to record directions and blocking.

3.1 *(Historical and Cultural Context)* Design and create masks, puppets, props, costumes, or sets in a selected theatrical style drawn from world cultures, such as Javanese shadow puppets or Kabuki masks.

3.2 *(Historical and Cultural Context)* Compare and contrast various theatre styles throughout history, such as those of Ancient Greece, Elizabethan Theatre, Kabuki theatre, Kathakali dance theatre, and commedia dell´arte.

4.2 *(Aesthetic Valuing)* Explain how cultural influences affect the content or meaning of works of theatre.

Visual Arts

1.4 *(Artistic Perception)* Analyze and describe how the elements of art and the principles of design contribute to the expressive qualities of their own works of art.

2.7 *(Creative Expression)* Create a series of works of art that express a personal statement demonstrating skill in applying the elements of art and the principles of design.

3.2 *(Historical and Cultural Context)* Compare and contrast works of art from various periods, styles, and cultures and explain how those works reflect the society in which they were made.

4.4 *(Aesthetic Valuing)* Develop and apply specific and appropriate criteria individually or in groups to assess and critique works of art.

5.3 *(Connections, Relationships, Applications)* Examine art, photography, and other two- and three-dimensional images, comparing how different visual representations of the same object lead to different interpretations of its meaning, and describe or illustrate the results.

Grade Seven Content Standards

Component Strand: *1.0 Artistic Perception*

Dance Processing, Analyzing, and Responding to Sensory Information Through the Language and Skills Unique to Dance	**Music** Processing, Analyzing, and Responding to Sensory Information Through the Language and Skills Unique to Music	**Theatre** Processing, Analyzing, and Responding to Sensory Information Through the Language and Skills Unique to Theatre	**Visual Arts** Processing, Analyzing, and Responding to Sensory Information Through the Language and Skills Unique to the Visual Arts
Students perceive and respond, using the elements of dance. They demonstrate movement skills, process sensory information, and describe movement, using the vocabulary of dance.	Students read, notate, listen to, analyze, and describe music and other aural information, using the terminology of music.	Students observe their environment and respond, using the elements of theatre. They also observe formal and informal works of theatre, film/video, and electronic media and respond, using the vocabulary of theatre.	Students perceive and respond to works of art, objects in nature, events, and the environment. They also use the vocabulary of the visual arts to express their observations.

<table>
<tr>
<td>

Development of Motor Skills, Technical Expertise, and Dance Movements

1.1 Demonstrate increased focus, physical control, coordination, skill, and accurate reproduction in performing locomotor and axial movement.

1.2 Demonstrate increased ability and skill to sustain longer and more complex movement sequences for expression in a variety of dance styles.

1.3 Demonstrate risk taking in generating bigger and stronger movements through space in rehearsal and performance.

Comprehension and Analysis of Dance Elements

1.4 Identify and use a wider range of space, time, and force/energy to manipulate locomotor and axial movements.

Development of Dance Vocabulary

1.5 Use appropriate dance vocabulary to describe everyday gestures and other movements observed in viewing live or recorded dance performances. (Descriptions may take the form of a drawing or video/computer documentation.)

</td>
<td>

Read and Notate Music

1.1 Read, write, and perform intervals, chordal patterns, and harmonic progressions.

1.2 Read, write, and perform rhythmic and melodic notation in duple, triple, and mixed meters.

1.3 Transcribe simple aural examples into rhythmic notation.

1.4 Sight-read melodies in the treble or bass clef (level of difficulty: 1 on a scale of 1–6).

Listen to, Analyze, and Describe Music

1.5 Analyze and compare the use of various genres, styles, and cultures, emphasizing tonality and intervals.

1.6 Describe larger music forms (canon, fugue, suite, ballet, opera, and oratorio).

</td>
<td>

Development of the Vocabulary of Theatre

1.1 Use the vocabulary of theatre, such as *playwright, rehearsal, dress rehearsal, run-through,* and *cold reading,* to describe theatrical experiences.

Comprehension and Analysis of the Elements of Theatre

1.2 Identify dramatic elements within a script, such as *foreshadowing, crisis, rising action, catharsis,* and *denouement,* using the vocabulary of theatre.

</td>
<td>

Develop Perceptual Skills and Visual Arts Vocabulary

1.1 Describe the environment and selected works of art, using the elements of art and the principles of design.

1.2 Identify and describe scale (proportion) as applied to two-dimensional and three-dimensional works of art.

Analyze Art Elements and Principles of Design

1.3 Identify and describe the ways in which artists convey the illusion of space (e.g., placement, overlapping, relative size, atmospheric perspective, and linear perspective).

1.4 Analyze and describe how the elements of art and the principles of design contribute to the expressive qualities of their own works of art.

</td>
</tr>
</table>

Indicates a key content standard for the grade level. See page 23 for information on key content standards.

Grade Seven Content Standards

Component Strand: *2.0 Creative Expression*

Dance Creating, Performing, and Participating in Dance	**Music** Creating, Performing, and Participating in Music	**Theatre** Creating, Performing, and Participating in Theatre	**Visual Arts** Creating, Performing, and Participating in the Visual Arts
Students apply choreographic principles, processes, and skills to create and communicate meaning through the improvisation, composition, and performance of dance.	Students apply vocal and instrumental musical skills in performing a varied repertoire of music. They compose and arrange music and improvise melodies, variations, and accompaniments, using digital/ electronic technology when appropriate.	Students apply processes and skills in acting, directing, designing, and scriptwriting to create formal and informal theatre, film/ videos, and electronic media productions and to perform in them.	Students apply artistic processes and skills, using a variety of media to communicate meaning and intent in original works of art.

Dance

Creation/Invention of Dance Movement

2.1 Create, memorize, and perform improvised movement sequences, dance studies, and choreography with dynamic range and fulfillment.

2.2 Demonstrate the ability to use personal discovery and invention through improvisation and choreography.

Application of Choreographic Principles and Processes to Creating Dance

2.3 Demonstrate the ability
🔊 **to use dance elements to develop dance phrases reflecting various musical rhythms, styles, and dynamics.**

2.4 Demonstrate skill in using ideas and themes to develop simple dance forms (e.g., rondo, ABA form).

Communication of Meaning in Dance Through Dance Performance

2.5 Demonstrate performance skill in the ability to interpret and communicate through dance.

2.6 Collaborate with others in preparing a dance presentation for an audience (short informal dance, lecture/demo, evening concert).

Development of Partner and Group Skills

2.7 Demonstrate increased originality in using partner or group relationships to define spatial floor patterns, shape designs, and entrances and exits.

Music

Apply Vocal and Instrumental Skills

2.1 Sing a repertoire of vocal
🔊 **literature representing various genres, styles, and cultures with expression, technical accuracy, tone quality, vowel shape, and articulation—written and memorized, by oneself and in ensembles (level of difficulty: 2 on a scale of 1–6).**

2.2 Sing music written in two and three parts

2.3 Perform on an instrument
🔊 **a repertoire of instrumental literature representing various genres, styles, and cultures with expression, technical accuracy, tone quality, and articulation, by oneself and in ensembles (level of difficulty: 2 on a scale of 1–6).**

Compose, Arrange, and Improvise

2.4 Compose short pieces in duple, triple, and mixed meters.

2.5 Compose and arrange
🔊 **simple pieces for voice and instruments, using traditional and nontraditional sound sources, including digital/electronic media.**

2.6 Improvise melodies and harmonic accompaniments.

2.7 Improvise melodic and rhythmic embellishments and variations on given pentatonic melodies.

Theatre

Development of Theatrical Skills

2.1 Use improvisation in rehearsal to discover character and motivation.

2.2 Maintain a
🔊 **rehearsal script/notebook to record directions and blocking.**

Creation/Invention in Theatre

2.3 Create characters, environments, and actions that exhibit tension and suspense.

Visual Arts

Skills, Processes, Materials, and Tools

2.1 Develop increasing skill in the use of at least three different media.

2.2 Use different forms of perspective to show the illusion of depth on a two-dimensional surface.

2.3 Develop skill in using mixed media while guided by a selected principle of design.

2.4 Develop skill in mixing paints and showing color relationships.

Communication and Expression Through Original Works of Art

2.5 Interpret reality and fantasy in original two-dimensional and three-dimensional works of art.

2.6 Create an original work of art, using film, photography, computer graphics, or video.

2.7 Create a series of
🔊 **works of art that express a personal statement demonstrating skill in applying the elements of art and the principles of design.**

🔊 Indicates a key content standard for the grade level. See page 23 for information on key content standards.

Grade Seven Content Standards

Component Strand: *3.0 Historical and Cultural Context*

Dance Understanding the Historical Contributions and Cultural Dimensions of Dance	**Music** Understanding the Historical Contributions and Cultural Dimensions of Music	**Theatre** Understanding the Historical Contributions and Cultural Dimensions of Theatre	**Visual Arts** Understanding the Historical Contributions and Cultural Dimensions of the Visual Arts
Students analyze the function and development of dance in past and present cultures throughout the world, noting human diversity as it relates to dance and dancers.	Students analyze the role of music in past and present cultures throughout the world, noting cultural diversity as it relates to music, musicians, and composers.	Students analyze the role and development of theatre, film/video, and electronic media in past and present cultures throughout the world, noting diversity as it relates to theatre.	Students analyze the role and development of the visual arts in past and present cultures throughout the world, noting human diversity as it relates to the visual arts and artists.

Dance

Development of Dance

3.1 Identify and perform dances from countries studied in the history–social science curriculum.

History and Function of Dance

3.2 Explain the function of dance in daily life during specific time periods and in countries being studied in history–social science (e.g., North African, Middle Eastern, and Central American dance in ceremonies, social events, traditional settings, and theatrical performances).

Diversity of Dance

3.3 Explain how dance functions among people of different age groups, including their own.

Music

Role of Music

3.1 Compare music from various cultures as to some of the functions music serves and the roles of musicians.

3.2 Identify and describe the development of music during medieval and early modern times in various cultures (e.g., African, Chinese, European, Islamic, Japanese, South American).

Diversity of Music

3.3 Identify and describe distinguishing characteristics of musical genres and styles from a variety of cultures.

3.4 Perform music from diverse genres and cultures.

3.5 Identify instruments from a variety of cultures visually and aurally.

3.6 Classify by style and genre exemplary musical works and explain the characteristics that make each work exemplary.

Theatre

Role and Cultural Significance of Theatre

3.1 Design and create masks, puppets, props, costumes, or sets in a selected theatrical style drawn from world cultures, such as Javanese shadow puppets or Kabuki masks.

History of Theatre

3.2 Compare and contrast various theatre styles throughout history, such as those of Ancient Greece, Elizabethan theatre, Kabuki theatre, Kathakali dance theatre, and commedia dell´arte.

Visual Arts

Role and Development of Visual Arts

3.1 Research and describe how art reflects cultural values in various traditions throughout the world.

Diversity of the Visual Arts

3.2 Compare and contrast works of art from various periods, styles, and cultures and explain how those works reflect the society in which they were made.

Indicates a key content standard for the grade level. See page 23 for information on key content standards.

Grade Seven Content Standards

Component Strand: 4.0 Aesthetic Valuing

Dance Responding to, Analyzing, and Making Judgments About Works of Dance	**Music** Responding to, Analyzing, and Making Judgments About Works of Music	**Theatre** Responding to, Analyzing, and Critiquing Theatrical Experiences	**Visual Arts** Responding to, Analyzing, and Making Judgments About Works in the Visual Arts

Students critically assess and derive meaning from works of dance, performance of dancers, and original works based on the elements of dance and aesthetic qualities.

Description, Analysis, and Criticism of Dance

4.1 Demonstrate understanding of the elements of dance and the craft of choreography when critiquing two kinds of dance (e.g., solo, duet).

4.2 Identify assessment criteria used for out-standing performances in different styles of dance (e.g., theatre, social, ceremonial).

Meaning and Impact of Dance

4.3 Explain and analyze the impact of live or recorded music on dance performances. (Recorded music is consistent. Live music can be altered.)

4.4 Explain how different venues influence the experience and impact of dancing (e.g., a studio setting, traditional stage, theater in the round).

Students critically assess and derive meaning from works of music and the performance of musicians in a cultural context according to the elements of music, aesthetic qualities, and human responses.

Analyze and Critically Assess

4.1 Use criteria to evaluate the quality and effectiveness of musical performances and compositions.

4.2 Apply criteria appropri-ate for the style or genre of music to evaluate the quality and effectiveness of performances, compo-sitions, arrangements, and improvisations by oneself and others.

Derive Meaning

4.3 Compare and contrast the differ-ences between one performance of a specific musical work and another perfor-mance of the same work.

Students critique and derive meaning from works of theatre, film/video, electronic media, and theatrical artists on the basis of aesthetic qualities.

Critical Assessment of Theatre

4.1 Design and apply appropriate criteria or rubrics for evaluating the effective use of masks, puppetry, makeup, and costumes in a theatrical presentation.

Derivation of Meaning from Works of Theatre

4.2 Explain how cultural influences affect the content or meaning of works of theatre.

Students analyze, assess, and derive meaning from works of art, including their own, according to the ele-ments of art, the principles of design, and aesthetic qualities.

Derive Meaning

4.1 Explain the intent of a personal work of art and draw possible parallels between it and the work of a recognized artist.

4.2 Analyze the form (how a work of art looks) and content (what a work of art communicates) of works of art.

Make Informed Judgments

4.3 Take an active part in a small-group discussion about the artistic value of specific works of art, with a wide range of the viewpoints of peers being considered.

4.4 Develop and apply specific and appropri-ate criteria individu-ally or in groups to assess and critique works of art.

4.5 Identify what was done when a personal work of art was reworked and explain how those changes improved the work.

Grade Seven Content Standards

Component Strand: 5.0 Connections, Relationships, Applications

Dance	Music	Theatre	Visual Arts
Connecting and Applying What Is Learned in Dance to Learning in Other Art Forms and Subject Areas and to Careers	Connecting and Applying What Is Learned in Music to Learning in Other Art Forms and Subject Areas and to Careers	Connecting and Applying What Is Learned in Theatre, Film/Video, and Electronic Media to Other Art Forms and Subject Areas and to Careers	Connecting and Applying What Is Learned in the Visual Arts to Other Art Forms and Subject Areas and to Careers

Dance

Students apply what they learn in dance to learning across subject areas. They develop competencies and creative skills in problem solving, communication, and management of time and resources that contribute to lifelong learning and career skills. They also learn about careers in and related to dance.

Connections and Applications Across Disciplines

5.1 Identify and use different sources to generate ideas for dance compositions (e.g., poetry, photographs, political/social issues).

5.2 Describe how dancing builds physical and emotional well-being (e.g., positive body imaging, physical goals, creative goals, focus/concentration).

Development of Life Skills and Career Competencies

5.3 Appraise how time management, listening, problem-solving, and teamwork skills used with other dancers in composing and rehearsing a dance can be applied to other group activities.

5.4 Research and compare careers in dance and dance-related fields.

Music

Students apply what they learn in music across subject areas. They develop competencies and creative skills in problem solving, communication, and management of time and resources that contribute to lifelong learning and career skills. They also learn about careers in and related to music.

Connections and Applications

5.1 Identify similarities and differences in the meanings of common terms used in various arts and other subject areas.

5.2 Identify and describe how music functions in the media and entertainment industries.

Careers and Career-Related Skills

5.3 Identify various careers for musicians in the entertainment industry.

Theatre

Students apply what they learn in theatre, film/video, and electronic media across subject areas. They develop competencies and creative skills in problem solving, communication, and time management that contribute to lifelong learning and career skills. They also learn about careers in and related to theatre.

Connections and Applications

5.1 Use theatrical skills to communicate concepts or ideas from other curriculum areas, such as creating a musical based on a piece of literature.

Careers and Career-Related Skills

5.2 Demonstrate projection, vocal variety, diction, gesture, and confidence in an oral presentation.

Visual Arts

Students apply what they learn in the visual arts across subject areas. They develop competencies and creative skills in problem solving, communication, and management of time and resources that contribute to lifelong learning and career skills. They also learn about careers in and related to the visual arts.

Connections and Applications

5.1 Study the music and art of a selected historical era and create a multi-media presentation that reflects that time and culture

5.2 Use various drawing skills and techniques to depict lifestyles and scenes from selected civilizations.

Visual Literacy

5.3 Examine art, photography, and other two- and three-dimensional images, comparing how different visual representations of the same object lead to different interpretations of its meaning, and describe or illustrate the results.

Careers and Career-Related Skills

5.4 Identify professions in or related to the visual arts and some of the specific skills needed for those professions.

Indicates a key content standard for the grade level. See page 23 for information on key content standards.

Grade Eight

Eighth-grade students have a foundation in each of the four arts disciplines that serves as a springboard into deeper study and broader views of the world and the role the arts play in people's lives. They also have the vocabulary needed to converse about the arts in school and in social settings. With their deepened understanding of the different cultural dimensions in the arts, they find their voice in an ever-changing world. And having ample opportunities to collaborate with other students with the same interests in the arts, they can determine more fully their own points of view and artistic choices. Given opportunities to apply their artistic abilities to creating and performing in the arts, they are prepared for constructive feedback from their teachers and their peers. In all the arts they are now prepared to compare how artists in each of the arts disciplines use their own source to convey an idea or emotion. For example, they might reflect on such things as patriotism or football as expressed in a song, a statue, a monologue, or a dance performance.

Dance

Students use their perceptual skills and dance vocabulary as they analyze gestures and movements they observe in live or recorded professional dance performances. What they learn from this analysis can be applied to their own creation, performance, and documentation of a personal repertoire of dance movements, patterns, and phrases. Using their analytical skills, they compare and contrast different kinds of dances that they learn and perform in class. And they can explain how dance provides positive health benefits.

Music

Students use their increased vocabulary to explore in depth how musical elements are used in music of different styles from various cultures, especially the use of chords and harmonic progressions. As they sing or perform on an instrument, they practice sight reading at a more difficult level and are evaluated for their accuracy and expressive quality. Now they have the musical background needed to compose short pieces in various meters.

Theatre

Students' increased vocabulary and ability to identify and analyze recurring themes and patterns in a script help the students make production choices as they design and direct a play. Because they have learned about various styles of theatre, such as melodrama and musical theatre, they can create short dramatizations in those styles. By practicing several different techniques of acting, they can improve their skills in character development. Further, they describe how theatre has portrayed moments in American history and explain how technological advances have changed American theatre. Because of their work in aesthetic valuing, they are prepared to write a formal review of a theatrical production.

Visual Arts

Students combine their skills in artistic perception and aesthetic valuing to analyze and justify the artistic choices they make about their own work and determine how those choices contribute to the expressive quality of the work. In both art media and processes, they demonstrate increased technical skills as they create works of art. Learning how art can make a social comment or protest a social condition in their research of art from various times and places affects their discussions of the effects on society of all visual communication, including television, videos, film, and the Internet. They also become aware of the power of the visual arts as they design a public artwork appropriate to and reflecting the location for which it is designed. Their ability to present a reasoned argument about the artistic value of a work of art can be applied to the works they create or the works of others past or present.

Key Content Standards
Grade Eight

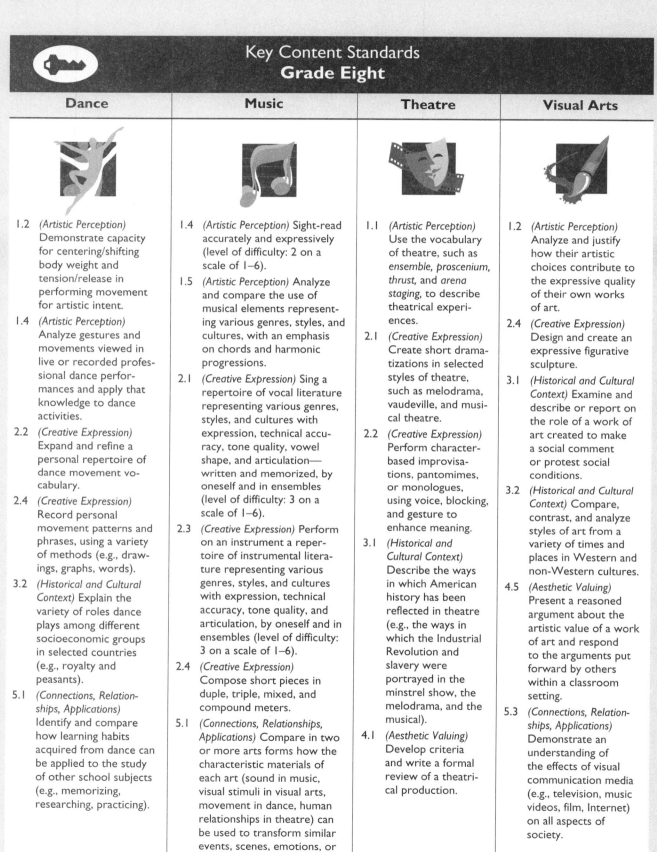

Dance	Music	Theatre	Visual Arts

Dance

1.2 *(Artistic Perception)* Demonstrate capacity for centering/shifting body weight and tension/release in performing movement for artistic intent.

1.4 *(Artistic Perception)* Analyze gestures and movements viewed in live or recorded professional dance performances and apply that knowledge to dance activities.

2.2 *(Creative Expression)* Expand and refine a personal repertoire of dance movement vocabulary.

2.4 *(Creative Expression)* Record personal movement patterns and phrases, using a variety of methods (e.g., drawings, graphs, words).

3.2 *(Historical and Cultural Context)* Explain the variety of roles dance plays among different socioeconomic groups in selected countries (e.g., royalty and peasants).

5.1 *(Connections, Relationships, Applications)* Identify and compare how learning habits acquired from dance can be applied to the study of other school subjects (e.g., memorizing, researching, practicing).

Music

1.4 *(Artistic Perception)* Sight-read accurately and expressively (level of difficulty: 2 on a scale of 1–6).

1.5 *(Artistic Perception)* Analyze and compare the use of musical elements representing various genres, styles, and cultures, with an emphasis on chords and harmonic progressions.

2.1 *(Creative Expression)* Sing a repertoire of vocal literature representing various genres, styles, and cultures with expression, technical accuracy, tone quality, vowel shape, and articulation—written and memorized, by oneself and in ensembles (level of difficulty: 3 on a scale of 1–6).

2.3 *(Creative Expression)* Perform on an instrument a repertoire of instrumental literature representing various genres, styles, and cultures with expression, technical accuracy, tone quality, and articulation, by oneself and in ensembles (level of difficulty: 3 on a scale of 1–6).

2.4 *(Creative Expression)* Compose short pieces in duple, triple, mixed, and compound meters.

5.1 *(Connections, Relationships, Applications)* Compare in two or more arts forms how the characteristic materials of each art (sound in music, visual stimuli in visual arts, movement in dance, human relationships in theatre) can be used to transform similar events, scenes, emotions, or ideas into works of art.

Theatre

1.1 *(Artistic Perception)* Use the vocabulary of theatre, such as *ensemble, proscenium, thrust,* and *arena staging,* to describe theatrical experiences.

2.1 *(Creative Expression)* Create short dramatizations in selected styles of theatre, such as melodrama, vaudeville, and musical theatre.

2.2 *(Creative Expression)* Perform character-based improvisations, pantomimes, or monologues, using voice, blocking, and gesture to enhance meaning.

3.1 *(Historical and Cultural Context)* Describe the ways in which American history has been reflected in theatre (e.g., the ways in which the Industrial Revolution and slavery were portrayed in the minstrel show, the melodrama, and the musical).

4.1 *(Aesthetic Valuing)* Develop criteria and write a formal review of a theatrical production.

Visual Arts

1.2 *(Artistic Perception)* Analyze and justify how their artistic choices contribute to the expressive quality of their own works of art.

2.4 *(Creative Expression)* Design and create an expressive figurative sculpture.

3.1 *(Historical and Cultural Context)* Examine and describe or report on the role of a work of art created to make a social comment or protest social conditions.

3.2 *(Historical and Cultural Context)* Compare, contrast, and analyze styles of art from a variety of times and places in Western and non-Western cultures.

4.5 *(Aesthetic Valuing)* Present a reasoned argument about the artistic value of a work of art and respond to the arguments put forward by others within a classroom setting.

5.3 *(Connections, Relationships, Applications)* Demonstrate an understanding of the effects of visual communication media (e.g., television, music videos, film, Internet) on all aspects of society.

Grade Eight Content Standards

Component Strand: *1.0 Artistic Perception*

Dance	Music	Theatre	Visual Arts
Processing, Analyzing, and Responding to Sensory Information Through the Language and Skills Unique to Dance	Processing, Analyzing, and Responding to Sensory Information Through the Language and Skills Unique to Music	Processing, Analyzing, and Responding to Sensory Information Through the Language and Skills Unique to Theatre	Processing, Analyzing, and Responding to Sensory Information Through the Language and Skills Unique to the Visual Arts

Dance

Students perceive and respond, using the elements of dance. They demonstrate movement skills, process sensory information, and describe movement, using the vocabulary of dance.

Development of Motor Skills, Technical Expertise, and Dance Movements

1.1 Demonstrate increased ability and skill to apply the elements of space, time, and force/energy in producing a wide range of dance sequences.

1.2 Demonstrate capacity for centering/shifting body weight and tension/release in performing movement for artistic intent.

1.3 Demonstrate greater technical control in generating bigger and stronger movements through space in rehearsal and performance.

Comprehension and Analysis of Dance Elements

1.4 Analyze gestures and movements *viewed* in live or recorded professional dance performances and apply that knowledge to dance activities.

Development of Dance Vocabulary

1.5 Identify and analyze the variety of ways in which a dancer can move, using space, time, and force/energy vocabulary.

Music

Students read, notate, listen to, analyze, and describe music and other aural information, using the terminology of music.

Read and Notate Music

1.1 Read, write, and perform augmented and diminished intervals, minor chords, and harmonic minor progressions.

1.2 Read, write, and perform rhythmic and melodic notation in duple, triple, compound, and mixed meters.

1.3 Transcribe aural examples into rhythmic and melodic notation.

1.4 Sight-read accurately and expressively (level of difficulty: 2 on a scale of 1–6).

Listen to, Analyze, and Describe Music

1.5 Analyze and compare the use of musical elements representing various genres, styles, and cultures, with an emphasis on chords *and* harmonic progressions.

1.6 Describe larger musical forms (e.g., symphony, tone poem).

1.7 Explain how musical elements are used to create specific music events in given aural examples.

Theatre

Students observe their environment and respond, using the elements of theatre. They also observe formal and informal works of theatre, film/video, and electronic media and respond, using the vocabulary of theatre.

Development of the Vocabulary of Theatre

1.1 Use the vocabulary of theatre, such as *ensemble, proscenium, thrust,* and *arena staging,* to describe theatrical experiences.

Comprehension and Analysis of the Elements of Theatre

1.2 Identify and analyze recurring themes and patterns (e.g., loyalty, bravery, revenge, redemption) in a script to make production choices in design and direction.

1.3 Analyze the use of figurative language and imagery in dramatic texts.

Visual Arts

Students perceive and respond to works of art, objects in nature, events, and the environment. They also use the vocabulary of the visual arts to express their observations.

Develop Perceptual Skills and Visual Arts Vocabulary

1.1 Use artistic terms when describing the intent and content of works of art.

Analyze Art Elements and Principles of Design

1.2 Analyze and justify how their artistic choices contribute to the expressive quality of their own works of art.

1.3 Analyze the use of the elements of art and the principles of design as they relate to meaning in video, film, or electronic media.

Grade Eight Content Standards

Component Strand: 2.0 Creative Expression

Dance	Music	Theatre	Visual Arts
Creating, Performing, and Participating in Dance	Creating, Performing, and Participating in Music	Creating, Performing, and Participating in Theatre	Creating, Performing, and Participating in the Visual Arts

Dance	Music	Theatre	Visual Arts
Students apply choreographic principles, processes, and skills to create and communicate meaning through the improvisation, composition, and performance of dance.	Students apply vocal and instrumental musical skills in performing a varied repertoire of music. They compose and arrange music and improvise melodies, variations, and accompaniments, using digital/electronic technology when appropriate.	Students apply processes and skills in acting, directing, designing, and script-writing to create formal and informal theatre, film/videos, and electronic media productions and to perform in them.	Students apply artistic processes and skills, using a variety of media to communicate meaning and intent in original works of art.
Creation/Invention of Dance Movement	*Apply Vocal or Instrumental Skills*	*Development of Theatrical Skills*	*Skills, Processes, Materials, and Tools*
2.1　Create, memorize, and perform dance studies, demonstrating technical expertise and artistic expression.	**2.1　Sing a repertoire of vocal** ⚷ **literature representing various genres, styles, and cultures with expression, technical accuracy, tone quality, vowel shape, and articulation—written and memorized—by oneself and in ensembles (level of difficulty: 3 on a scale of 1–6).**	**2.1　Create short** ⚷ **dramatizations in selected styles of theatre, such as melodrama, vaudeville, and musical theatre.**	2.1　Demonstrate an increased knowledge of technical skills in using more complex two-dimensional art media and processes (e.g., printing press, silk screening, computer graphics software).
2.2　Expand and refine a ⚷ **personal repertoire of dance movement vocabulary.**	2.2　Sing music written in two, three, or four parts.	*Creation/Invention in Theatre*	2.2　Design and create maquettes for three-dimensional sculptures.
Application of Choreographic Principles and Processes to Creating Dance	**2.3　Perform on an instrument** ⚷ **a repertoire of instrumental literature representing various genres, styles, and cultures with expression, technical accuracy, tone quality, and articulation, by oneself and in ensembles (level of difficulty: 3 on a scale of 1–6).**	**2.2　Perform** ⚷ **character-based improvisations, pantomimes, or monologues, using voice, blocking, and gesture to enhance meaning.**	*Communication and Expression Through Original Works of Art*
2.3　Apply basic music elements to the making and performance of dances (e.g., rhythm, meter, accents).			2.3　Create an original work of art, using film, photography, computer graphics, or video.
2.4　Record personal move- ⚷ **ment patterns and phrases, using a variety of methods (e.g., drawings, graphs, words).**	*Compose, Arrange, and Improvise*		**2.4　Design and create** ⚷ **an expressive figurative sculpture.**
Communication of Meaning Through Dance Performance	**2.4　Compose short pieces in** ⚷ **duple, triple, mixed, and compound meters.**		2.5　Select a medium to use to communicate a theme in a series of works of art.
2.5　Demonstrate performance skill in the ability to project energy and express ideas through dance.	2.5　Arrange simple pieces for voices or instruments other than those for which the pieces were written, using traditional and nontraditional sound sources, including digital/electronic media.		2.6　Design and create both additive and subtractive sculptures.
2.6　Demonstrate the use of personal images as motivation for individual and group dance performances.	2.6　Improvise melodic and rhythmic embellishments and variations in major keys.		2.7　Design a work of public art appropriate to and reflecting a location.
Development of Partner and Group Skills	2.7　Improvise short melodies to be performed with and without accompaniment.		
2.7　Demonstrate originality in using partner or group relationships to define spatial patterns and the use of overall performing space.			

⚷ Indicates a key content standard for the grade level. See page 23 for information on key content standards.

Grade Eight Content Standards

Component Strand: *3.0 Historical and Cultural Context*

Dance Understanding the Historical Contributions and Cultural Dimensions of Dance	**Music** Understanding the Historical Contributions and Cultural Dimensions of Music	**Theatre** Understanding the Historical Contributions and Cultural Dimensions of Theatre	**Visual Arts** Understanding the Historical Contributions and Cultural Dimensions of the Visual Arts
Students analyze the function and development of dance in past and present cultures throughout the world, noting human diversity as it relates to dance and dancers.	Students analyze the role of music in past and present cultures throughout the world, noting cultural diversity as it relates to music, musicians, and composers.	Students analyze the role and development of theatre, film/video, and electronic media in past and present cultures throughout the world, noting diversity as it relates to theatre.	Students analyze the role and development of the visual arts in past and present cultures throughout the world, noting human diversity as it relates to the visual arts and artists.

Dance

Development of Dance

3.1 Compare and contrast specific kinds of dances (e.g., work, courtship, ritual, entertainment) that have been performed.

History and Function of Dance

3.2 Explain the variety
🔑 **of roles dance plays among different socioeconomic groups in selected countries (e.g., royalty and peasants).**

Diversity of Dance

3.3 Describe the roles of males and females in dance in the United States during various time periods.

Music

Role of Music

3.1 Compare and contrast the functions music serves and the place of musicians in society in various cultures.

3.2 Identify and explain the influences of various cultures on music in early United States history.

3.3 Explain how music has reflected social functions and changing ideas and values.

Diversity of Music

3.4 Compare and contrast the distinguishing characteristics of musical genres and styles from a variety of cultures.

3.5 Perform music from diverse genres, cultures, and time periods.

3.6 Classify exemplary musical works by style, genre, and historical period and explain why each work is considered exemplary.

Theatre

Role and Cultural Significance of Theatre

3.1 Describe the ways
🔑 **in which American history has been reflected in theatre (e.g., the ways in which the Industrial Revolution and slavery were portrayed in the minstrel show, the melodrama, and the musical).**

History of Theatre

3.2 Identify and explain how technology has changed American theatre (e.g., how stage lighting has progressed from candlelight to gaslight to limelight to electrical light to digital light).

Visual Arts

Role and Development of the Visual Arts

3.1 Examine and describe
🔑 **or report on the role of a work of art created to make a social comment or protest social conditions.**

3.2 Compare, contrast,
🔑 **and analyze styles of art from a variety of times and places in Western and non-Western cultures.**

Diversity of the Visual Arts

3.3 Identify major works of art created by women and describe the impact of those works on society at that time.

3.4 Discuss the contributions of various immigrant cultures to the art of a particular society.

🔑 Indicates a key content standard for the grade level. See page 23 for information on key content standards.

Grade Eight Content Standards

Component Strand: 4.0 Aesthetic Valuing

Dance Responding to, Analyzing, and Making Judgments About Works of Dance	Music Responding to, Analyzing, and Making Judgments About Works of Music	Theatre Responding to, Analyzing, and Critiquing Theatrical Experiences	Visual Arts Responding to, Analyzing, and Making Judgments About Works in the Visual Arts
Students critically assess and derive meaning from works of dance, performance of dancers, and original works based on the elements of dance and aesthetic qualities.	Students critically assess and derive meaning from works of music and the performance of musicians in a cultural context according to the elements of music, aesthetic qualities, and human responses.	Students critique and derive meaning from works of theatre, film/video, electronic media, and theatrical artists on the basis of aesthetic qualities.	Students analyze, assess, and derive meaning from works of art, including their own, according to the elements of art, the principles of design, and aesthetic qualities.

Dance

Description, Analysis, and Criticism of Dance

4.1 Identify preferences for choreography and discuss those preferences, using the elements of dance.

Meaning and Impact of Dance

4.2 Explain the advantages and disadvantages of various technologies in the presentation of dance (e.g., video, film, computer, DVD, recorded music).

4.3 Describe and analyze how differences in costumes, lighting, props, and venues can enhance or detract from the meaning of a dance.

Music

Analyze and Critically Assess

4.1 Use detailed criteria for evaluating the quality and effectiveness of musical performances and compositions and apply the criteria to personal listening and performing.

4.2 Apply detailed criteria appropriate for the genre and style of the music to evaluate the quality and effectiveness of performances, compositions, arrangements, and improvisations, by oneself and others.

Derive Meaning

4.3 Explain how and why people use and respond to specific music from different musical cultures found in the United States.

4.4 Compare the means used to create images or evoke feelings and emotions in musical works from a minimum of two different musical cultures found in the United States.

Theatre

Critical Assessment of Theatre

4.1 **Develop criteria and write a formal review of a theatrical production.**

Derivation of Meaning from Works of Theatre

4.2 Compare and contrast how works of theatre from different cultures or time periods convey the same or similar content or plot.

Visual Arts

Derive Meaning

4.1 Define their own points of view and investigate the effects on their interpretation of art from cultures other than their own.

4.2 Develop a theory about the artist's intent in a series of works of art, using reasoned statements to support personal opinions.

4.3 Construct an interpretation of a work of art based on the form and content of the work.

Make Informed Judgments

4.4 Develop and apply a set of criteria as individuals or in groups to assess and critique works of art.

4.5 **Present a reasoned argument about the artistic value of a work of art and respond to the arguments put forward by others within a classroom setting.**

4.6 Select a grouping of their own works of art that reflects growth over time and describe the progression.

Grade Eight Content Standards

Component Strand: 5.0 Connections, Relationships, Applications

Dance	Music	Theatre	Visual Arts
Connecting and Applying What Is Learned in Dance to Learning in Other Art Forms and Subject Areas and to Careers	Connecting and Applying What Is Learned in Music to Learning in Other Art Forms and Subject Areas and to Careers	Connecting and Applying What Is Learned in Theatre, Film/Video, and Electronic Media to Other Art Forms and Subject Areas and to Careers	Connecting and Applying What Is Learned in the Visual Arts to Other Art Forms and Subject Areas and to Careers

Dance

Students apply what they learn in dance to learning across subject areas. They develop competencies and creative skills in problem solving, communication, and management of time and resources that contribute to lifelong learning and career skills. They also learn about careers in and related to dance.

Connections and Applications Across Disciplines

5.1 Identify and compare how learning habits acquired from dance can be applied to the study of other school subjects (e.g., memorizing, researching, practicing).

5.2 Describe how dancing builds positive mental, physical, and health-related practices (e.g., discipline, stress management, anatomic awareness).

Development of Life Skills and Career Competencies

5.3 Research and explain how dancers leave their performing careers to enter into alternative careers.

Music

Students apply what they learn in music across subject areas. They develop competencies and creative skills in problem solving, communication, and management of time and resources that contribute to lifelong learning and career skills. They also learn about careers in and related to music.

Connections and Applications

5.1 Compare in two or more arts forms how the characteristic *materials* of each art (sound in music, visual stimuli in visual arts, movement in dance, human relationships in theatre) can be used to transform similar events, scenes, emotions, or ideas into works of art.

5.2 Describe how music is composed and adapted for use in film, video, radio, and television.

Careers and Career-Related Skills

5.3 Describe the skills necessary for composing and adapting music for use in film, video, radio, and television.

Theatre

Students apply what they learn in theatre, film/video, and electronic media across subject areas. They develop competencies and creative skills in problem solving, communication, and time management that contribute to lifelong learning and career skills. They also learn about careers in and related to theatre.

Connections and Applications

5.1 Use theatrical skills to present content or concepts in other subject areas, such as creating a video on cellular mitosis.

Careers and Career-Related Skills

5.2 Identify career options in the dramatic arts, such as cinematographer, stage manager, radio announcer, or dramaturg; and research the education, training, and work experience necessary in that field.

Visual Arts

Students apply what they learn in the visual arts across subject areas. They develop competencies and creative skills in problem solving, communication, and management of time and resources that contribute to lifelong learning and career skills. They also learn about careers in and related to the visual arts.

Connections and Applications

5.1 Select a favorite artist and some of his or her works of art and create a music video that expresses personal ideas and views about the artist.

5.2 Create a painting, satirical drawing, or editorial cartoon that expresses personal opinions about current social or political issues.

Visual Literacy

5.3 Demonstrate an understanding of the effects of visual communication media (e.g., television, music videos, film, Internet) on all aspects of society.

Careers and Career-Related Skills

5.4 Work collaboratively with a community artist to create a work of art, such as a mural, and write a report about the skills needed to become a professional artist.

Indicates a key content standard for the grade level. See page 23 for information on key content standards.

Grades Nine Through Twelve

Choices, choices, and more choices! Graduation is around the corner, and participation in the arts will have a lifelong impact on careers, higher education, and community involvement. Having established a firm foundation in all of the arts from kindergarten through grade eight, high school students choose a yearlong course of study in dance, music, theatre, or the visual arts. All will take at least one arts course to meet high school graduation and college entrance requirements. Some will continue expanding their knowledge and skills through additional courses in an arts discipline of special interest; others may be interested in the arts as a career path and want to spend as much time as possible involved in the arts inside and outside school.

In a yearlong beginning course of study in a chosen art form, students may reach a proficiency level that allows them to progress to an advanced course, meet a graduation requirement, and, if the course has been approved, meet the new visual and performing arts requirement for freshman admission to the University of California and the California State University (see Appendix B). In this course students read about, write about, talk about, reflect on, and make connections and choices while creating and performing in dance, music, theatre, or the visual arts. Their study provides fluency, skills, and deeper comprehension in their chosen arts discipline.

After completing a beginning-level high school course in one of the arts disciplines, a student may continue in that art form or pursue study in other arts disciplines. For those who want to go forward, additional courses in an art form provide them with opportunities to continue discovering and expressing themselves through the arts. In an advanced course of study, students research, analyze, question, clarify, evaluate, refine, plan, and create a body of work that reflects complex ideas, personal points of view, and technical skills.

**Grades Nine
Through Twelve**

Dance

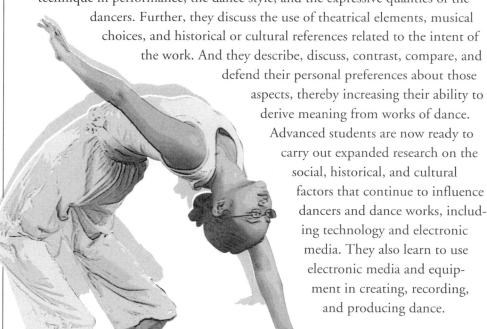

High school students develop and refine their physical conditioning, control of movement, and technical ability. They perceive the body more accurately as an instrument for self-expression through dance. At the beginning level and in advanced dance courses, students build on the knowledge and skills they gained in kindergarten through grade eight.

As their knowledge of dance elements expands, students demonstrate their ability to communicate through improvised and choreographed movement. Using the vocabulary of dance, they distinguish how movement looks physically in space, time, and force or energy. They learn a variety of dance movements, forms, and styles from various traditions and strive toward maintaining a respectful and professional attitude toward their own work and that of others.

Students learn, develop, and perform a body of work in dance ranging from original dance sequences to fully choreographed works. Building on their knowledge of dance elements, principles, and choreography, they can expand their ability to incorporate a wider range of musical forms and theatrical components. In performing, they can communicate the original intent of dance works by various artists and maintain the integrity of dances from specific cultures and historical periods. They also analyze the function of dance in past and present cultures throughout the world.

In describing, analyzing, and critiquing their own works of dance and those of others, they focus on the artistic choices in the choreography, the level of technique in performance, the dance style, and the expressive qualities of the dancers. Further, they discuss the use of theatrical elements, musical choices, and historical or cultural references related to the intent of the work. And they describe, discuss, contrast, compare, and defend their personal preferences about those aspects, thereby increasing their ability to derive meaning from works of dance. Advanced students are now ready to carry out expanded research on the social, historical, and cultural factors that continue to influence dancers and dance works, including technology and electronic media. They also learn to use electronic media and equipment in creating, recording, and producing dance.

High School Arts Content Standards—Dance

Component Strand: *1.0 Artistic Perception*

Students perceive and respond, using the elements of dance. They demonstrate movement skills, process sensory information, and describe movement, using the vocabulary of dance.

**Grades Nine
Through Twelve**

Proficient	Advanced
Processing, Analyzing, and Responding to Sensory Information Through the Language and Skills Unique to Dance	Processing, Analyzing, and Responding to Sensory Information Through the Language and Skills Unique to Dance

Development of Motor Skills, Technical Expertise, and Dance Movements

1.1 Demonstrate refined physical coordination when performing movement phrases (e.g., alignment, agility, balance, strength).

1.2 Memorize and perform works of dance, demonstrating technical accuracy and consistent artistic intent.

1.3 Perform in multiple dance genres (e.g., modern, ballet, jazz, tap, traditional/recreational).

Comprehension and Analysis of Dance Elements

1.4 Demonstrate clarity of intent while applying kinesthetic principles for all dance elements.

Development of Dance Vocabulary

1.5 Apply knowledge of dance vocabulary to distinguish how movement looks physically in space, time, and force/energy.

Development of Motor Skills, Technical Expertise, and Dance Movements

1.1 Demonstrate highly developed physical coordination and control when performing complex locomotor and axial movement phrases from a variety of genres (e.g., refined body articulation, agility, balance, strength).

1.2 Perform in multiple dance genres, integrating an advanced level of technical skill and clear intent.

1.3 Memorize and perform complicated works of dance at a level of professionalism (i.e., a high level of refinement).

Comprehension and Analysis of Dance Elements

1.4 Apply a wide range of kinesthetic communication, demonstrating clarity of intent and stylistic nuance.

Development of Dance Vocabulary

1.5 Select specific dance vocabulary to describe movement and dance elements in great detail.

Chapter 3
Visual and
Performing Arts
Content
Standards

Grades Nine
Through Twelve

High School Arts Content Standards—Dance

Component Strand: 2.0 Creative Expression

Students apply choreographic principles, processes, and skills to create and communicate meaning through the improvisation, composition, and performance of dance.

Proficient	**Advanced**
Creating, Performing, and Participating in Dance	Creating, Performing, and Participating in Dance

Creation/Invention of Dance Movement

2.1 Create a body of works of dance demonstrating originality, unity, and clarity of intent.

Application of Choreographic Principles and Processes to Creating Dance

2.2 Identify and apply basic music elements (e.g., rhythm, meter, tempo, timbre) to construct and perform dances.

2.3 Design a dance that utilizes an established dance style or genre.

Communication of Meaning in Performance of Dance

2.4 Perform original works that employ personal artistic intent and communicate effectively.

2.5 Perform works by various dance artists communicating the original intent of the work while employing personal artistic intent and interpretation.

Development of Partner and Group Skills

2.6 Collaborate with peers in the development of choreography in groups (e.g., duets, trios, small ensembles).

2.7 Teach movement patterns and phrases to peers.

Creation/Invention of Dance Movement

2.1 Create a diverse body of works of dance, each of which demonstrates originality, unity, clarity of intent, and a dynamic range of movement.

Application of Choreographic Principles and Processes to Creating Dance

2.2 Use dance structures, musical forms, theatrical elements, and technology to create original works.

2.3 Notate dances, using a variety of systems (e.g., labanotation, motif writing, personal systems).

Communication of Meaning in Performance of Dance

2.4 Perform a diverse range of works by various dance artists, maintaining the integrity of the work while applying personal artistic expression.

Development of Partner and Group Skills

2.5 Collaborate with peers in the development of complex choreography in diverse groupings (e.g., all male, all female, people standing with people sitting).

2.6 Teach to peers a variety of complex movement patterns and phrases.

Chapter 3
Visual and
Performing Arts
Content
Standards

Grades Nine
Through Twelve

High School Arts Content Standards—Dance

Component Strand: 3.0 Historical and Cultural Context

 Students analyze the function and development of dance in past and present cultures throughout the world, noting human diversity as it relates to dance and dancers.

 Students recognize dance in past and present cultures throughout the world.

Proficient	Advanced
Understanding the Historical Contributions and Cultural Dimensions of Dance	Understanding the Historical Contributions and Cultural Dimensions of Dance

Proficient

Development of Dance

3.1 Identify and perform folk/traditional, social, and theatrical dances with appropriate stylistic nuances.

3.2 Describe ways in which folk/traditional, social, and theatrical dances reflect their specific cultural context.

History and Function of Dance

3.3 Explain how the works of dance by major choreographers communicate universal themes and sociopolitical issues in their historical/cultural contexts (e.g., seventeenth-century Italy, eighteenth-century France, the women's suffrage movement, dance in the French courts, Chinese cultural revolution).

Diversity of Dance

3.4 Explain how dancers from various cultures and historical periods reflect diversity and values (e.g., ethnicity, gender, body types, and religious intent).

Advanced

Development of Dance

3.1 Identify, analyze, and perform folk/traditional, social, and theatrical dances with technical accuracy and appropriate stylistic nuances.

3.2 Analyze the role dancers and choreographers play in the interpretation of dances in various historical and cultural settings.

History and Function of Dance

3.3 Compare and contrast universal themes and sociopolitical issues in a variety of dances from different cultural contexts and time periods.

Diversity of Dance

3.4 Explain how dancers and choreographers reflect roles, work, and values in selected cultures, countries, and historical periods.

**Grades Nine
Through Twelve**

High School Arts Content Standards—Dance
Component Strand: *4.0 Aesthetic Valuing*

Students critically assess and derive meaning from works of dance, performance of dancers, and original works based on the elements of dance and aesthetic qualities.

Proficient	**Advanced**
Responding to, Analyzing, and Making Judgments About Works of Dance	Responding to, Analyzing, and Making Judgments About Works of Dance

Description, Analysis, and Criticism of Dance

4.1 Describe how the qualities of a theatrical production contribute to the success of a dance performance (e.g., music, lighting, costuming, text, set design).

4.2 Apply criteria-based assessments appropriate to various dance forms (e.g., concert jazz, street, liturgical).

4.3 Defend personal preferences about dance styles and choreographic forms, using criteria-based assessment.

Meaning and Impact of Dance

4.4 Research and identify dances from different historic periods or cultures and make connections between social change and artistic expression in dance.

4.5 Identify and evaluate the advantages and limitations of viewing live and recorded dance performances.

Description, Analysis, and Criticism of Dance

4.1 Critique dance works to improve choreographic structure and artistic presence.

4.2 Use selected criteria to compare, contrast, and assess various dance forms (e.g., concert jazz, street, liturgical).

4.3 Analyze evolving personal preferences about dance styles and choreographic forms to identify change and development in personal choices.

Meaning and Impact of Dance

4.4 Research and assess how specific dance works change because of the impact of historic and cultural influences on their interpretations (e.g., because of the loss of lives in war, Fancy Dancing, once performed only by men, is now also performed by women).

4.5 Evaluate how aesthetic principles apply to choreography designed for technological media (e.g., film, video, TV, computer imaging).

High School Arts Content Standards—Dance

Component Strand: *5.0 Connections, Relationships, Applications*

Students apply what they learn in dance to learning across subject areas. They develop competencies and creative skills in problem solving, communication, and management of time and resources that contribute to lifelong learning and career skills. They also learn about careers in and related to dance.

**Grades Nine
Through Twelve**

Proficient	Advanced
Connecting and Applying What Is Learned in Dance to Learning in Other Art Forms and Subject Areas and to Careers	Connecting and Applying What Is Learned in Dance to Learning in Other Art Forms and Subject Areas and to Careers

Connections and Applications Across Disciplines

5.1 Demonstrate effective use of technology for recording, analyzing, and creating dances.

5.2 Apply concepts from anatomy, physiology, and physics to the study and practice of dance techniques.

Development of Life Skills and Career Competencies

5.3 Explain how dancing presents opportunities and challenges to maintain physical and emotional health and how to apply that information to current training and lifelong habits.

5.4 Explain how participation in dance develops creative skills for lifelong learning and well-being that are interpersonal and intrapersonal.

5.5 Examine the training, education, and experience needed to pursue dance career options (e.g., performer, choreographer, dance therapist, teacher, historian, critic, filmmaker).

Connections and Applications Across Disciplines

5.1 Demonstrate effective knowledge and skills in using audiovisual equipment and technology when creating, recording, and producing dance.

5.2 Compare the study and practice of dance techniques to motion, time, and physical principles from scientific disciplines (e.g., muscle and bone identification and usage; awareness of matter, space, time, and energy/force).

Development of Life Skills and Career Competencies

5.3 Synthesize information from a variety of health-related resources to maintain physical and emotional health.

5.4 Determine the appropriate training, experience, and education needed to pursue a variety of dance and dance-related careers.

**Grades Nine
Through Twelve**

Music

High school students develop and refine their ability to read, play, and compose music. Immersed in all aspects of music, they transcribe songs, sight-read accurately and expressively, and analyze music as to musical elements, expressive devices, compositional devices and techniques, and use of form. Focusing on vocal or instrumental skills, they perform by themselves and in ensembles a more complex repertoire of music with technical accuracy and expression. Composing, arranging, and improvising music require application of musical elements and perhaps the use of various digital or electronic instruments. They also study musicians and the historical aspects of music developed in the United States and in various cultures and time periods. For example, they may explain the role of various musicians in the culture, describe differences in musical styles, and classify and compare stylistic features of music.

As students gain the ability to develop and apply specific criteria for judging and evaluating the quality and effectiveness of music and performances, they are better able to apply criteria to improving their own work, realizing that the same criteria may not apply to music from other cultures and time periods. They also gain insights into why and how people from different parts of the world create and respond to music. Further, they analyze the role and function of music in American culture as related to the other arts disciplines, examine the function of music in radio, television, and advertising, and research musical careers.

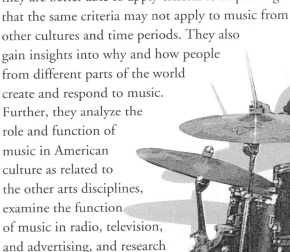

High School Arts Content Standards—Music

Component Strand: *1.0 Artistic Perception*

Students read, notate, listen to, analyze, and describe music and other aural information, using the terminology of music.

Proficient	**Advanced**
Processing, Analyzing, and Responding to Sensory Information Through the Language and Skills Unique to Music	Processing, Analyzing, and Responding to Sensory Information Through the Language and Skills Unique to Music

Read and Notate Music

1.1 Read an instrumental or vocal score of up to four staves and explain how the elements of music are used.

1.2 Transcribe simple songs when presented aurally into melodic and rhythmic notation (level of difficulty: 1 on a scale of 1–6).

1.3 Sight-read music accurately and expressively (level of difficulty: 3 on a scale of 1–6).

Listen to, Analyze, and Describe Music

1.4 Analyze and describe the use of musical elements and expressive devices (e.g., articulation, dynamic markings) in aural examples in a varied repertoire of music representing diverse genres, styles, and cultures.

1.5 Identify and explain a variety of compositional devices and techniques used to provide unity, variety, tension, and release in aural examples.

1.6 Analyze the use of form in a varied repertoire of music representing diverse genres, styles, and cultures.

Read and Notate Music

1.1 Read a full instrument or vocal score and describe how the elements of music are used.

1.2 Transcribe simple songs into melodic and rhythmic notation when presented aurally (level of difficulty: 2 on a scale of 1–6).

1.3 Sight-read music accurately and expressively (level of difficulty: 4 on a scale of 1–6).

Listen to, Analyze, and Describe Music

1.4 Analyze and describe significant musical events perceived and remembered in a given aural example.

1.5 Analyze and describe the use of musical elements in a given work that makes it unique, interesting, and expressive.

1.6 Compare and contrast the use of form, both past and present, in a varied repertoire of music from diverse genres, styles, and cultures.

**Grades Nine
Through Twelve**

High School Arts Content Standards—Music

Component Strand: *2.0 Creative Expression*

Students apply vocal and instrumental musical skills in performing a varied repertoire of music. They compose and arrange music and improvise melodies, variations, and accompaniments, using digital/electronic technology when appropriate.

Proficient	**Advanced**
Creating, Performing, and Participating in Music	Creating, Performing, and Participating in Music

Apply Vocal or Instrumental Skills

2.1 Sing a repertoire of vocal literature representing various genres, styles, and cultures with expression, technical accuracy, tone quality, vowel shape, and articulation—written and memorized, by oneself and in ensembles (level of difficulty: 4 on a scale of 1–6).

2.2 Sing music written in three or four parts, with and without accompaniment.

2.3 Sing in small ensembles, with one performer for each part.

2.4 Perform on an instrument a repertoire of instrumental literature representing various genres, styles, and cultures with expression, technical accuracy, tone quality, and articulation, by oneself and in ensembles (level of difficulty: 4 on a scale of 1–6).

2.5 Perform on an instrument in small ensembles, with one performer for each part.

Compose, Arrange, and Improvise

2.6 Compose music, using musical elements for expressive effect.

2.7 Compose and arrange music for voices or various acoustic or digital/electronic instruments, using appropriate ranges for traditional sources of sound.

2.8 Arrange pieces for voices and instruments other than those for which the pieces were originally written.

2.9 Improvise harmonizing parts, using an appropriate style.

2.10 Improvise original melodies over given chord progressions.

Apply Vocal or Instrumental Skills

2.1 Sing a repertoire of vocal literature representing various genres, styles, and cultures with expression, technical accuracy, tone quality, vowel shape, and articulation—written and memorized, by oneself and in ensembles (level of difficulty: 5 on a scale of 1–6).

2.2 Sing music written in four parts, with and without accompaniment.

2.3 Sing in small ensembles, with one performer for each part (level of difficulty: 5 on a scale of 1–6).

2.4 Perform on an instrument a repertoire of instrumental literature representing various genres, styles, and cultures with expression, technical accuracy, tone quality, and articulation, by oneself and in ensembles (level of difficulty: 5 on a scale of 1–6).

2.5 Perform in small instrumental ensembles with one performer for each part (level of difficulty: 5 on a scale of 1–6).

Compose, Arrange, and Improvise

2.6 Compose music in distinct styles.

2.7 Compose and arrange music for various combinations of voice and acoustic and digital/electronic instruments, using appropriate ranges and traditional and nontraditional sound sources.

2.8 Create melodic and rhythmic improvisations in a style or genre within a musical culture (e.g., gamelan, jazz, and mariachi).

High School Arts Content Standards—Music

Component Strand: *3.0 Historical and Cultural Context*

Students analyze the role of music in past and present cultures throughout the world, noting cultural diversity as it relates to music, musicians, and composers.

**Grades Nine
Through Twelve**

Proficient	**Advanced**
Understanding the Historical Contributions and Cultural Dimensions of Music	Understanding the Historical Contributions and Cultural Dimensions of Music

Role of Music

3.1 Identify the sources of musical genres of the United States, trace the evolution of those genres, and cite well-known musicians associated with them.

3.2 Explain the various roles that musicians perform, identify representative individuals who have functioned in each role, and explain their activities and achievements.

Diversity of Music

3.3 Describe the differences between styles in traditional folk genres within the United States.

3.4 Perform music from various cultures and time periods.

3.5 Classify, by genre or style and historical period or culture, unfamiliar but representative aural examples of music and explain the reasoning for the classification.

Role of Music

3.1 Analyze how the roles of musicians and composers have changed or remained the same throughout history.

3.2 Identify uses of music elements in nontraditional art music (e.g., atonal, twelve-tone, serial).

3.3 Compare and contrast the social function of a variety of music forms in various cultures and time periods.

Diversity of Music

3.4 Perform music from a variety of cultures and historical periods.

3.5 Compare and contrast instruments from a variety of cultures and historical periods.

3.6 Compare and contrast musical styles within various popular genres in North America and South America.

3.7 Analyze the stylistic features of a given musical work that define its aesthetic traditions and its historical or cultural context.

3.8 Compare and contrast musical genres or styles that show the influence of two or more cultural traditions.

**Grades Nine
Through Twelve**

High School Arts Content Standards—Music

Component Strand: *4.0 Aesthetic Valuing*

Students critically assess and derive meaning from works of music and the performance of musicians in a cultural context according to the elements of music, aesthetic qualities, and human responses.

Proficient	**Advanced**
Responding to, Analyzing, and Making Judgments About Works of Music	Responding to, Analyzing, and Making Judgments About Works of Music

Analyze and Critically Assess

4.1 Develop specific criteria for making informed critical evaluations of the quality and effectiveness of performances, compositions, arrangements, and improvisations and apply those criteria in personal participation in music.

4.2 Evaluate a performance, composition, arrangement, or improvisation by comparing each with an exemplary model.

Derive Meaning

4.3 Explain how people in a particular culture use and respond to specific musical works from that culture.

4.4 Describe the means used to create images or evoke feelings and emotions in musical works from various cultures.

Analyze and Critically Assess

4.1 Compare and contrast how a composer's intentions result in a work of music and how that music is used.

Derive Meaning

4.2 Analyze and explain how and why people in a particular culture use and respond to specific musical works from their own culture.

4.3 Compare and contrast the musical means used to create images or evoke feelings and emotions in works of music from various cultures.

High School Arts Content Standards—Music

Component Strand: *5.0 Connections, Relationships, Applications*

Students apply what they learn in music across subject areas. They develop competencies and creative skills in problem solving, communication, and management of time and resources that contribute to lifelong learning and career skills. They also learn about careers in and related to music.

**Grades Nine
Through Twelve**

Proficient	Advanced
Connecting and Applying What Is Learned in Music to Learning in Other Art Forms and Subject Areas and to Careers	Connecting and Applying What Is Learned in Music to Learning in Other Art Forms and Subject Areas and to Careers

Connections and Applications

5.1 Explain how elements, artistic processes, and organizational principles are used in similar and distinctive ways in the various arts.

5.2 Analyze the role and function of music in radio, television, and advertising.

Careers and Career-Related Skills

5.3 Research musical careers in radio, television, and advertising.

Connections and Applications

5.1 Explain ways in which the principles and subject matter of music and various disciplines outside the arts are interrelated.

5.2 Analyze the process for arranging, underscoring, and composing music for film and video productions.

Careers and Career-Related Skills

5.3 Identify and explain the various factors involved in pursing careers in music.

**Grades Nine
Through Twelve**

Theatre

High school students apply their understanding of the vocabulary of theatre as they document the production elements of theatrical performances, thereby increasing their ability to write, design, produce, and perform. They base their acting choices on script analysis, character research, reflection, and revision, writing dialogues and scenes and applying their knowledge of dramatic structure. From at first playing theatrical games to now describing ways in which playwrights reflect and influence their culture, students grasp the power of theatre to present and explore complex ideas and issues in forms that range from comedy to tragedy. They also examine how a specific actor uses or has used drama to convey meaning and analyze the impact of traditional and nontraditional theatre, film, television, and electronic media on societies. They understand the value of the knowledge and skills they learned in theatre as related to careers in theatre and elsewhere. By participating in theatre, they continue to improve their time-management skills, meet deadlines, and learn the professional standards required in the world of theatre.

High School Arts Content Standards—Theatre

Component Strand: *1.0 Artistic Perception*

Students observe their environment and respond, using the elements of theatre. They also observe formal and informal works of theatre, film/video, and electronic media and respond, using the vocabulary of theatre.

**Grades Nine
Through Twelve**

Proficient	**Advanced**
Processing, Analyzing, and Responding to Sensory Information Through the Language and Skills Unique to Theatre	Processing, Analyzing, and Responding to Sensory Information Through the Language and Skills Unique to Theatre

Development of the Vocabulary of Theatre

1.1 Use the vocabulary of theatre, such as *acting values, style, genre, design,* and *theme,* to describe theatrical experiences.

Comprehension and Analysis of the Elements of Theatre

1.2 Document observations and perceptions of production elements, noting mood, pacing, and use of space through class discussion and reflective writing.

Development of the Vocabulary of Theatre

1.1 Use the vocabulary of theatre, such as *genre, style, acting values, theme,* and *design* to describe theatrical experiences.

Comprehension and Analysis of the Elements of Theatre

1.2 Research, analyze, or serve as the dramaturg for a play in collaboration with the director, designer, or playwright.

1.3 Identify the use of metaphor, subtext, and symbolic elements in scripts and theatrical productions.

112

Chapter 3
Visual and
Performing Arts
Content
Standards

High School Arts Content Standards—Theatre

Component Strand: *2.0 Creative Expression*

Students apply processes and skills in acting, directing, designing, and scriptwriting to create formal and informal theatre, film/videos, and electronic media productions and to perform in them.

Proficient	**Advanced**
Creating, Performing, and Participating in Theatre	Creating, Performing, and Participating in Theatre

Development of Theatrical Skills

2.1 Make acting choices, using script analysis, character research, reflection, and revision through the rehearsal process.

Creation/Invention in Theatre

2.2 Write dialogues and scenes, applying basic dramatic structure: exposition, complication, conflict, crises, climax, and resolution.

2.3 Design, produce, or perform scenes or plays from a variety of theatrical periods and styles, including Shakespearean and contemporary realism.

Development of Theatrical Skills

2.1 Make acting choices, using script analysis, character research, reflection, and revision to create characters from classical, contemporary, realistic, and nonrealistic dramatic texts.

Creation/Invention in Theatre

2.2 Improvise or write dialogues and scenes, applying basic dramatic structure (exposition, complication, crises, climax, and resolution) and including complex characters with unique dialogue that motivates the action.

2.3 Work collaboratively as designer, producer, or actor to meet directorial goals in scenes and plays from a variety of contemporary and classical playwrights.

113

Chapter 3
Visual and
Performing Arts
Content
Standards

Students analyze the role and development of theatre, film/video, and electronic media in past and present cultures throughout the world, noting diversity as it relates to theatre.

Proficient	**Advanced**
Understanding the Historical Contributions and Cultural Dimensions of Theatre	Understanding the Historical Contributions and Cultural Dimensions of Theatre

*Role and Cultural Significance
of Theatre*

3.1 Identify and compare how film, theatre, television, and electronic media productions influence our values and behaviors.

3.2 Describe the ways in which playwrights reflect and influence their culture in such works as *Raisin in the Sun, Antigone,* and the *Mahabarata.*

History of Theatre

3.3 Identify key figures, works, and trends in world theatrical history from various cultures and time periods.

*Role and Cultural Significance
of Theatre*

3.1 Research and perform monologues in various historical and cultural contexts, using accurate and consistent physical mannerisms and dialect.

History of Theatre

3.2 Analyze the impact of traditional and nontraditional theatre, film, television, and electronic media on society.

3.3 Perform, design, or direct theatre pieces in specific theatrical styles, including classics by such playwrights as Sophocles, Shakespeare, Lope de Vega, Aphra Behn, Moliere, and Chekhov.

3.4 Compare and contrast specific styles and forms of world theatre. For example, differentiate between Elizabethan comedy and Restoration farce.

**Grades Nine
Through Twelve**

High School Arts Content Standards—Theatre

Component Strand: *4.0 Aesthetic Valuing*

 Students critique and derive meaning from works of theatre, film/video, electronic media, and theatrical artists on the basis of aesthetic qualities.

Proficient	**Advanced**
Responding to, Analyzing, and Critiquing Theatrical Experiences	Responding to, Analyzing, and Critiquing Theatrical Experiences

Critical Assessment of Theatre

4.1 Compare a traditional interpretation of a play with a nontraditional interpretation and defend the merits of the different interpretations.

Derivation of Meaning from Works of Theatre

4.2 Report on how a specific actor used drama to convey meaning in his or her performances.

Critical Assessment of Theatre

4.1 Use complex evaluation criteria and terminology to compare and contrast a variety of genres of dramatic literature.

4.2 Draw conclusions about the effectiveness of informal and formal productions, films/videos, or electronic media on the basis of intent, structure, and quality of the work.

Derivation of Meaning from Works of Theatre

4.3 Develop a thesis based on research as to why people create theatre.

High School Arts Content Standards—Theatre

Component Strand: *5.0 Connections, Relationships, Applications*

Students apply what they learn in theatre, film/video, and electronic media across subject areas. They develop competencies and creative skills in problem solving, communication, and time management that contribute to lifelong learning and career skills. They also learn about careers in and related to theatre.

Proficient	Advanced
Connecting and Applying What Is Learned in Theatre, Film/Video, and Electronic Media to Other Art Forms and Subject Areas and to Careers	Connecting and Applying What Is Learned in Theatre, Film/Video, and Electronic Media to Other Art Forms and Subject Areas and to Careers

Connections and Applications

5.1 Describe how skills acquired in theatre may be applied to other content areas and careers.

Careers and Career-Related Skills

5.2 Manage time, prioritize responsibilities, and meet completion deadlines for a production as specified by group leaders, team members, or directors.

5.3 Demonstrate an understanding of the professional standards of the actor, director, scriptwriter, and technical artist, such as the requirements for union membership.

Connections and Applications

5.1 Create projects in other school courses or places of employment, using tools, techniques, and processes from the study and practice of theatre, film/video, and electronic media.

Careers and Career-Related Skills

5.2 Demonstrate the ability to create rehearsal schedules, set deadlines, organize priorities, and identify needs and resources when participating in the production of a play or scene.

5.3 Communicate creative, design, and directorial choices to ensemble members, using leadership skills, aesthetic judgment, or problem-solving skills.

5.4 Develop advanced or entry-level competencies for a career in an artistic or technical field in the theatrical arts.

**Grades Nine
Through Twelve**

Visual Arts

High school students deepen and broaden their investigation of the subject while improving their techniques and developing a style. Building on their previous work with the elements of art and principles of design, they now discuss, analyze, and synthesize the use of those elements and principles and apply them to create their own work. Recognizing that an artist's style and materials influence the artwork, they compare work created with traditional and electronic media. Their artwork now reflects refined craftsmanship and technical skill, extending into the manipulation of digital imagery and reflecting refined observational drawing skills.

Students know how to communicate to others through their artwork as artists from all cultures have done through the ages. Focusing on contemporary artists, they discuss the role and purpose of art being produced. They also discuss how art historians determine the time, place, context, value, and culture of works from the past. Going further, they research the skills required by those working in all fields related to the visual arts—the artist, the gallery owner, or aesthetician—who might ponder the question What is art? or speculate on how advances in technology might change the definition and function of the visual arts.

High School Arts Content Standards—Visual Arts
Component Strand: *1.0 Artistic Perception*

Students perceive and respond to works of art, objects in nature, events, and the environment. They also use the vocabulary of the visual arts to express their observations.

Grades Nine Through Twelve

Proficient	**Advanced**
Processing, Analyzing, and Responding to Sensory Information Through the Language and Skills Unique to the Visual Arts	Processing, Analyzing, and Responding to Sensory Information Through the Language and Skills Unique to the Visual Arts

Develop Perceptual Skills and Visual Arts Vocabulary

1.1 Identify and use the principles of design to discuss, analyze, and write about visual aspects in the environment and in works of art, including their own.

1.2 Describe the principles of design as used in works of art, focusing on dominance and subordination.

Analyze Art Elements and Principles of Design

1.3 Research and analyze the work of an artist and write about the artist's distinctive style and its contribution to the meaning of the work.

1.4 Analyze and describe how the composition of a work of art is affected by the use of a particular principle of design.

Impact of Media Choice

1.5 Analyze the material used by a given artist and describe how its use influences the meaning of the work.

1.6 Compare and contrast similar styles of works of art done in electronic media with those done with materials traditionally used in visual arts.

Develop Perceptual Skills and Visual Arts Vocabulary

1.1 Analyze and discuss complex ideas, such as distortion, color theory, arbitrary color, scale, expressive content, and real versus virtual in works of art.

1.2 Discuss a series of their original works of art, using the appropriate vocabulary of art.

1.3 Analyze their works of art as to personal direction and style.

Analyze Art Elements and Principles of Design

1.4 Research two periods of painting, sculpture, film, or other media and discuss their similarities and differences, using the language of the visual arts.

1.5 Compare how distortion is used in photography or video with how the artist uses distortion in painting or sculpture.

1.6 Describe the use of the elements of art to express mood in one or more of their works of art.

Impact of Media Choice

1.7 Select three works of art from their art portfolio and discuss the intent of the work and the use of the media.

1.8 Analyze the works of a well-known artist as to the art media selected and the effect of that selection on the artist's style.

**Grades Nine
Through Twelve**

High School Arts Content Standards—Visual Arts

Component Strand: 2.0 Creative Expression

Students apply artistic processes and skills, using a variety of media to communicate meaning and intent in original works of art.

Proficient	**Advanced**
Creating, Performing, and Participating in the Visual Arts	Creating, Performing, and Participating in the Visual Arts

Skills, Processes, Materials, and Tools

2.1 Solve a visual arts problem that involves the effective use of the elements of art and the principles of design.

2.2 Prepare a portfolio of original two- and three-dimensional works of art that reflects refined craftsmanship and technical skills.

2.3 Develop and refine skill in the manipulation of digital imagery (either still or video).

2.4 Review and refine observational drawing skills.

Communication and Expression Through Original Works of Art

2.5 Create an expressive composition, focusing on dominance and subordination.

2.6 Create a two- or three-dimensional work of art that addresses a social issue.

Skills, Processes, Materials, and Tools

2.1 Create original works of art of increasing complexity and skill in a variety of media that reflect their feelings and points of view.

2.2 Plan and create works of art that reflect complex ideas, such as distortion, color theory, arbitrary color, scale, expressive content, and real versus virtual.

2.3 Assemble and display objects or works of art as a part of a public exhibition.

Communicate and Express Through Original Works of Art

2.4 Demonstrate in their own works of art a personal style and an advanced proficiency in communicating an idea, theme, or emotion.

2.5 Use innovative visual metaphors in creating works of art.

2.6 Present a universal concept in a multi-media work of art that demonstrates knowledge of technology skills.

119

Chapter 3
Visual and
Performing Arts
Content
Standards

High School Arts Content Standards—Visual Arts

Component Strand: 3.0 Historical and Cultural Context

Students analyze the role and development of the visual arts in past and present cultures throughout the world, noting human diversity as it relates to the visual arts and artists.

Proficient	**Advanced**
Understanding the Historical Contributions and Cultural Dimensions of the Visual Arts	Understanding the Historical Contributions and Cultural Dimensions of the Visual Arts

Role and Development of the Visual Arts

3.1 Identify similarities and differences in the purposes of art created in selected cultures.

3.2 Identify and describe the role and influence of new technologies on contemporary works of art.

Diversity of the Visual Arts

3.3 Identify and describe trends in the visual arts and discuss how the issues of time, place, and cultural influence are reflected in selected works of art.

3.4 Discuss the purposes of art in selected contemporary cultures.

Role and Development of the Visual Arts

3.1 Identify contemporary styles and discuss the diverse social, economic, and political developments reflected in the works of art examined.

3.2 Identify contemporary artists worldwide who have achieved regional, national, or international recognition and discuss ways in which their work reflects, plays a role in, and influences present-day culture.

Diversity of the Visual Arts

3.3 Investigate and discuss universal concepts expressed in works of art from diverse cultures.

3.4 Research the methods art historians use to determine the time, place, context, value, and culture that produced a given work of art.

**Grades Nine
Through Twelve**

High School Arts Content Standards—Visual Arts

Component Strand: *4.0 Aesthetic Valuing*

Students analyze, assess, and derive meaning from works of art, including their own, according to the elements of art, the principles of design, and aesthetic qualities.

Proficient	**Advanced**
Responding to, Analyzing, and Making Judgments About Works in the Visual Arts	Responding to, Analyzing, and Making Judgments About Works in the Visual Arts

Derive Meaning

4.1 Articulate how personal beliefs, cultural traditions, and current social, economic, and political contexts influence the interpretation of the meaning or message in a work of art.

4.2 Compare the ways in which the meaning of a specific work of art has been affected over time because of changes in interpretation and context.

Make Informed Judgments

4.3 Formulate and support a position regarding the aesthetic value of a specific work of art and change or defend that position after considering the views of others.

4.4 Articulate the process and rationale for refining and reworking one of their own works of art.

4.5 Employ the conventions of art criticism in writing and speaking about works of art.

Derive Meaning

4.1 Describe the relationship involving the art maker (artist), the making (process), the artwork (product), and the viewer.

4.2 Identify the intentions of artists creating contemporary works of art and explore the implications of those intentions.

4.3 Analyze and articulate how society influences the interpretation and message of a work of art.

Make Informed Judgments

4.4 Apply various art-related theoretical perspectives to their own works of art and the work of others in classroom critiques.

4.5 Construct a rationale for the validity of a specific work of art—artwork that falls outside their own conceptions of art.

4.6 Develop written criteria for the selection of a body of work from their portfolios that represents significant achievements.

High School Arts Content Standards—Visual Arts

Component Strand: *5.0 Connections, Relationships, Applications*

Students apply what they learn in the visual arts across subject areas. They develop competencies and creative skills in problem solving, communication, and management of time and resources that contribute to lifelong learning and career skills. They also learn about careers in and related to the visual arts.

Proficient	**Advanced**
Connecting and Applying What Is Learned in the Visual Arts to Other Art Forms and Subject Areas and to Careers	Connecting and Applying What Is Learned in the Visual Arts to Other Art Forms and Subject Areas and to Careers

Connections and Applications

5.1 Design an advertising campaign for a theatre or dance production held at a school, creating images that represent characters and major events in the production.

5.2 Create a work of art that communicates a cross-cultural or universal theme taken from literature or history.

Visual Literacy

5.3 Compare and contrast the ways in which different media (television, newspapers, magazines) cover the same art exhibition.

Careers and Career-Related Skills

5.4 Demonstrate an understanding of the various skills of an artist, art critic, art historian, art collector, art gallery owner, and philosopher of art (aesthetician).

Connections and Applications

5.1 Speculate on how advances in technology might change the definition and function of the visual arts.

Visual Literacy

5.2 Compare and contrast works of art, probing beyond the obvious and identifying psychological content found in the symbols and images.

Careers and Career-Related Skills

5.3 Prepare portfolios of their original works of art for a variety of purposes (e.g., review for postsecondary application, exhibition, job application, and personal collection).

5.4 Investigate and report on the essential features of modern or emerging technologies that affect or will affect visual artists and the definition of the visual arts.

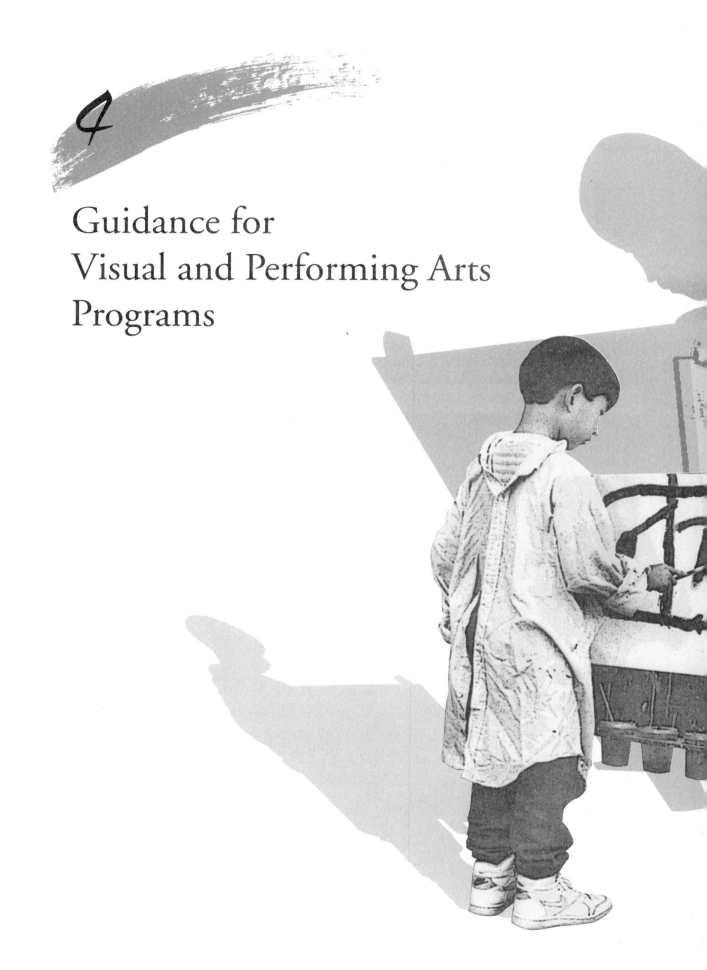

4

Guidance for
Visual and Performing Arts
Programs

Guidance for Visual and Performing Arts Programs

All students can learn and benefit from arts education. All teachers and administrators, not just those who specialize in the arts, must support and be involved in arts education and must have opportunities to participate in well-designed preservice and in-service arts education programs. Time, staff, facilities, materials, and equipment must be provided to support arts education programs.

—Arts Work

This chapter focuses in turn on each of the four arts disciplines, providing a clear picture of the many factors that contribute to a successful standards-based education program for dance, music, theatre, and the visual arts. Some factors are similar for each discipline; others are unique. A standards-based program, kindergarten through high school, should be guaranteed for all students and prepare them for educational, career, and life choices beyond high school. However, for many reasons some disciplines may be more fully available than others.

All of the descriptions in this chapter represent best practices recommended for program implementation. With that ideal program in mind, a school district, in partnership with the community, can develop a multiyear plan for building a high-quality standards-based program in each of the arts that provides all students with equal access.

125

Chapter 4
Guidance
for Visual and
Performing Arts
Programs

Dance

Dancing is an experience in movement. Whether accompanied by words, music, sounds, or silence, bodily movement represents an important means of expression. For many generations and in many cultures, people have danced socially to entertain one another, communicate their deepest feelings and emotions, and celebrate their humanity. Although some may think that dance amounts merely to "learning the steps," they should acknowledge that to become conversant with the ideas and expressions that embody dance, students must develop certain skills.

Dance embodies control, perception, flexibility, and rhythm along with an awareness of one's movements within an environment and in combination with other dancers. When controlled,

That which cannot be spoken can be sung; that which cannot be sung can be danced.

—Old French saying

shaped, and elaborated, movements produce dance. As students define, embellish, pattern, exaggerate, repeat, and coordinate their ordinary bodily movements with other movements and gestures, they become more skillful in dancing. Those experiences help to transform the students into purposeful, expressive beings.

The vocabulary of dance includes the basic elements of *time, space,* and *force* or *energy.* In a well-planned dance education program, students grow in understanding dance and its elements through direct experience. The craft, skill, and knowledge they gain as they advance through the grades constitute a discipline distinct and separate from physical education.

Standards-Based Curriculum for Dance

All students should recognize that they dance somewhere every day through gesture, body language, and nonverbal communication. Accordingly, dance should be made part of the school curriculum. In the primary grades students explore and experiment with movement, becoming aware of their kinesthetic intelligence. With continued sequential study as described in the content standards, they acquire increased bodily awareness and control and develop confidence as they make their own choices.

A well-planned curriculum for a standards-based dance program is articulated from kindergarten through grade twelve. Such a curriculum provides opportunities for students to dance, create dances, and observe and appreciate dances. By reading about, writing about, talking about, and reflecting on dances from a variety of cultures and historical periods, they become aware of

Dance

how dance connects to the world around them, to other curriculum areas, and to careers.

The dance curriculum at each grade level incorporates all five arts strands in the content standards: artistic perception, creative expression, historical and cultural context, aesthetic valuing, and connections, relationships, and applications (see Chapter 3). The standards in each strand align with the motor, social, emotional, and cognitive developmental levels of the students at each grade level. Using the strands as the basis for instruction, the teacher should recognize that for students to create works in dance, they must view dance and respond to it in ways that enable them to understand the nature and power of aesthetic experiences.

Artistic Perception

The physical experiences that students encounter when they practice dance techniques increase their artistic perception of the elements of dance, including time, space, and force or energy. In this strand instruction focuses on kinesthetic awareness, movement communication skills, capacity for movement response, and motor efficiency through multisensory activities. Also inherent in this strand is an appreciation of dance as an art form accessible to all students.

Creative Expression

Students use intuition and imagination to express emotion and communicate meaning as they participate in dance. Improvising and forming movement patterns and compositions lead to the development of choreographic skills to create culturally authentic or personally original works in dance. Individual creativity is encouraged and developed as students explore movement in spontaneous and structured assignments. As they learn to express their feelings and ideas through movement, they grow in ability to develop choreography. Through shared experiences students develop respect and appreciation for the uniqueness of each individual's expression. Communicating through physical movement, they learn more about the body as an instrument of artistic expression.

Students learn to appreciate their bodies and care for them through proper conditioning, warm-ups, dance technique, rest, and nutrition. Correct anatomical alignment, effective warm-up and rest of muscles, proper nutrition, and a safe environment for movement should be emphasized in every lesson. Through increased knowledge of the natural laws governing human movement, students become increasingly aware of the uniqueness of each individual's expressions.

Historical and Cultural Context

The deep, complex heritage of dance is derived from the contributions of all cultural groups, past and present. An understanding of dance history helps students recognize and appreciate the cultural differences and commonalities that

127

Chapter 4
Guidance
for Visual and
Performing Arts
Programs

make up the human experience. By studying the historical, cultural, social, and contemporary expressions of dance, students uncover the influence of one cultural style on another. As they share personal cultural experiences and ideas, they can connect elements of individual traditions with those of shared cultures. Through the study of the history of dance, students can examine historical and cultural concepts, events, and themes in diverse contexts.

An Example of Historical and Cultural Context in High School Dance

Many cultures have long traditions of formal dance performance. For example, casino-style dancing came to California after being adapted from music and movement that originated in West Africa. First, the dance and music of West Africa migrated to Cuba. The remarkable melting pot of cultures on the island contributed to a unique cultural experience in the Americas. In the 1930s a dance form called *Rueda de Casino* raged throughout Cuba and eventually reached Miami and the rest of the United States. Couples dance together in pairs or with other couples. Through calls and signals different movement combinations cause pairs to turn and switch partners. Dancing to salsa timing (stepping on the first beat) results in a fast-paced, beautifully synchronized, exciting dance that inspires young people to be part of a community and celebrate their individual skills. This is just one example of how dance defines the historic influences of different cultures within the state.

Aesthetic Valuing

Aesthetic valuing enables students to make critical judgments about the quality and success of dance compositions and performances based on their own knowledge, experiences, and perceptions. Through oral and written analyses, they reveal their opinions, newly acquired knowledge, and criteria for evaluating dance. The criteria for making critical judgments emerging from discussions between students and teachers are often guided by professional examples and expert opinion. When viewing a dance performance in class, on video, or at a live concert, students critique the performance, using appropriate aesthetic criteria. They might consider, for example, whether the performer exhibits proper posture, balance, and coordination or maintains consistent and appropriate rhythm throughout the performance.

Connections, Relationships, Applications

Described as an exciting, vibrant art useful in an educational setting, dance helps students develop by unifying their physical, mental, and emotional lives. Dance education programs include opportunities for the development of critical thinking and analytical skills, cooperation and teamwork, self-expression and self-awareness, organization and problem solving, cultural literacy, and communication of emotions through movement. These important abilities can be applied to situations occurring in the workplace and throughout life.

Dance

The elements of dance (time, space, and force or energy) can be applied to other subject areas, such as the language arts, writing, mathematics, science, history–social science, and physics. Opportunities for connections, relationships, and applications in the curriculum can be found in the mathematics of geometric shapes and spatial maps; the physics of energy and force; the use of vocabulary, such as rhythm and character; the study of history and culture through the study of dance from other time periods and locations around the world; and the choreographic process as it relates to writing.

Levels of Dance Instruction

In elementary school dance instruction is a part of classroom experiences. Teachers at this level should participate regularly in professional development in dance provided by, for example, teachers involved in The California Arts Project or dance artists working in the schools. At the middle school and high school levels, the dance program, offered in a visual and performing arts department, is available to all students. At that level at least one teacher of dance trained in teaching the knowledge, skills, and art of dance should be employed.

Elementary School Level

All elementary school students in California should receive dance instruction in which, learning through creative movement, they create and perform dance. Movement employs three modes: (1) auditory—the dancer listens to the teacher or to an accompanying drum or music; (2) visual—children observe and imitate the teacher, watch other dancers, and recognize spatial relationships; and (3) kinesthetic—children, moving in both new and familiar ways, develop a greater awareness of their bodies.

By practicing movements and viewing performance videos and live performances, students can identify and experience a variety of dance forms. Instruction is also focused on helping students understand dance vocabulary and the historical and cultural contexts of dances, dance styles (see *genre-d* in the glossary), and group expressions.

By emphasizing the creative process as well as the final performance, the elementary curriculum provides opportunities for students to experience and develop their creative potential and original expressions. In turn, this ability leads students to accept and appreciate the work of others.

Middle School Level

The middle school dance program expands elementary school learning and experiences through broader explorations and deeper study. Students acquire more extensive knowledge of dance, develop dance skills, and expand their creative potential. By attending regular dance classes and participating in other

Chapter 4
Guidance
for Visual and
Performing Arts
Programs

Dance

dance education programs, including before- or after-school programs, auxiliary periods, daytime standards-based curriculum, community dance artist residencies, summer school, or intersessions, students advance in knowledge and skills.

Through their own dance compositions and expressions, students explore the creative process, translating ideas, thoughts, and feelings into original pieces of choreography. They also study dance forms from many cultures and time periods in cultural and historical context. By performing and attending the performances of professional dancers and dance companies, they develop the skills needed for making aesthetic judgments and engaging in thoughtful discussions of their reasoning in the classroom. Because young adolescents often participate in describing an artistic problem, the teacher can focus on the students' interests, inspiring them and giving them the confidence to continue their study of dance. These experiences can make them aware of the many career opportunities in and related to dance.

High School Level

The dance program should be an integral part of the high school's visual and performing arts department. Standards-based high school dance instruction provides opportunities for students to create a body of dance works, conduct in-depth studies of major dance forms from various cultures, delve into the meaning and impact of dance, gain skills to improve their everyday lives, enhance opportunities for higher education, and develop competency leading to successful careers. At a minimum, instruction should provide a variety of learning opportunities in dance to meet the needs of all students toward achieving the content standards at the beginning or proficient level.

As they learn the language of dance, students advance to innovative and challenging experiences. At this level creative thinking in the five strands of the dance content standards should be intertwined through a sequence of appropriate introductory, intermediate, and advanced dance courses. The courses should be approved by the University of California and the California State University to meet the new visual and performing arts requirements for freshman admission to those institutions. To be approved, dance courses must include all five strands of the content standards. (Standards-based courses approved for admission and those that will not be accepted as college preparatory dance courses are listed in Appendix B.)

Instruction describing connections between dance and other subjects expands and enhances the scope of students' educational experiences. At this level students should have frequent contacts with professional dancers and view or attend professional dance performances. They should also create electronic, video, or computer-based portfolios to track their individual growth, prepare for high school exit exams, apply for college entrance and scholarships, or audition for employment opportunities in the field of dance.

Dance

Dance

Sample Standards-Based Unit of Study
Grades Nine Through Twelve

Standards-based instruction reinforces the importance of a rigorous, comprehensive arts education. Recognizing that performance classes are not intended to focus on appreciation, teachers should provide a variety of opportunities to meet standards while preparing students to perform quality works in dance. The following unit of study is an example of how to maintain the integrity of performance classes by focusing on developing dancing skills while providing a comprehensive approach to dance education. It also recognizes that many high school dance classes have both beginning and advanced students in one class and provide different opportunities according to experience.

This unit of study helps students to create individualized movement patterns, work with partners, and combine movement patterns. Revising and refining a choreographic approach based on good decision-making skills, they develop fully realized dance documentation for use inside and outside class.

PROFICIENT LEVEL	ADVANCED LEVEL
First year of instruction	Two or more years of additional instruction
Students view the dance productions of two different dance companies and compare and contrast the styles and production qualities (e.g., the Pilobolus Dance Theatre and the San Francisco Ballet).	Students research and view the dance productions of two different dance companies and compare and contrast the styles and production qualities. Reading and analyzing program notes from both companies, they determine cultural influences, stylistic nuances, and clarity of intent.
Students explain and defend their personal preference for one of the styles and choreographic forms by using a criteria-based assessment.	Students analyze their own preferences for one of the styles and choreographic forms as to how their own preferences and criteria for dance performance and choreography have evolved over time.

Chapter 4
Guidance
for Visual and
Performing Arts
Programs

Dance

PROFICIENT LEVEL (Continued)	ADVANCED LEVEL (Continued)
In collaborative groups students develop criteria for a dance they will choreograph, stage, and perform involving solos, duets, or ensembles based on, or in response to, the work of one of the dance companies studied.	In collaborative groups students develop criteria for a complex dance they will choreograph, stage, and perform involving solos, duets, or ensembles based on or in response to the work of one of the dance companies studied. The criteria include originality, unity, clarity of intent, and dynamic range of movement.
In collaborative groups students choreograph, practice, and perform a dance involving solos, duets, or ensembles based on, or in response to, the work of one of the dance companies studied. They videotape their performances.	In collaborative groups students choreograph, practice, and perform a complex dance involving solos, duets, or ensembles according to or in response to the work of one of the dance companies studied. The performance should demonstrate an advanced level of technical skill, clear intent, and professionalism. The students videotape their performances.
Students critique their own collaborative dance piece and the work of other groups in the class by using the criteria they have developed.	Students critique their own collaborative dance piece and the work of other groups in the class by using the criteria they have developed and specific dance vocabulary to describe movement and dance elements in great detail.
Students refine their dance performances, drawing on their own work, that of their peers, and an examination of the video of their performances.	Students refine their dance performances, drawing on their own work, that of their peers, and an examination of the video of their performances, and document the reasons for each change.

Dance

PROFICIENT LEVEL (Continued)	ADVANCED LEVEL (Continued)
Students identify and evaluate the advantages and limitations of viewing live and recorded dance performances.	Students identify and evaluate the advantages and limitations of viewing live and recorded dance performances and evaluate the use of video in recording their own performances.
Students discuss the training, education, and experience they called on to complete their dance performance and the potential use of that knowledge and skill in various dance careers, such as performer, choreographer, teacher, critic, or filmmaker.	On the basis of their investigation of dance companies, students research and determine the appropriate training, experience, and education needed to pursue a variety of dance and dance-related careers, including becoming an artistic director or a manager of a dance company.

Role of Student Dance Performances

Inventive, careful planning can make beginning performances shared experiences rather than "show" activities. When such performances represent an outgrowth of the students' capacity to move expressively and knowingly according to their age and physical ability, schools can overcome the tendency to produce high-powered performances with a few select students. The dance material should be appropriate for the level, skills, learning situation, knowledge, and understanding of the participants and the audience. Through these performing experiences, students can exhibit their own choreographic ideas and get feedback.

Students may present their beginning-level performances informally in a classroom or studio. Applying their newly acquired skills, they demonstrate their solution to a problem or evaluate a particular experience or technique in dance. Next, as students become skillful, they may present more formal dances outside the classroom or studio.

The visibility and popularity of performance groups may lead to consequences not related directly to dance education. Often, schools receive requests for their dance groups to perform, for example, at athletic events, assemblies, student productions, parent meetings, community clubs, conferences, and civic events. Although providing entertainment may be a valid activity for performance groups, it should never interfere with the students' dance education or

133

Chapter 4
Guidance
for Visual and
Performing Arts
Programs

understanding of the importance of presenting dance solely for its own recognition and aesthetic analysis.

Collections of student work in dance may include documentation of their learning through journal writing; reflections on dance performances or master classes; videos of work; research papers on California choreographers, for example; and charts of lighting designs. The collections may then be put on a CD and serve the students well in their continuing academic or professional pursuits. By creating portfolios and audition tapes, students can track their individual growth, prepare themselves for graduation, and use when applying for college entrance, scholarships, or employment in dance or when pursuing a dance-related career.

Resources for the Dance Program

A wide variety of experiences provide students with opportunities to improve personal and cultural understanding and insights and develop the knowledge and skills required to be considered proficient in the dance content standards. Vital to the success of such a standards-based program are appropriate equipment, instructional materials, and facilities as well as community resources and parent involvement.

Equipment and Instructional Materials

Equipment and instructional materials for dance classes may include some or all of the following:

- *Instructional equipment and materials.* The dance program should have access to instructional and presentation equipment and materials, including video cameras and playback equipment, films, audiotapes and videos, prints, photographs, rhythm instruments, body mats, and literature appropriate for each grade level, kindergarten through grade twelve. The library media teacher should serve as a fundamental partner in identifying and providing access to those resources.

- *Musical instruments.* Percussion instruments, essential to any creative movement class, are used for rhythmic training, locomotor activities, and dance composition. Instruments having a pleasing timbre and played by hand, such as bongo or plastic drums, are excellent choices.

  Other percussion sound sources and instruments provide accompanying sounds varying in tone, timbre, duration, and intensity. In most dance studios students can find a piano as standard equipment and use it effectively when working on movement qualities, rhythmic materials, and phrasing. Additional material and equipment may include multiple-speed CD or tape players.

Dance

- *Costumes and props.* Materials for composition work may include scarves, streamers, balls, balloons, paper bags, newspapers, ropes, elastics, a variety of costume items, pieces of fabric, and masks.
- *Access to contemporary media.* Study of the history and culture of dance and aesthetic valuing require access to new media and electronic technology, including the Internet and audiovisual resources. Students use the Internet to do research in dance, computer programs to develop choreography, and video cameras to record their performances for the critique process.

Suggested Facilities

Implementing a dance program requires adherence to safety regulations. Adequate open floor space must be provided for students to participate in creative expression. In the elementary school dancing may be done in classrooms provided it can be done safely. At the middle school and high school levels, use of a resilient wood floor is highly recommended because injuries commonly occur on hard surfaces. To accommodate partnering work at the secondary level, such as occurs when one partner lifts the other overhead, the teacher must ensure that the ceiling is high enough to prevent injuries.

In addition, the teacher should require a room that is well ventilated and equipped with adjustable heating and cooling systems. If the room contains folding or collapsible benches, they can be pushed back so that the space can be used for demonstrations and performances. Storage space is needed for materials and equipment, and, at the secondary level, dressing rooms should also be provided. To meet higher dance standards, students need access to proper performance and theatre technology. As students progress in dance from elementary school to high school, they require more complex and flexible equipment.

Dance facilities for high schools should include (1) small and large dance studios; (2) sprung floors with wood or Marley covering that can be placed over an existing floor, providing an adequate surface for dancing; (3) theatre or performance space; (4) theatrical lighting; (5) stagecraft areas; (6) sound systems; (7) costume shops; (8) set design and construction areas; and (9) technology labs for editing and recording.

Community Resources and Parent Involvement

Community resources can provide assistance to the dance program. Examples are as follows:

- Articulated partnerships between the local university dance department and elementary school, middle school, and high school classes, providing university students opportunities to develop teaching skills in dance as they instruct students in kindergarten through grade twelve

- Local dance studio companies and classes at the school site
- Field trips to see dance companies that come to perform in their local areas
- Districtwide master classes or even districtwide or citywide dance performances organized by dance teachers and dance specialists
- Classes for students at local dance studios, particularly for those students who at the advanced level continue to take classes to further their dance training

Parent advocacy and support are critical in developing and sustaining an active dance program. For example, parents with a strong folk and traditional dance background can contribute to the vitality of dance programs within the school as well as in the larger community. Other ways they may offer assistance are by:

- Providing supervision on field trips
- Selling or collecting tickets for dance performances
- Assisting with costumes and props (shopping, designing, sewing)
- Serving as liaisons to business and community organizations
- Providing services, such as copying, printing, and decorating
- Providing assistance in securing and using new technology and electronic media
- Supporting their children's continuing dance study in and outside school

Music

Music is an integral part of human experience. Used in celebrations, rituals, and everyday life, it expresses the heights and depths of human feelings and emotions, the joys and the sorrows encountered by all. Significantly, the study of music combines human emotional experience and intellectual cognition.

One of the greatest values of a comprehensive music education program is that it allows all students to develop fully those qualities that will help them understand and enjoy life. It provides a means for creativity and self-expression. Through music they learn that their thoughts and feelings can be communicated nonverbally by composing and improvising original music involving higher-order thinking processes, such as those involved in skill mastery, analysis, and synthesis.

After silence, that which comes nearest to expressing the inexpressible is music.

—Aldous Huxley

Standards-Based Curriculum for Music

The curriculum for a standards-based music program should be well planned and articulated from kindergarten through grade twelve. In addition to musical performance, the curriculum provides opportunities for students to learn musical notation and compose music. By studying the history and cultural context of works of music, students can understand aesthetic concepts as they gain a foundation for aesthetic valuing and criticism. At all levels they learn how music connects to the world around them, to other curriculum areas, and to careers. An effective music curriculum at each grade level incorporates all five component strands in the content standards: artistic perception, creative expression, historical and cultural context, aesthetic valuing, and connections, relationships, and applications (see Chapter 3).

Artistic Perception

Artistic perception includes listening to, reading, and composing and performing music of various cultures and time periods. The perception of sound and sound patterns is the first step in this process. Then the learner develops concepts and understanding about music based on active listening experiences.

As students study the musical elements of melody, harmony, rhythm, form, tempo, dynamics, and timbre, they use critical listening skills and appropriate music vocabulary. They are able to use traditional, nontraditional, and created symbols to read and write rhythm, pitch, dynamics, tempo, articulation, and expression.

Chapter 4
Guidance
for Visual and
Performing Arts
Programs

Music

2 Creative Expression

Creative expression occurs when students perform, improvise, compose, and arrange music. Their understanding of music grows out of frequent experiences with music and sequential development of their musical skills. Singing is one of the most natural, intimate ways for students to experience music. Through regular instruction and practice, beginning in kindergarten, students develop the skills to sing on pitch, in rhythm, and with expression. Group singing should include a wide repertoire of music from various styles and cultures.

Playing instruments, individually or in ensembles, from various parts of the world provides students with a powerful medium for learning music. By using melodic, harmonic, and rhythmic instruments, young students develop musical concepts and the skills needed to perform accurately on pitch, in rhythm, and with expression. Ensemble experiences should include a wide repertoire of appropriate musical literature.

Musical skills should include performing from written music and participating in creative processes. Students need opportunities to learn to improvise rhythms and melodies, harmonizing parts consistent with the style, meter, and tonality of the music being studied. By composing and arranging their own works, they can use music to communicate their ideas, feelings, and responses to their cultural and natural environments.

3 Historical and Cultural Context

Time and place influence music. The study of the history of music reveals a rich resource of outstanding examples of the power of music to inspire and reach the depths of human emotion. Because to a large degree an individual's artistic life is shaped by the surrounding culture, its history, and its traditions, music can best be understood and appreciated when presented within its cultural context. By studying music from many cultures, students can enjoy the music of the whole world and raise their cultural and social awareness.

4 Aesthetic Valuing

Aesthetic valuing extends beyond acquiring knowledge and skills to understanding the wide range of values in music. As students respond emotionally to music and reflect on what they are performing, listening to, and composing, they develop their affective and cognitive abilities. Aesthetic valuing begins with artistic perception and extends to critical judgments about music, including judging one's own performances and compositions and those of others.

5 Connections, Relationships, Applications

Learning is reinforced when music instruction is carefully connected with other disciplines—likely a long-term effort. Those connections also allow for the effective teaching of correlations between music and dance, theatre, and the

Chapter 4
Guidance
for Visual and
Performing Arts
Programs

Music

visual arts. Musically literate students can find numerous realistic applications for their knowledge and skills. In this strand students can explore career possibilities in music and learn about many jobs within the music industry.

Levels of Music Instruction

Comprehensive music instruction, offered best by credentialed music teachers, includes general music classes ranging from classroom music at the elementary school level to music appreciation, theory, song-writing courses, keyboard instruction, and music history classes at higher levels. Exploratory music courses, such as music appreciation and general music, should include hands-on music making and reading, writing, and talking about music. In addition, students may participate in choral and instrumental performance ensembles. To ensure full access to the content standards, students in kindergarten through grade eight and high school students receiving music instruction need standards-based instruction regularly during the school day.

Elementary School Level

In a general music curriculum at the primary level, activities include singing, rhythmic speech, movement, playing of pitched and nonpitched percussion, and the use of instruments, recorders, or keyboards. To help students achieve proficiency in the content standards, teachers often use such instructional methodologies as those of Orff, Schulwerk, Kodály, and Dalcroze. For information on those and other methodologies available through the National Association for Music Education, visit the Web site *http://www.menc.org*. Sequential instruction in general music continues in grades four through six. In addition, all students should have opportunities to explore their musical development by participating in performance groups.

Music instruction according to the five strands allows young students to use a variety of instructional resources in exploring music experiences: singing, moving, playing an instrument, listening, responding, and reflecting. Included among the resources are age-appropriate musical instruments, written literature on music, CDs, computer software, Internet resources, audiotapes, videos, DVDs, and photographs, all of which are often obtained through the school library. In addition to learning from high-quality resources, students benefit from visiting artists and performances at school or in the community.

General, choral, and instrumental music instruction allows students to identify a variety of musical elements from many cultures. Using the vocabulary of music in their discussions of composers and their works, they learn about and practice musical works and performances. Instruction helps students understand the historical and cultural contexts of music, styles, and periods and the expressions of cultural groups. In addition, they have opportunities to

139

Chapter 4
Guidance
for Visual and
Performing Arts
Programs

Music

identify and discuss the characteristics of master performances and composi-tions as they work toward achieving the content standards in the aesthetic valu-ing strand. This process enables students to learn about their own responses to music and to assess those responses in relation to the music.

Middle School Level

Music instruction in the middle school continues with general music expe-riences available to all students and includes elective performance classes in orchestra, band, choir, and other ensembles. A standards-based program pro-vides instruction for beginning, intermediate, and advanced levels of student participation. Through singing and playing, students are challenged to develop their performance skills as they receive subject-centered, standards-based music instruction. Incorporated into other subjects as appropriate, music helps stu-dents, for example, gain a deeper realization of the emotional and social impact of the U.S. Civil War as they study the music of the period. And as they apply the concept of fractions to musical notation, they become aware of connections, relationships, and applications.

According to the content standards, students are to develop a heightened perceptual awareness of the aesthetic qualities of the music from cultures throughout the world and of major works of music. They develop listening skills and become more perceptive and observant. Through school music pro-grams students have opportunities to apply the elements of music and extend their knowledge of the language of music and their ability to use it.

By composing music and other expressions, students explore the creative process. This work is enhanced as they study music compositions from many cultures and time periods. By participating in performances and attending pro-fessional performances, they develop the skills needed for making aesthetic judgments and applying thoughtful reasoning and criteria to those judgments. Their experiences also make them aware of many careers in and related to the field of music.

High School Level

Standards-based music instruction provides opportunities for students to do in-depth studies in one or more areas of concentration, delve into the mean-ing and impact of music, and develop life skills and career competencies. At the high school level, instruction prepares students to enter the university music program.

Music instruction provides an opening for students to participate in choral and instrumental ensembles. These classes offer instruction at the beginning, intermediate, and advanced levels to meet the needs of all students in achieving the standards at the beginning or proficient level or higher. Other classes that also benefit students include music appreciation, music theory, the history and

Chapter 4
Guidance
for Visual and
Performing Arts
Programs

Music

literature of music, piano and electronic music, instrumental music, and the recording arts.

High school music courses should be approved by the University of California and the California State University to meet the new visual and performing arts requirements for freshman admission to those institutions. (Standards-based courses approved for entrance and courses that would not be accepted as college preparatory music courses are listed in Appendix B.) According to the five component strands of the music content standards, creative thinking should be promoted through instruction in a sequence of appropriate music courses. In addition, students should have frequent opportunities to work with professional musicians and attend professional performances at school and in the community. Community college, university, or community programs in music often may be open to students with particular interests or talents. As students recognize connections between music and other curriculum areas, they can expand and enrich the scope of their educational experience.

Music teachers need to communicate with their colleagues throughout their school district and with university music departments and professional music groups to enhance their programs and support continuity of instruction.

Music

Sample Standards-Based Unit of Study Grades Nine Through Twelve

Standards-based instruction reinforces the importance of a rigorous, comprehensive arts education program. Understanding that performance classes are not intended to be appreciation courses, teachers should provide a variety of opportunities for students to meet standards while preparing students to perform quality works of music. The following unit of study is an example of how teachers can maintain the integrity of performance classes by focusing on development of skills in music while providing a comprehensive approach to music education. It also recognizes that many high school performance classes have both beginning and advanced students in one class and provides for differentiated opportunities based on experience.

Chapter 4
Guidance
for Visual and
Performing Arts
Programs

Music

This unit provides choral music students at the proficient level with an opportunity to improvise original melodies while students at the advanced level can create melodies in a blues style. At each level students apply a set of criteria to establish indicators of success, and the teacher uses the recorded improvised examples to document student achievement.

PROFICIENT LEVEL	ADVANCED LEVEL
First year of instruction	Two or more years of additional instruction
Students listen to and research familiar types of vocal improvisation from familiar music (e.g., bends, slides).	Students examine and study a variety of vocal improvisation styles from familiar music (e.g., Stevie Wonder, Ella Fitzgerald, Mel Torme, Bobby McFerrin) and learn style names, including the term *scat singing*.
The choir sings an arrangement of a familiar selection in a popular style, discussing and trying stylistically correct embellishments (e.g., bends, slides).	While the choir sings an arrangement of a familiar selection in a popular style, individual students improvise solos to selected sections of the arrangement.
Independently, students listen to local radio stations and note the names of the songs that include vocal improvisations and attempt to classify the styles supporting their classifications. In class students discuss their classifications in small groups.	Students listen to recorded music chosen by the choir teacher and placed on reserve in the school library, including selections using a blues progression. Students note styles used and discuss differences and similarities between blues progression styles and popular music styles. In class students discuss what they found and give a personal demonstration for each characteristic discovered.
Students learn the blues progression. While half of the choir sings chord tones, the other half improvises a melody over the chord progression. They then switch roles.	While the choir sings a blues chord progression, individual choir members improvise a melody over the chord progression. Groups of two (duet) or three (trio) create improvised melodies.

Music

PROFICIENT LEVEL (Continued)	ADVANCED LEVEL (Continued)
Students record themselves improvising over a blues progression and listen to the recording, applying criteria for evaluating blues improvisation. Students discuss areas of success and areas to work on. (The teacher assesses student's understanding of the criteria and keeps the recordings on file to compare to later improvisations.)	Small groups of students record themselves in pairs or peer groups, listening to and coaching each other using more complex and refined criteria. (The teacher assesses students' comprehension of the criteria and keeps the recordings on file to compare to later improvisations.)

As a culminating task students listen to several unfamiliar professional-quality performances of improvisation and classify them by style, explaining why they chose the labels they did (i.e., demonstrate understanding of various improvisation vocal styles).

Possible scoring criteria:

1. Identification of style characteristics
2. Ability to improvise, using more than two vocal styles (match between pitches in improvised melody and accompanying tonality and chord progression)
3. Use of appropriate musical vocabulary to describe various aspects of improvisation and performance styles

As a culminating task students listen to nonprofessional blues performances (self, anonymous peer, partner) and critique improvisations in light of criteria/dimension.

Possible scoring criteria:

1. Appropriate blues style (meter and phrasing)
2. Use of appropriate rhythmic ideas that include but go beyond those heard in the accompaniment
3. Match between pitches in improvised melody and accompanying tonality and chord progression
4. Introduction of appropriate blue notes and passing tones
5. Use of contour or direction
6. Development of a motif or other idea

143

Chapter 4
Guidance
for Visual and
Performing Arts
Programs

Music

Role of Student Music Performances

Student performances provide opportunities for young musicians to demonstrate musical growth, gain personal satisfaction from achievement, and experience the joy of making music. They can motivate students to learn and stimulate careful rehearsing and self-discipline. However, although they are an important part of the music curriculum and promote student learning, performances should be an outcome rather than the basic objective of music instruction.

Public performances allow students to reflect on and refine their musical understanding, showcasing individual or group achievement. Formal performances, such as concerts, music festivals, and stage productions, may serve as culminating experiences in which students are challenged to perform at their best. Through informal performances in the classroom or for the community, students can demonstrate the learning process at different stages and in greater detail.

The visibility and popularity of student performance groups may lead to expectations not directly related to music education. Demands are often made on school music ensembles to perform at athletic events, assemblies, student productions, parent meetings, community club meetings, conferences, and civic events. Although providing entertainment may be a valid activity for music groups, the demands should never interfere with the students' music education.

Music programs should pay attention to educating the audience in addition to the student musicians and performers. For example, providing program notes is helpful and may include a description of the content standards students are working to achieve. And in all aspects of music performance, diversity must be considered, including diversity in selecting the music to be played and the soloists to perform.

Resources for the Music Program

Appropriate, up-to-date equipment, instructional materials, and facilities as well as community resources and parent involvement are vital to the standards-based music program.

Equipment and Instructional Materials

Music instruction requires an adequate budget for the purchase, maintenance, repair, and replacement of equipment and instruments. An adequate number of musical instruments should be available to ensure balanced instrumentation at all levels of instruction. At the elementary school and middle school levels, a variety of pitched and nonpitched classroom instruments should be available for general music.

Chapter 4
Guidance
for Visual and
Performing Arts
Programs

Music

Music supplies made available to students may include reeds, valve oil, instrument swabs, rosin, cork grease, and strings. An instrument repair kit should be made available to the teacher. Musical instruments should be of high quality and maintained in good condition. And sound equipment, such as CD players, amplifiers, microphones, and speakers, must be of good quality and kept in good repair.

The resources used in teaching and learning music include a variety of traditional and new media. Quickly becoming the standard for the music industry, CD and DVD technology is playing an increasingly important role in music education. When teachers have access to both digital and analog technologies, they are better able to make use of the best in video and audio productions.

Along with necessary playback equipment, a well-equipped music library is essential for teaching and learning. To learn about music, teachers and students should use videos and audiotapes, CD and DVD recordings, musical scores and sheet music, computer programs, and books. These resources bring to life the music of many cultures, the work of great composers, and the connections between music and the other arts.

When teachers and students acquire and share information with colleagues and peers, they must observe federal copyright laws pertaining to reproduction, such as those governing fair use and public domain. Information regarding copyright laws and issues, including those governing the use of music in performances, is available on the Internet or from the school district's legal counsel (see also Appendix E).

Suggested Facilities

Decisions regarding music facilities should be driven by the instructional needs of the program. At each site a dedicated space for music instruction should be identified; it should accommodate such needs as a sound system, a piano, risers, movement space, and secure storage. Vocalists and instrumentalists need room to move and perform, and instrumentalists need space to use and store their instruments, equipment, and music stands. Because the traffic of students in music rooms is often concentrated and takes place under time constraints, the floor plan must provide enough space to eliminate congestion and ensure excellent traffic flow.

A music room also needs to have an appropriate amount of space and ceiling height to provide good acoustics. For the hearing of students and the teacher not to be affected, rooms should be built of acoustically appropriate materials in the walls, floors, and ceilings. Existing rooms should be acoustically enhanced to prevent any disruption to neighboring classrooms and keep levels of sound in the room to acceptable industry standards to avoid harm or distortion.

145

Chapter 4
Guidance
for Visual and
Performing Arts
Programs

Music

A well-equipped music facility at the middle school and high school levels may typically include:

- Rehearsal areas for a large group
- Practice rooms for rehearsals by individuals or a small ensemble
- Sound system, including audio and visual recording equipment
- Music stands and risers
- Storage areas for musical instruments, printed music, sound systems, and other equipment
- Storage area for uniforms and choral robes
- Student desks or tables for general music, theory, history, and appreciation courses
- Keyboard lab for piano and keyboard classes
- A faculty or administrative office
- A performance space or theatre

Community Resources and Parent Involvement

A standards-based music curriculum communicates an open invitation to community musicians to assist in promoting a lifelong love of music among students. Music educators can survey their communities for musicians willing to work and perform with students. Visits by professional and amateur musicians enhance and bring into focus concepts already introduced in the regular instructional program and can provide additional professional development for teachers. In turn, music students can be encouraged to attend or participate in musical performances in the community. Local performing groups, arts councils, and professional musicians are all resources for the music educator. And the music faculty and students at colleges and universities can provide a wealth of musical resources.

As in other curricular areas, parents are often active supporters of the music program. Music teachers welcome parental partnerships that bring parents into the classroom. By providing additional support to meet student and program needs, attending performances, and encouraging their student's musical experiences, parents who are not musicians can aid the program. The inclusion of community and parent resources does not, however, substitute for the sequential, comprehensive music program but does strengthen it.

Theatre

As revealed in the earliest recorded history, theatre reflects the time and place of its origins. The creations of theatre artists come from perceptions of nature, from relationships and interactions with others, and from the artists' inner selves. Through storytelling and other oral traditions, cultures define themselves and educate their members down through the ages. In contemporary and historical commemorations, celebrations, and dramatizations, theatre gives voice to culture. Theatre, pageant, entertainment, new media, and electronic technology continue to serve many social functions. Theatre unifies groups, expresses important knowledge, reinforces group values, strengthens the individual, and defines and commemorates events. It provides a powerful multisensory mirror reflecting social issues, challenges, and accomplishments.

To break through language in order to touch life is to create or re-create the theatre.

—Antonin Artaud (1896–1948)

The elements of theatre in stage, film, and video productions include scriptwriting, acting, technical production, management, and design. In a well-planned theatre education program, students engage directly in each of the elements during grade-by-grade study of theatre, enabling them to learn time management, solve problems, work collaboratively, and exhibit leadership skills. Their participation in theatre helps them gain an increased understanding of self and the world, empathy for others, and self-confidence. They learn to make critical judgments about television, radio, electronic media, and live performance.

Standards-Based Curriculum for Theatre

Pretend! Imagine! Imitate! Role-play! Unknowingly, kindergarten students practice theatrical skills, such as characterization, pantomime, improvisation, story development, and costuming. In grades one through three, students place these activities in the context of theatre, film, and video as they dramatize or improvise familiar stories and learn the vocabulary of theatre and ways to work cooperatively and develop a commitment to purpose. In grades four through six, they gain more in-depth knowledge of the elements of theatre as they analyze a character's motives and develop criteria to apply to the quality of performances. Middle school students continue to develop skills as they compare and contrast various theatre styles from the past and become more aware of the influence of theatre and the entertainment industry on their lives. And in high school students read, write, research, reflect, and synthesize to deepen their

Chapter 4
Guidance
for Visual and
Performing Arts
Programs

Theatre

understanding of all aspects of theatre and to strengthen their skills in acting, directing, designing, and scriptwriting. All instruction is designed to help students create and perform formal and informal productions in theatre, film, video, and media.

The sequential curriculum for a standards-based theatre program needs to be well planned and articulated from kindergarten through grade twelve. It should provide opportunities for students to develop skills, use the language of theatre, and create works in theatre. By studying the history and cultural context of theatre, students can perceive and understand concepts providing a foundation for aesthetic valuing and criticism. At all levels they learn how theatre connects to the world around them, to other curriculum areas, and to careers. At each grade level an effective theatre curriculum should incorporate the five component strands of the theatre content standards: artistic perception, creative expression, historical and cultural context, aesthetic valuing, and connections, relationships, and applications (see Chapter 3).

Artistic Perception

Artistic perception in theatre involves observing the environment and constructing meaning from it, thereby developing the acuity of all the senses. Whether improvised or scripted, a theatrical production expresses the perceptions of the writer, the director, the actors, and the designers. The audience's response to it requires perception based on knowledge of theatrical skills and an appreciation of imagination and creativity. Through direct experiences with theatrical terms and concepts, students learn the vocabulary of theatre. Engagement in theatre experiences heightens students' sensitivity to their own potential for creation and that of others.

Creative Expression

Students express themselves creatively as they plan, prepare, and carry out a theatrical performance. Through exercises, improvisation, rehearsal, production, evaluation, revision, and self-reflection, they develop theatrical skills. All students should participate and experience success as individuals and as part of a group. And in their purposeful activities they should focus on understanding the language, elements, and tools of theatre.

Historical and Cultural Context

Capturing time and a culture, theatre can provide a rich historical context for students. It allows them to look at a culture through the lens of a particular time and place and introduces them to other cultures through theatrical activities in which world dramatic literature, folklore, personal histories, film, video, electronic media, and puppetry are used. Informing and inspiring students, theatrical activities will help them discover the wide spectrum of theatrical forms.

Chapter 4
Guidance
for Visual and
Performing Arts
Programs

Theatre

Theatre itself is an important part of culture and history. Through its study students gain a greater understanding of the role theatre has played and continues to play in society. By learning the history of dramatic literature, technology, architecture, acting styles, and theatre conventions that have developed into contemporary world theatre, they gain a broader perspective from which to create their own works.

4 Aesthetic Valuing

In theatre education aesthetic valuing is the ability to analyze the feelings and thoughts elicited by theatrical experiences. To express their reactions to theatrical works, students apply what they have learned in artistic perception, creative expression, and historical and cultural context. Opportunities to observe and practice across a broad range of experiences help students make informed judgments, which depend on understanding the intent, structure, effectiveness, and worth of a play, movie, television drama, or other theatrical presentation. The valuing process, cyclical and cumulative, may start, for example, when students reflect on, analyze, and evaluate their own work. It gives them the experience and confidence to assess the work of others. By critiquing the work of others, they gain new perspectives from which to review their own work.

In a standards-based theatre program, students learn the difference between theatrical reviews, personal perspective, dramatic criticism, and theory-based analysis. They also acquire the ability to think and speak about aspects of theatre reasonably and intelligently and discuss multifaceted theatre experiences from a variety of viewpoints.

5 Connections, Relationships, Applications

Today, theatre is more influential than ever, reaching millions of people worldwide and affecting people's lives through technology. Because of the impact of the media on students and society, students are provided the help they need through standards-based theatre instruction to become media literate, analytical, and critical. Instruction in the theatre arts helps students become responsible and creative workers, informed consumers, and effective communicators.

Through playmaking, improvising, creating scenes, and scriptwriting, students can demonstrate their understanding of important concepts in other subject areas. And by dramatizing events from history–social science or current events or a concept from another subject area, they can develop story comprehension, helpful in developing scriptwriting and acting skills, such as character development. As they learn and experience theatre, they discover the many career opportunities in theatre and the prominent role theatre plays in the entertainment industry in California, a world leader in the production of film and electronic media.

The history–social science and theatre curricula emphasize the ideas, values, and beliefs of people from many lands who have contributed to a vast body of knowledge. Students should recognize that literature and the arts reflect the inner life of a culture. To support this learning, the theatre content standards introduce stories, fables, and formal and informal dramatizations incorporating conflict and raising value issues both interesting and age appropriate.

Because theatre and the language arts are interrelated, oral and literacy skills are integral to the theatrical process. Learning verbal and nonverbal communication, students experience the value and application of both. They are taught that the sequence of skill development in the language arts is the body and soul of theatre.

In mathematics and the arts, students learn how to analyze problems and select strategies. Accordingly, in theatre students apply mathematical concepts and skills in making a model, drawing a picture, organizing information on a table or chart, finding a simpler related problem, acting out a situation, restating a problem, looking for patterns, estimating and predicting, and working on a problem with the end always in mind. They should feel free to take risks and recognize that many ways exist to arrive at the "right" answer.

Theatre

Levels of Theatre Instruction

The standards-based theatre program promotes the development of each student's imagination, knowledge, problem-solving ability, understanding of human relationships, and communication skills. To accomplish that purpose, school administrators, theatre arts specialists, and teachers need to establish a carefully planned program of instruction for each elementary school, middle school, and high school student.

Elementary School Level

Students in California elementary schools should all have opportunities for theatre instruction in their regular classrooms. At this level students work toward achieving the theatre content standards through a variety of instructional strategies, including creative dramatics, improvisation, pantomime, storytelling, and the acting out of stories. Students should explore their creative potential by participating in theatre.

Teachers should have instructional materials and resources on theatre, including films, audiotapes, videos, DVDs, prints, photographs, props, and literature, that are appropriate for elementary school students. To obtain those materials and resources, teachers should find the library media teacher helpful.

Theatre

By practicing, performing, and viewing a variety of theatrical forms in live performances at school or in the community, students will develop skills as performers and as members of the audience. Exposing students to a variety of experiences in theatre helps them gain personal, historical, and cultural insights.

Middle School Level

Exploration is the hallmark of middle school theatre. Instruction inspires students to become self-confident, empathetic individuals and competent group members. As they identify with a group in meeting common goals, they develop a strong sense of camaraderie. And they become more adventurous in acting and production as they encounter materials from varied sources, periods, and styles of theatre. Texts might include scripts, magazines, news articles, books, lyrics, and personal experiences. (*Note:* Scripted materials for middle school students should be age appropriate.)

The school's schedule should include a variety of electives in theatre to meet students' interests and educational needs. Standards-based instruction provides students with more advanced training and deeper study of the five strands. In addition to discrete instruction, theatre activities may be applied or related to instruction in other content areas.

High School Level

Instruction in the standards-based high school theatre program, an integral part of the school curriculum, meets the needs of students working to achieve the proficient or beginning level of the theatre content standards at a minimum. It also provides opportunities to achieve the advanced or optimum level in one or more additional classes. Instruction may be provided in play production, stagecraft, scriptwriting, children's theatre, oral interpretation, videography, design, and theatre management. Those completing a high school theatre program have a general understanding of all aspects of theatre as an art form, enabling them to begin advanced studies in specific areas at a college or university.

Performance is an integral part of the high school theatre instruction. Whether produced or attended, plays and scenes should be carefully selected for educational worth, literary merit, diversity, community values, and cultural contribution. Students should experience the full spectrum of theatre in performance, such as formal and informal productions, improvisations, mime, puppetry, children's theatre, film, video, and other electronic media. Taking part in theatre festivals, playwriting contests, field trips, and other realistic applications, students have opportunities to work with theatre professionals and attend professional performances. In addition, community college, university, or community theatre intern programs may be open to students. Documented for reflection and evaluation, student work may be used in a portfolio in preparation for higher education or a career.

151

Chapter 4
Guidance
for Visual and
Performing Arts
Programs

Theatre

High school theatre courses should be approved by the University of California and California State University systems to meet the entrance requirement of a one-year course in a visual or performing art. To be accepted, theatre courses must include all five strands of the content standards. Traditional and new media courses may be acceptable provided they are standards based. For more information on course requirements, visit the Web site *http://www.ucop.edu.* Examples of theatre courses that may be acceptable for admission include acting, directing, oral interpretation, and dramatic production; dramaturgy, history, and theory; and stage lighting and costume design.

Creating traditional or electronic portfolios of one's work is a powerful tool to track individual growth, prepare for high school graduation, and use when applying for college entrance, scholarships, or employment in the theatre or a theatre-related career.

Theatre

Sample Standards-Based Unit of Study
Grades Nine Through Twelve

Standards-based instruction reinforces the importance of a rigorous, comprehensive arts education. Understanding that performance classes are not intended to be theatre appreciation courses, teachers should provide a variety of opportunities to meet standards while preparing students to perform quality theatrical works. The following unit of study is an example of how to maintain the integrity of performance classes by focusing on developing theatrical skills while providing a comprehensive approach to theatre education. Many high school theatre classes with both beginning and advanced students in one class provide for differentiated opportunities based on experience.

To develop a depth of knowledge and theatre skills in such areas as acting, design, styles, dramatic literature, directing, promotion, lighting, and costuming, the theatre teacher should develop a unit of study that includes plays in specific styles, genres, or periods.

Theatre

PROFICIENT LEVEL	ADVANCED LEVEL
First year of instruction	Two or more years of additional instruction
Students read, view, and research the theatre of a specific period, playwright, genre, or style (e.g., Restoration, Shaw, post-colonial). Research includes the function of theatre in the culture.	After studying theatre from several different periods or cultures, students explain the social, cultural, and political influences on several different styles of theatre and the influence of each style on society. In addition, they compare how one period of theatre influenced another.
Students learn and present teacher-directed scenes from the plays of a given period, playwright, genre, or style.	In class students learn and present teacher-directed scenes from plays of a given period, playwright, genre, or style, using highly developed acting techniques.
Students choose a monologue from a given period, playwright, genre, or style and use research information to present it in an appropriate style.	Students develop a presentation for their portfolio that includes a director's concept for the production of a play from a given period, playwright, genre, or style. They then choose two production areas, such as costumes, lighting, or blocking, and develop a complete design or director's production notes.
Students and teacher develop a rubric to evaluate the scenes and monologues. The performance is videotaped and assessed by the student, classmates, and teacher.	Students demonstrate the ability to achieve a director's stylized concept by serving as director, actor, or designer in a play from a given period, playwright, genre, or style.

Chapter 4
Guidance
for Visual and
Performing Arts
Programs

Theatre

Role of Student Theatre Performances

Although performances should be an integral part of theatre at all levels, not all theatre activities need to culminate in a public performance. A large part of a theatre curriculum is focused on skill development. Plays and scenes should be carefully selected for educational worth, literary merit, diversity, community values, and cultural contribution.

An active theatre arts program promotes the development of students as theatre artists and audience members. They should experience the full spectrum of theatre, such as formal and informal production, improvisation, mime, puppetry, film, video, and other electronic media. They should also offer student-written and commercial plays to students and parents and, when appropriate, take part in theatre festivals, playwriting contests, field trips to community performances, and other realistic applications. In addition to being educated as theatre artists, all students should learn to respond appropriately as members of the audience during theatrical performances, an ability that requires knowledge of etiquette and theatre appreciation. The theatre program should offer plays demonstrating a variety of theatre styles and origins and provide program notes containing information regarding the style and objectives of the production as related to the achievement of the theatre content standards.

Student performances in nonprofessional or professional theatre productions should be viewed as an extension of classroom training. Any student in a theatre arts program who demonstrates a commitment to the art and accepts the discipline required of a performer may take advantage of opportunities to perform outside school.

Resources for the Theatre Program

To help students achieve the content standards in theatre, school districts should adopt long-range plans providing for appropriate equipment, instructional materials, and facilities and including the assistance of community resources and parent involvement.

Equipment and Instructional Materials

Although theatre has been performed with a minimal amount of equipment and facilities, students in the school's theatre program will benefit from the use of proper theatre technology (lighting, sound) to meet theatre arts standards. As students progress from elementary school to high school, the equipment appropriate for each level increases in complexity and capability.

Equipment for the theatre program at the elementary school and middle school levels may include CD players, DVD player/recorders, audio player/recorders, video cameras, videocassette recorder/players, television monitors, and computers for research, design, and word processing. Other

Theatre

resources recommended for a school theatre space, especially for middle schools and high schools, include the following:

- An adequate sound system to allow the actors' voices, sound effects, and mood music to be heard comfortably by the audience. The system should include microphones, speakers, CD players, sound mixers, tape players, and cables. An appropriate number of assistive hearing devices and audio describers should also be provided to ensure equal access.

- A theatrical lighting system that at least illuminates the stage, actors, and sets and at best creates mood and special effects. To be included are lighting instruments, a lighting control board, cables, dimmer packs, a power supply, color media, and hardware.

- Stagecraft capabilities that are age appropriate and allow for increasing sophistication in constructing sets and props, using costumes and makeup, and operating, for example, power tools, sewing machines, painting equipment, air brushes, glue guns, and staple guns. Other items might include hand tools and basic construction tools, cutting tables, and irons. Although lower-grade students may have very little involvement with design and construction, they must, to meet the standards, be taught the elements of stagecraft.

- Computers and computer software for producing video programs. In middle schools and high schools, camcorders, TV studios, and editing capabilities should be available for video productions.

- A resource center, especially at the high school level. In addition, for classroom and production activities, reference materials available in the school library enrich learning with historical and cultural contexts. These resources may be used by teachers and students and can include a variety of materials, such as textbooks, plays, scenes, monologues, and screenplays; history of the theatre, historical references, and biographies; resources for researching aspects of theatre (dialects, costumes, historical events or periods, music, plays, and literature); the professional theatre; and media journals and magazines.

155

Chapter 4
Guidance
for Visual and
Performing Arts
Programs

- Videos of master plays, documentaries, educational lectures, and examples of master works in films and demonstrations. Also enhancing instruction would be a library of CDs, DVDs, and audiotapes of sound effects; music, plays, and screenplays; and resources for researching aspects of theatre (dialects, costumes, historical events or periods, music, plays, and literature).
- Other resources, such as capabilities for Internet research, computer publishing, digital recording, and editing.

Suggested Facilities

Elementary schools need flexible classroom areas or large, open indoor spaces for theatre activities and storage for props, costumes, and curriculum materials. In addition to storage, middle schools need assembly halls or other large rooms with stages or platforms equipped with lighting, high ceilings to allow for lighting angles, sound equipment, masking curtains, and seating for an audience. Theatres or auditoriums at the high school level should be designed to present plays and musicals. Some school districts work with city or theatre organizations to build theatres on high school campuses and share their use, staffing, and maintenance.

A high school theatre or auditorium should be equipped with the following:

- Stage area, offstage area, wing space, light booth, fly space, wooden (paintable) floor, drapes, curtains, teasers, light grid, catwalk, pipes, baton, and pin rail, with all areas handicap accessible
- Set construction area, with secure storage of tools to build sets and equipment to paint and decorate them
- Storage area for furniture, costumes, props, set pieces, drapes, drops, cycloramas, and makeup
- Costume construction area, with a sewing machine, sink, full-length mirrors, an iron and ironing board, cutting tables, and storage for tools used in sewing and designing
- Separate dressing rooms for male and female students, with showers, toilets, and several well-lighted mirror stations for applying makeup
- Television and film studio and editing facilities

Community Resources and Parent Involvement

Many individuals, professional actors, performing groups, and organizations in the community can become valuable resources for a theatre arts program. Identifying and locating those resources will differ for each school.

Parent involvement in the theatre program can range from simply being a member of an audience to organizing a parent booster club. Including parents in the entire process enhances the program and engages the parents in the arts.

Visual Arts

The visual arts, part of the human experience since prehistoric times, began with images painted or scratched on cave walls, small sculpted objects, and huge structural forms. Those works illustrate that artists at the dawn of human history, like other artists throughout the ages, were creative, imaginative, and self-expressive. As stated by Jensen, the "visual arts are a universal language with a symbolic way of representing the world. But they also allow us to understand other cultures and provide for healthy emotional expression."[1] They have been vital to all cultures and civilizations, communicating ideas, customs, traditions, and beliefs by providing a window through which the visual record of the peoples, places, and circumstances in the past can be observed.

The visual arts help human beings organize and make sense of what they observe and experience. The arts appear in many forms, including traditional and contemporary painting and drawing, sculpture and installations, photography, ceramics, folk arts and crafts of all kinds, and new media and electronic technology.

Art is both love and friendship and understanding; it is the desire to give. It is not charity, which is the giving of things. It is more than kindness, which is the giving of self. It is both the taking and giving of beauty. . . .

—Letter to Cedric Wright from Ansel Adams

Also included are cutting-edge experiments and performance art that cross the boundaries between the several arts.

Through study and the experience of producing works of art, students learn the basic visual arts vocabulary, based on the elements of art and the principles of design. Artists and art students at any grade level work with those elements: line, color, shape, texture, form, and space. With the application of the principles of design, such as harmony, balance, rhythm, dominance, and subordination, artists can create unique and original statements through endless combinations, variations, and innovations. The resulting art can be joyous or sad, funny or somber, calm or powerful and can depict everyday reality or the imagination or dreams of the artist.

Standards-Based Curriculum for the Visual Arts

Through visual arts education images become part of human language. For example, the marks made by young children are part of their first attempts at communication and language. Building on a child's natural inclination to

---

[1] Eric Jensen, *Arts with the Brain in Mind.* Alexandria, Va.: Association for Supervision and Curriculum Development, 2001, p. 49.

157

Chapter 4
Guidance
for Visual and
Performing Arts
Programs

communicate beyond those first marks, visual arts education supports the exchange of ideas that continues throughout life.

Kindergarten students are eager to get their hands on paints, clay, and other art materials that inspire them to explore and create. All hands are raised enthusiastically when they are asked, Who is an artist? In grades one through three, they learn more about what becoming an artist requires as they view and describe the art around them, including art from various cultures. Through hands-on experiences they learn ways to use line, color, shape, and texture in their artwork on paper and in three-dimensional form.

In grades four through six, students explore deeper applications of the elements of art and the principles of design, such as rhythm and balance. They are fascinated to learn that they, too, like the artists they study, can create pictures with spatial depth by using what they learn about perspective. Their ability to analyze, assess, and find meaning in works of art leads them to a deeper understanding and appreciation of artists and artworks from around the world and from different time periods. By using traditional and new media and electronic technology, they can expand their skills and ability to communicate. They also participate in discussions about the merits of certain works of art and identify professions in or related to the visual arts.

High school students create works of art, developing a more focused style and message that incorporates what they have learned about the history of art. Reflecting on the comments of their teachers and peers, they express their own ideas in visual form.

A comprehensive visual arts curriculum provides opportunities for students to develop and use the language of the visual arts and apply that knowledge to creating works of art. As they experience and study the visual arts of various cultures and historical periods, they begin to understand the aesthetic concepts needed to gain a foundation for aesthetic valuing and criticism. They are thereby able to respond to works of art in ways that enable them to grasp the power and nature of the aesthetic experience.

At all levels students learn how the visual arts connect to the world around them, to other curriculum areas, and to careers. The curriculum for a standards-based visual arts program should be well planned and articulated through the grade levels. An effective curriculum incorporates all five of the arts component strands in the content standards (see Chapter 3).

Visual Arts

Visual Arts

1 Artistic Perception

Students perceive the visual world according to their individual experiences and the opportunities they have to develop those perceptions. Gradually, they learn to recognize the universal structures of the natural world and the ways in which those structures inform art and art making. Further, they recognize the elements of art everywhere and the links between the principles of design and natural and created environments. As they work toward becoming proficient in each of the five component strands, they draw upon their developed perceptual skills and become increasingly able to point out and analyze the formal qualities of the visual arts.

2 Creative Expression

Creating original works of art involves translating thoughts, perceptions, and ideas into visual form through a variety of media and techniques. To communicate, understand, and appreciate the visual arts, students must work in expressive modes, recognizing the originality of their own expressions and the importance of respecting those of others. They thereby gain an understanding of the various media and the technical proficiency used to create works of art. And they develop their skills in the visual arts and improve their visual literacy as they work in traditional and electronic media and two- and three-dimensional art. Examples here might include painting, drawing, graphic arts, printmaking, sculpture, ceramics, photography, video and computer-generated art, architecture, product design and advertising art, textiles, jewelry, fiber arts, and glass.

Students should work on forms that combine many media, such as performance art installations, environmental art, site-specific works, and multimedia pieces. For those activities to be a part of the visual arts curriculum, they must help students communicate their ideas and feelings and appreciate their own and others' creativity. Through a carefully structured visual arts curriculum, beginning at the kindergarten level, students can develop their own artistic style and vision.

3 Historical and Cultural Context

Through the study of the visual arts from a variety of cultures, students gain an understanding and appreciation of the creative expressions of peoples across time and place. They understand artists and artworks in relation to their role and social context and the significance of the visual arts within world cultures, including the historical development of the visual arts in the United States and in California. Able to place their own work in its historical and cultural context, they also emphasize cross-cultural studies of common art forms and the distinguishing characteristics and history of works of art. They learn what art historians and aestheticians do and what role they play in society's understanding and appreciation of the visual arts.

159

Chapter 4
Guidance
for Visual and
Performing Arts
Programs

4 Aesthetic Valuing

Aesthetic valuing in the visual arts involves analysis of and informed critical response to the intent, purpose, and technical proficiency of works of art. Together with others students learn to make sound critical judgments about the quality and success of works of art by relying on their own experiences in and perceptions about the visual arts. Expressing their responses in oral, written, and electronic forms, they also discuss such aesthetic questions as, What is art for? or What makes an object a work of art? Analyzing and responding to their own artwork and that of others help students understand the feelings and ideas expressed in two-dimensional and three-dimensional works of art created by artists of many cultures, places, and times.

5 Connections, Relationships, Applications

By connecting, applying, and observing the relationships of the visual arts to the other arts disciplines, to their own world, and, gradually, to the world at large, students understand that the visual arts do not exist in isolation. Through visual arts instruction students learn to discover, appreciate, and value the contributions of the visual arts to culture, society, and the economy, particularly in California. They recognize that visual and graphic images and imagery support most global communication. They also begin to realize that, whether in fine art paintings or Internet animations, billboards or children's book illustrations, car design or kinetic sculpture, logos or iconography, cinemagraphic epics or video installations, visual art is connected to their everyday lives. Recognizing that everyone from birth is influenced by visual communication, the teacher of the standards-based visual arts can empower students to become media literate, analytical, and critical.

Today, the visual arts are providing new career opportunities for students. They are learning new ways of seeing the world and making art and recognizing that new media are changing and expanding the role of the artist in ways no one could have imagined a decade ago. What students learn in the visual arts now helps them in numerous careers in and related to the expanded visual arts. (See Appendix C, "Careers in the Visual and Performing Arts.")

When students improve their visual and media literacy, they may also improve their ability to obtain, evaluate, interpret, and communicate information in a variety of media, a form of literacy crossing all curricular boundaries and applying to all aspects of life. Students can probe beyond the obvious, identify the psychological content found in symbols and icons, and, through the Internet, learn about the changing roles of the twenty-first century artist. Using a variety of new media and electronic technology, students can prepare portfolios of original works of art for evaluations, exhibitions, applications for college entrance and jobs, and personal collections. By being visually and media literate, students have the tools needed to make sense of the profusion of images constantly bombarding them.

Visual Arts

Levels of Visual Arts Instruction

All students in California elementary schools should be participating in standards-based visual arts instructional programs carefully designed and implemented. Effective instruction calls for regular, planned, cumulative learning opportunities from kindergarten through high school and is characterized by spiraling, expanding content and diverse instructional strategies.

Elementary School Level

Whenever possible, classroom teachers in elementary schools should plan a sequential instructional program in the visual arts in cooperation with a visual arts specialist, lead teachers in the arts within the school district, and members of the community. They should base their instruction and design of instructional units on the visual arts content standards. In that way students can begin to grasp the larger picture of what those engaged in the visual arts know and do.

By strongly emphasizing instruction in the creative process rather than the product, the elementary school program provides opportunities for students to explore and appreciate their own creative and original expressions. Through discussion they begin to understand their own expressions and those of others and are given opportunities to experience a wide variety of media.

At this level students begin to learn the language of the visual arts by discussing the world around them and, more specifically, their own artwork and that from many other time periods and cultures. They also practice using that language. Through this instruction students begin to understand the historical and cultural contexts of works of art, the styles and periods of art, and the expressions of different cultural groups.

In addition, they are given opportunities to identify and discuss the characteristics of master works of art found in museums and galleries in the community. For example, Content Standard 3.2 for grade four in the historical and cultural context component strand states that the study of California history is enriched as students "identify and discuss the content of works of art in the past and present, focusing on the different cultures that have contributed to California's history and art heritage."

Middle School Level

The standards-based visual arts program in the middle schools extends the learning and experience gained by students at the elementary school level and prepares them for further visual arts courses. Through this comprehensive instruction students are able to acquire further knowledge of the visual arts, continue to develop artistic skills, and expand their creative potential. Visual arts programs promote lifelong involvement in and appreciation of the arts and an awareness of career opportunities. At this level students might begin to compile portfolios of their work that can be maintained on a CD-ROM or another form of electronic media.

Middle schools should provide instruction in the visual arts for all students through exploratory, elective, and special-interest classes, enabling students to make connections, observe relationships, and apply what they learn to all other content areas. Visual arts instruction at this level relates to the stages of development and interests of young adolescents and includes experiences for individual students and collaborating groups of students. Often, students assist in defining an artistic problem, allowing instruction to be focused on their interests, thereby inspiring in students the confidence they need to continue in the study of the visual arts.

High School Level

The high school visual arts program is an integral part of the school's visual and performing arts department. At this level students may explore one or more areas of concentration in depth or investigate a broad range of knowledge and skills in the visual arts.

The instructional program should provide students with a variety of learning opportunities in two-dimensional, three-dimensional, and electronic media at the beginning and advanced levels. Innovative and challenging experiences promote creative thinking so that all students achieve at least the beginning or proficient level of the visual arts content standards. Through such foundation courses in the visual arts, students can gain the knowledge and skills that apply to other curriculum areas along with careers in or related to the visual arts.

The course content of visual arts classes must include increasingly meaningful lessons and units in all five strands to meet the new visual and performing arts requirements for freshman admission to the University of California and the California State University. Both traditional and new media courses may be accepted provided they are based on the standards. Examples of acceptable standards-based courses and of unacceptable courses are listed in Appendix B.

By the time students reach high school, they will have become more articulate and reasoned in their judgment about art because of previous instruction in the visual arts. They can articulate their own opinions about works of art on the basis of informed judgments, recognizing that art is created for a wide variety of

Visual Arts

Visual Arts

purposes and that the observer does not have to like a work of art to understand that it is successful. Further, they notice that some art can be powerful or playful, challenging, or even disturbing and that not all visual art is intended to be beautiful.

When instructional strategies include opportunities for high school students to work with professional artists and visit art exhibits in museums and galleries, the ability of students is strengthened. Instruction that includes the study of many kinds of art deepens the students' understanding of the intent different artists bring to their work. The more artwork students see, the more accepting and appreciative they will be toward art from all cultures and from many historical and contemporary time periods. Often, programs for interns in design and gallery management sponsored by community colleges, universities, or communities may be offered to high school students with particular interests or talents.

High school students may create traditional or electronic portfolios to track their own artistic growth, prepare for high school graduation, apply for college entrance and scholarships, or obtain employment in the visual arts. At the end of a series of lessons or a visual arts course, students should evaluate their portfolios according to specified criteria and rubrics. During a series of lessons, advanced students should display their artwork and discuss technical aspects and individual progress. At the conclusion of the lessons, they should examine their own portfolio, determine their growth over time, and write a final evaluation. Then they can select works to be exhibited and included in their final, year-end portfolio.

Instruction is enhanced when high school visual arts teachers communicate continually with their colleagues in the school district, in college and university visual arts departments, and in professional organizations. That communication will enhance their programs and support the continuity and articulation of instruction.

Beginning/Advanced Drawing and Painting

Sample Standards-Based Unit of Study
Grades Nine Through Twelve

Standards-based instruction in the visual arts reinforces the importance of a rigorous, comprehensive arts education. Understanding that studio classes are not intended to be art appreciation courses, teachers should provide students with a variety of opportunities to meet the content standards and help students prepare portfolios of their work for personal use, for use in applying to postsecondary institutions, or for career presentations and exhibitions. The following unit of study is an example of how to maintain the integrity of studio classes by focusing on skill development while providing a comprehensive approach to art education. Many high school studio art classes enroll students at the proficient and advanced levels in one class and provide for differentiated opportunities based on experience.

This unit of study for beginning and advanced students focuses on creating a series of original drawings and paintings reflecting contemporary California artists and their works of art.

Visual Arts

PROFICIENT LEVEL	ADVANCED LEVEL
First year of instruction	Two or more years of additional instruction
Students research Wayne Thiebaud, a contemporary California artist. The students study the artist's works of art and the ways in which they reflect contemporary culture.	Students research Richard Diebenkorn, a contemporary California artist, and discuss ways in which his landscapes reflect, play a role in, and influence contemporary culture. Students visit local museums and galleries displaying the artist's works, view videos, and use the Internet to *see* the artist's landscapes.
Students analyze the artist's artwork according to composition and principles of design.	Students analyze the artist's works according to composition, the use of elements of art and principles of design, the art media selected, and the effect of the media selection on the artist's style.
Students complete a series of still-life drawings in their sketchbooks, reflecting Thiebaud's food themes and artifacts of the abundance of the American culture, particularly their own.	Students plan and complete a series of abstract landscape paintings of a selected landscape site, incorporating Diebenkorn's diverse use of media and abstraction.

Visual Arts

PROFICIENT LEVEL (Continued)	ADVANCED LEVEL (Continued)
In sketches students demonstrate and explore Thiebaud's ideas of formal compositional units (e.g., regimentation and variation, geometric organization, positive and negative space, and color use).	Students articulate an understanding of Diebenkorn's use of interlocking colors, bold lines, scale, observation of nature, and architectonic structures.
Students create a series of tempera paintings based on their research of Thiebaud's themes, compositional units, and color theories.	Students identify their intentions as contemporary artists in writing and peer reviews. They discuss their use of elements of art, principles of design, media, and the effect of the media on their artwork.
Students write about their own Thiebaud portfolio and assess their artwork according to their understanding of the content standards and an appropriate rubric that measures growth over time.	Students prepare their works of art for exhibition and inclusion in their portfolios and write about their works, identifying psychological content found in the images.
Students display their works of art in an exhibition and write about their understanding of the importance of art criticism.	Students apply various art-related theoretical perspectives to their own works of art.

165

Chapter 4
Guidance
for Visual and
Performing Arts
Programs

Visual Arts

Role of Student Visual Arts Exhibitions

Exhibitions of student work in the visual arts provide opportunities for students to share accomplishments and educate the community about the visual arts program, perhaps thereby increasing support for the program. Another reason to organize such exhibitions is to communicate to young artists the value placed on their artwork and artistic achievements. Awards and prizes are not necessary because students will be satisfied with the opportunities provided to exhibit their work.

A statement providing background about a work of art is valuable in communicating to the public the intention of the work and to locate it in the context of the visual arts program and content standards. It may include lesson objectives, descriptions of lessons or assignments, and the relation between the work and the visual arts content standards. Often, photographs of the students at work and the inclusion of works in progress may help clarify the context of what is on display. When several examples of particular lessons are grouped together, parents and other viewers may understand the uniqueness of each student's work. The exhibits should also demonstrate the variety of media in which students are working. When students are responsible for designing and installing an exhibit, they gain additional skill and experience relating to such careers as serving as a curator, working in an art gallery, or managing a museum.

Resources for the Visual Arts Program

To enable students to explore ideas, think innovatively, and participate in creating visual art in all its forms, school districts should adopt long-range plans providing for appropriate equipment, instructional materials, and facilities and including the assistance of community resources and parent involvement. Library media centers and teachers can also provide important resource materials to support the activities of visual arts students and teachers.

Equipment and Instructional Materials

The State Office of Environmental Health Hazard Assessment provides an advisory on legislation regulating the purchase of art and craft materials and guidelines for the safe use of the materials. The advisory includes a list titled "Art and Craft Materials Which Cannot Be Purchased for Use in Kindergarten and Grades One Through Six." Updated regularly, the list is available at *http://www.oehha.ca.gov/education/art/getart.html.* (See also Appendix F, "Guidelines for the Safe Use of Art and Craft Materials.")

The advisory further informs school personnel about precautions to be taken when purchasing art and craft materials for use in grades seven through twelve, and *Education Code* Section 32064 mandates labeling standards for those materials when they contain toxic substances. The mandate is based on the

Visual Arts

assumption that students in grades seven through twelve can read and understand warning labels on art products and, once aware of the hazard, can take the necessary precautions to minimize exposure to the hazard. That assumption makes it incumbent on teachers to ensure that all students in grades seven through twelve are aware of hazardous materials and resources and know the steps to be taken should they become exposed to those materials. Purchasing products that do not contain toxic ingredients will provide an additional measure of safety in the classroom.

Students using tools and equipment in design-craft classes, jewelry classes, and most other classes in additive and subtractive sculpture must be instructed on safety. Furthermore, they should be tested regularly on safety, and the results of the tests should be filed. When working with selected materials and equipment, such as toxic dyes, airbrushes, spray-glaze equipment, loud drills, and band saws, they must wear goggles, dust masks, and protection for their ears. All equipment handled by students should be appropriate to their age and monitored when in use.

Care should also be taken to ensure that the equipment is used in accordance with the manufacturer's directions and that all safeguards are observed. When not in use, equipment should be stored safely and securely. Electrical equipment that cannot be stored in a secure manner (e.g., band saws, motorized sanders, and grinders) should be connected to a central master breaker so that power to the machinery is cut when it is not in use. A safety zone should be set up around the equipment.

Suggested Facilities

A well-designed learning environment enhances the visual arts program in elementary schools, middle schools, and high schools. The facility should be aesthetic and spacious and provide a safe space in which students can work on a variety of art projects. It must be large enough for the number of students who will be working and moving around in the space. The visual arts room should provide storage space for materials, equipment, and works in progress tailored to the specific media being used. The facility must also be easily accessible for the delivery of equipment and materials, have space for working outdoors, allow ample natural light, and have good ventilation of fumes and vapors. Also required are large, deep sinks with individual faucets providing at least one source of hot water. For exhibitions of student work, every available wall surface should be covered with stain-resistant tackboard. All cabinets and drawers should have security locks, and a secure cabinet is needed for the VCR, DVD player, and other electronic equipment.

167

Chapter 4
Guidance
for Visual and
Performing Arts
Programs

Other equipment requires deep cabinets for storage. A counter should be provided at which students can sit and use computers with network access. Worktables must be wide enough for students to be situated on both sides and not interfere with other students at work. Storage areas and drying racks for student work must provide for a variety of paper sizes. Flat files or storage drawers must accommodate large paper, mat board, and posters at least 42 inches by 36 inches. There should also be an adjacent storage room.

Special needs concerning safety, energy, lighting, location, sound control, and maintenance must be considered. For example, access to the facility by students with physical disabilities and those with exceptional needs must be ensured. In addition, the space for the display and exhibition of two-dimensional and three-dimensional artwork should be available to students and accessible by the entire student body for viewing displays.

Safety issues are important in visual arts education. A clean environment is essential for health and safety; it must include sinks for clean-up and adequate ventilation to exhaust all fumes, dust, or odors. (*Note: Design Standards for School Art Facilities,* published by the National Art Education Association, details specifications for safe and effective visual arts rooms.)

Community Resources and Parent Involvement

A comprehensive visual arts program incorporates community resources, such as galleries, museums, arts commissions, arts councils, nonprofit organizations, Rotary clubs, PTAs, county offices of education, artists, special exhibitions, businesses that support the arts, internships, site docents, and colleges and universities. Educators should take advantage of the visual arts resources in their immediate community that may be available on request. For example, local galleries are often willing to allow a class visit at their sites and discuss how their galleries are operated, and artists living in the area may be willing to speak to students or even demonstrate their art form to a class. In addition, community arts councils or organizations may have visiting artist programs or a list of artists in the area.

If asked, many parent organizations will donate money for arts supplies. Some even sponsor training for individuals to become art docents in the classrooms. Local colleges may have large collections of art prints in their library available for checkout, and postsecondary educators are often more than willing to give advice or help with a class project. The more the involvement of parents and community members in local arts education occurs, the more students will benefit, and the more valuable the program will become. (See also "Promoting Partnerships and Collaborations" in Chapter 2.)

5

Assessment in the Arts

Assessment in the Arts

Throughout California the visual and performing arts content standards provide teachers, administrators, students, and the community with a clear set of expectations as to what students should know and be able to perform in dance, music, theatre, and the visual arts in elementary school, middle school, and high school.

Purpose of Student Assessment

Assessment of student work in the arts helps teachers determine how they should adapt their instruction so that their students can achieve the content standards. It also helps teachers build a profile for each student that can be used to communicate progress. At the school district level, the assessment data help administrators make effective decisions about instruction, personnel, and resources for the arts education program.

Assessment and instruction should be aligned within the curriculum. The key to using assessment effectively and efficiently is to recognize that, above all, no single assessment tool meets all assessment needs. Assessment can be used to inform instruction, monitor student progress, provide feedback to students and parents, summarize students' learning over a given period of time, and provide additional information to qualify students for special programs.

Assessment of student work in the arts may be accomplished through thoughtfully designed performances, critiques, and analyses, just as artists are constantly assessing their own performances and products and asking others to assess or critique their work. If the visual and performing arts curriculum and instructional materials fully integrate assessment, most assessment activities, especially the monitoring of progress, will contribute to learning and maximize instructional time.

Wolf and Pistone enumerate five assumptions about the efficacy of assessment in the arts. First, students and teachers insist on excellence as exhibited in performances and portfolios. High standards having been set, studio and classroom discussions involve ways to reach those standards. Second, much discussion takes place about judgment—opinions on a range of qualitative issues—and decisions based on insight, reason, and craft. Third, self-assessment is important for all artists. That is, students need to learn how to understand and appraise their own work and that of their peers and other artists. Fourth, varied forms of assessment must be used to obtain information about individual and group performances. And fifth, ongoing assessment allows students to reflect on their own creations and use the insight gained to enrich their work. When viewed in that way, assessment is an episode of learning. [1] (See "Selected References and Resources" at the back of this publication for additional resources on assessment.)

Types of Assessment

Regular assessment of student progress in mastering grade-level standards is essential to the success of an instructional program based on the visual and performing arts content standards and framework. It should be informative and timely and contribute appropriately to student learning and development. The three types of student assessment are described as follows:

- *Entry-level assessment.* Do students possess crucial prerequisite skills and knowledge? Do they already know some of the material being taught? If so, the teacher can more easily determine the most efficient starting point for learning. Some entry-level assessments should measure mastery of foundational standards; others should measure the degree to which students have mastered some portion of what is to be learned next. Teachers should use the information from the entry-level assessment to ensure that students receive support in specific areas. Entry-level assessments might consist of vocabulary pretests, open-ended conceptual questions, performance opportunities for students to show current mastery of theory or technique, or opportunities to demonstrate current level of skill by using a set of material or prompts.

- *Progress monitoring.* Are students progressing adequately toward achieving standards? Monitoring, which should occur regularly, helps guide instruction in the right direction. In standards-based classrooms monitoring becomes a crucial component of instruction for every student. It signals when alternative routes need to be taken or when students need to review material before moving forward. Only through such monitoring can teachers focus instruction continually so that all students are constantly progressing.

   Everything students do during instruction provides opportunities for monitoring. Ongoing assessment allows student artists to reflect on their own creations, using the insights gained to enrich their own work. They need to learn how to appraise their own work and that of peers and professional artists. Therefore, monitoring, whether internal or external, should reflect the essential nature of the knowledge or skill being assessed, direct student learning, and establish expectations for achievement.

---

[1] Dennie Palmer Wolf and Nancy Pistone, *Taking Full Measure: Rethinking Assessment Through the Arts.* New York: College Entrance Examination Board, 1991.

Internal monitoring (self-assessment) helps students determine their level of mastery according to a set of clear criteria. External monitoring helps teachers, also using a set of clear criteria, determine the students' level of mastery. External monitoring should (1) document performance; (2) help teachers make instructional decisions and adjustments according to documented performance; (3) identify student performance in relationship to the standards; and (4) include a variety of strategies to determine students' level of knowledge and skills.

Monitoring of progress in the arts may also be formal or informal. Formal monitoring might appear as questions or prompts to be answered by students or the performance of a prescribed set of skills on demand. Informal monitoring might include a conference or conversational analysis centered on a work in progress and determination of the next steps needed for completion.

- *Summative evaluation.* Have students achieved the goals defined by a given standard or group of standards? Summative evaluation helps determine whether students have achieved the goals defined in a standard or group of standards. It answers the following questions: Do students know and understand the material? Can they apply the material in another situation? Are they ready to move on? Typically, this type of assessment comes at the end of an instructional unit or school year. The most important aspect of summative evaluation is that it measures the students' long-term growth and mastery of grade-level standards.

Considerations in Arts Assessment

The visual and performing arts content standards focus on developing the knowledge and skills required to create successful artwork and performances. They also include the study of the arts and artists and their influence on culture. Comprehensive assessment relies on a variety of means to create a complete evaluation of students' progress. Assessments include student works of art and performances, open-ended projects or questions, research assignments, constructed response items, or multiple-choice items.

Scoring Rubrics

Whenever a performance assessment tool is used, explicit criteria for evaluating students' work should be determined and shared with the students before the evaluation occurs. Because the arts encourage enthusiasm or novelty, students enjoy a variety of ways to solve artistic problems. Therefore, an assignment or performance task may produce a result far different from what was envisioned yet meet the stated criteria for assessment. Students can express their creativity fully according to the accepted criteria when they and their parents or guardians are familiar with the criteria and scoring rubrics that teachers use to identify the students' levels of success in meeting the content standards. To help students focus on their work, teachers may attach to assignments or performance tasks sample scoring rubrics describing levels of accomplishment.

Assessment of Performances and Exhibitions

Student performances and exhibitions can lend themselves to formal or informal assessment. Through careful planning the teacher may allow beginning performances to be shared and critiqued to help students gain mastery of the skills being developed. Such a supportive and creative environment helps students build confidence. To satisfy the entrance requirements of the University of California and California State University systems, performance course criteria should include appropriate cocurricular work, such as performances and exhibitions. Teachers should encourage students to make presentations at school board and parent meetings.

Student Portfolios

One way to assess student learning is to examine collections of students' work. Student artists should maintain portfolios of formal and informal work to monitor progress and display the depth and breadth of their skills over time, as do professional artists. Portfolios help students observe improvement in their work and assist teachers in evaluating student progress and the effectiveness of their teaching strategies. When the portfolios have been reviewed according to predetermined criteria, teachers and students can establish the levels of content mastery already achieved. Portfolios can also be used to demonstrate to parents how far students have advanced toward the goal of content mastery.

Assessment portfolios might include examples of draft sketches, technique development, and finished work as well as documentation of artwork or performances, including photographs, audios, videos, digitally formatted compilations, and reflective writings. Some types of such portfolios are as follows:

- *Process portfolios.* These portfolios demonstrate student mastery over time. They may include rough sketches or drafts, preliminary plans for staging, scores or scripts, choreography notes and diagrams, and more refined and finished works. In addition, they may contain written reflections on works in progress, the process for completing the work, influences on the work, and critiques of self and peers. During the course teachers and students should discuss the work periodically to determine progress and areas needing improvement.

- *Portfolios of assessment tasks.* These portfolios include a series of specific tasks or assignments usually related to the mastery of a set of specific content standards in each of the strands. A middle school portfolio of the assessment tasks has been developed by the California Art Education Association: In task one students compare and contrast two works of portrait art; in task two they create self-portraits; and in task three they use a scoring rubric to evaluate their own artwork.

- *Best-work portfolios.* These portfolios are intended to showcase the best work students have completed in a course. Usually selected jointly by students and teachers, they are typically used in formal and informal reviews of student progress.

- *Competition or high-stakes portfolios.* Portfolios of this type are developed by students for competitions, applications for advanced study, or admission to special programs. Works included should be of the highest quality and demonstrate advanced technical skills and conceptual awareness. Further, they should show evidence of accomplishment in a variety of media, including reflective statements written by the students regarding their work.

Ensemble Assessment

Ensemble products provide a different set of challenges and opportunities. The members of an orchestra, the dancers in a troupe, the actors in a play, and the singers in a quartet all need their own clear assessment criteria because the role of the individual student, whether as a soloist or as a member of the group, is vital to the overall success of the ensemble. That factor should be part of the assessment of a student's progress.

New Media and Electronic Technology

Using new media and electronic technologies for assessment is increasingly valuable to visual and performing arts educators and students. To deliver constructed response items, a school or school district may select exemplary work by teachers who are artists or by students to be digitally photographed or recorded. For example, virtual-reality software facilitates a 360-degree view of an object or performance by a simple command on the computer. Once burned onto a CD, the items may be used by the entire school or school district as part of an assessment.

In any arts discipline portfolios of student work can be burned onto a CD or DVD, stored, and shared with others for assessment. Students may send their portfolios to colleges or universities for entrance into a program or use them to apply for employment. In creating portfolios, students develop

Multiple Measures of Student Progress in the Arts

Selected response items: Multiple choice, true-false, matching, enhanced choice

Brief constructed responses: Fill in the blanks (words, phrases); write short answers (sentences, paragraphs); label a diagram or visual representation (Web, concept map, flowchart, graph or table, illustration).

Products: Produce an essay, a research paper, a log or journal, a report, a story or play, an exhibit, a project, artwork, a model, a dance, a video or audiotape, or a portfolio.

Performances: Make an oral presentation; dance; sing or play an instrument; offer a demonstration, dramatic reading, enactment, debate, recital; teach a lesson.

Process-focused: Perform oral questioning, an observation, an interview, a conference, a process description or demonstration; think aloud; write a learning log.

—Adapted from Ferrara and McTighe,
Assessing Learning in the Classroom

skills in critiquing their own work, a sense of accomplishment, marketable technology skills, insight into their body of work, and a portable record of that work. Students who are performance artists will find videos, CDs, or DVDs especially valuable in documenting and critiquing their work.

An electronic process for assessing student work and providing professional development for arts teachers involves a Web site with an interactive digital interface. In this process teachers first upload a standards-based assessment task with an accompanying scoring rubric and then add examples of student work so that other teachers can evaluate to what extent that work meets the criteria on the scoring rubric. To provide observations and comments, teachers from different schools and school districts may have access to the site. The multiple reviews of the work provide insights and establish anchor or benchmark performances for the task.

Arts Assessment: From the Classroom to the School District

Assessment data help schools and school districts to be accountable for the quality of standards-based arts education programs. A school district moving toward establishing districtwide assessment in the arts might first conduct an arts program assessment to determine the extent to which the arts are taught at each school level. Then the district might consider what students need to know to attain the visual and performing arts standards and how to report their progress. As school districts move toward student assessment in the arts and share their processes and results, arts education programs throughout the state will be expanded and improved.

Assessment Outside the Classroom

Students can venture outside the classroom to test their knowledge and skills. They can share their works in progress and completed artwork or performances away from the classroom and in doing so gain an invaluable source of new ideas. For example, schoolwide student exhibitions and performances provide a supportive first step in sharing artwork with the community. In time the scope of this sharing can widen to include the school district; the local community; the city, the county, and the state; and national festivals and competitions. But it should be noted that participation in those events is not an end in itself but an integral part of a larger learning objective.

Participation in festivals, competitions, and public exhibitions provides opportunities for the assessment of individuals and ensembles. In those educational events experienced adjudicators provide constructive feedback to teachers and their students and valuable insight that reinforces and extends classroom learning.

Teachers must balance opportunities to share student work and students' need for practicing their skills without having to provide entertainment at events, assemblies, meetings, clubs, and conferences. Although the visibility and popularity of student performing groups can build widespread support for arts programs, those activities should not interfere with the students' overall education.

Advanced placement (AP) courses also provide opportunities for students to challenge the depth of their understanding of the conceptual and historical arts nationally. Rankings from AP examinations can benefit a student's placement in college and chances of winning scholarships and grant entitlements. International baccalaureate programs provide a standardized program that focuses on critical thinking and exposure to a variety of points of view and is designed to encourage intercultural understanding by young people. (More information can be found online at *http://www.ibo.org.*)

Arts Assessment in California

The California arts education community has been exploring the assessment of student work in the arts for many years. For that purpose the Towards Arts Assessment Project of the California Department of Education and the

Sacramento County Office of Education has issued *Prelude to Performance Assessment in the Arts.* [2] Assessment projects have also been initiated by the following organizations:

- The California Arts Project (TCAP) is attempting to involve more teachers in multiple measures of arts assessment.
- The California professional arts teacher associations provide resources on arts assessment.
- The California Art Education Association (CAEA) has published two documents on portfolio assessment in the visual arts.
- The California Music Educators Association (CMEA) offers publications on assessing students in music and sponsors regional and state-wide-adjudicated festivals and competitions.
- The California Dance Educators Association (CDEA) and the California Educational Theatre Association (CETA) also provide information in their publications and at annual conferences offer professional development in assessing student work.
- CETA and CAEA also offer students opportunities to participate in adjudicated festivals, competitions, and shows.

In 1998 the California Department of Education initiated the California Arts Assessment Network (CAAN) to assist school districts in developing and piloting appropriate assessment of student work in the arts at the school district level. The network activities include a project with *TeachingArts.org,* the California online arts resource center, to evaluate student work interactively online. CAAN is also collaborating with a variety of educational agencies in other states to develop an online pool of assessment items.

Arts Assessment Nationally

In 1997 the National Assessment Governing Board (NAGB) developed assessment tools and items for grades four, eight, and twelve in dance, music, theatre, and the visual arts. The National Assessment of Education Progress (NAEP), administered to eighth-grade students throughout the nation, measured students' knowledge and skills only in music, theatre, and the visual arts. Although an assessment was developed for dance, it was not administered because of the lack of a suitable national sample. The next arts assessment will be administered in 2008. Further information is available online at *http://nces.ed.gov/nationsreportcard/arts/* or from the NAGB at 800 North Capitol Street, NW, Suite 825, Washington, DC 20002-4233.

---

[2] *Prelude to Performance Assessment in the Arts: Kindergarten Through Grade Twelve.* Sacramento: California Department of Education, 1994.

6

Professional Development
in the Arts

Professional Development in the Arts

Successful implementation of the visual and performing arts content standards depends on effective teacher preparation (i.e., preservice training) and long-term professional development. Two important findings about professional development in the arts were revealed in a survey published by the California Department of Education.[1] The survey indicated that teachers trained in the arts are more likely to teach the arts. It serves as a reminder that many classroom teachers have not received training or professional development in how to teach the arts. The survey also confirmed that, in addition to the teachers, community members with artistic skills are involved in teaching the arts in the schools.

Teacher Preparation in the Arts

To accomplish the goals of this framework, teacher education programs should design the curriculum for the benefit of those pursuing multisubject credentials and those planning to teach single-subject courses in the visual and performing arts. The curriculum should provide a foundation in the arts that addresses the visual and performing arts content standards and the five related strands.

Future teachers of the visual and performing arts should major in a specific arts discipline at the college or university level and develop their own artistic skills and knowledge. In preservice arts education they should have opportunities to (1) plan and assess arts learning systematically; (2) gain an understanding of arts pedagogy, including processes and strategies for arts instruction appropriate to the ages and abilities of students; (3) develop strategies for working with diverse student populations; and (4) gain experience in the use of new media and electronic technology relevant to teaching, learning, or performing the arts.

---

[1] *The Results of the Arts Work Survey of California Public Schools.* Sacramento: California Department of Education, 2001.

Organization of Professional Development in the Arts

Implementing standards-based visual and performing arts programs challenges school district administrators planning professional development for teachers. The sequential nature of the standards in each of the arts and the comprehensive approach of including the five strands require many teachers at all levels to become more knowledgeable about the arts and effective ways in which to teach them.

Ongoing professional development should be planned for both generalists who teach the arts and arts specialists and should be offered locally and regularly. Because effective professional development requires long-term efforts, it should be focused on increasing teachers' knowledge of and practice in the arts and their ability to teach the arts. All professional development programs in the arts should be based on the content standards and guidelines presented in the *Visual and Performing Arts Framework*. Training should prepare teachers to use the state-adopted arts instructional materials effectively in kindergarten through grade eight. The training can be particularly useful for teachers in schools with limited resources and access to only a few district specialists. Those who provide professional development programs must be able to demonstrate the effectiveness of their recommendations for the typically diverse California classroom and be competent to instruct teachers.

Schools and school districts should support teachers' lifelong learning with released time and funding in ongoing, planned professional development programs coordinated at the district level. Professional development may include courses at institutions of higher education; participation in meetings and conferences of regional, state, and national education and arts education organizations; and institutes and workshops offered by The California Arts Project (TCAP) and professional arts organizations. (See Selected References and Resources for information on contacting arts education organizations.)

Resources for Professional Development in Arts Education

The resources listed in Selected References and Resources include information on organizations that identify or provide professional development programs in arts education. Often, they are as close as the regional site of The California Arts Project, the state professional development project in the visual and performing arts, or one of the four professional arts teacher associations: the California Dance Educators Association, the California Association for Music Education, the California Educational Theatre Association, and the California Arts Education Association.

Some communities have city or county arts agencies that can also be valuable resources, and some colleges and universities have outreach programs providing assistance to schools in teaching the arts. Often, institutions of higher education provide special programs for teachers to advance their learning in and teaching of the arts and include courses in the arts in their teacher preparation programs as requirements for receiving teaching credentials.

Throughout the state arts education consultants and arts providers (e.g., museums, symphonies, music centers, opera and dance companies, folk art providers) employ education and outreach personnel who may be helpful in professional development. And nonprofit arts organizations often focus their work on advocating arts education in the schools and provide professional development for teachers and instruction for students. The California online resource center for the arts at *http://www.TeachingArts.org* provides valuable help in planning professional development programs.

Workshops, demonstrations, and peer reviews provide useful information for arts specialist teachers and classroom teachers. Teachers can participate in workshops with peers; view and analyze demonstration lessons or exchange classroom visits; receive coaching and mentoring from district lead teachers or specialists; and work with resident or visiting artists. It is important that those receiving professional development in the arts are provided with time to discuss with their peers ways to implement the concepts and techniques presented in professional development programs. Often, county offices of education offer professional development opportunities for teachers from several school districts. They may bring in professional artists to work with students in the classroom setting while the classroom teacher observes the techniques being taught.

Professional development also benefits guest or resident artists working at any level to extend and enrich the arts curriculum. They too require orientation to the arts content standards and the curriculum together with information on effective teaching strategies matched to intended curriculum outcomes. Many artists working in the schools appreciate professional development that will help them adapt their knowledge of content and artistic processes.

Content of Professional Development in the Arts

If the vision of a standards-based arts education for all students in every grade is to be achieved, teachers of the arts must be trained in critical areas. During preservice education and through long-term professional development, those areas are further developed, refined, and expanded throughout the teachers' careers.

Teachers should engage in ongoing professional development to acquire knowledge of (1) the strands of the arts content standards, including, when appropriate, training related to state-adopted visual and performing arts instructional materials; (2) processes and products in arts education; (3) the interdependence and independence of the arts; (4) the arts and learning across the curriculum; (5) affective and cognitive aspects of the arts; (6) world arts and cultures; (7) collaboration and articulation; (8) student assessment; and (9) the uses of new media and electronic technology.

1. Strands of the Arts Content Standards

Instruction in the arts content standards should center on the five strands of the arts content standards. Therefore, generalists teaching the arts should understand and have experience with the strands: artistic perception, creative expression, historical and cultural context, aesthetic valuing, and connections, relationships, and applications. For kindergarten through grade eight, a set of key standards in each of the five strands has been identified in this framework. A professional development program may begin by emphasizing the key standards and training related to the state-adopted visual and performing arts instructional materials.

Teachers must determine what students learned in the arts in prior grades because the standards for dance, music, theatre, and the visual arts are based on those earlier experiences. Because growth in knowledge and skills is cumulative, students are continually constructing meaning. They are able, through the five strands and the content standards, to gain the breadth of knowledge and skills needed to experience an arts discipline from varied perspectives. In the same manner teachers who have learned an arts discipline as creators and thoughtful critics are better prepared to teach that discipline.

2. Processes and Products in Arts Education

Focusing on the arts processes (how) and products or performances (what), arts teachers should explore the learning involved in producing a product or performance because it is important to student achievement. Achievement is accomplished through purposeful teacher-guided reflection during the learning process and completion of a product or performance.

Through experimentation or exploration students engaged in the arts learn by doing and gain an understanding of the depth of the knowledge and skills required in each of the arts disciplines. Examples of beginning work and works in progress captured in photographs and portfolios or on audiocassettes can be presented in concerts or exhibitions. And videos of students' performances can be shown, together with the culminating works, to demonstrate hard work, discipline, progress, and the artistic process.

3. **Interdependence and Independence of the Arts**

Professional development for teachers needs to include acquisition of knowledge and skills in specific arts disciplines and recognition of the connections between the various disciplines. This knowledge and these skills will provide a means for teachers to deepen their understanding of particular disciplines and recognize points of contact and areas of contrast in relation to the other arts and other content areas.

4. **The Arts Across the Curriculum**

When teachers begin to understand the arts and become proficient in teaching them, they become aware of natural connections to learning across the curriculum. Together, arts specialist teachers, classroom teachers of the arts, and teachers of other content areas are responsible for helping students make such connections. Therefore, professional development programs should inform teachers of appropriate, successful strategies to help students apply what they have learned.

5. **Affective and Cognitive Aspects of the Arts**

Arts education requires the use of all the cognitive processes commonly needed to master other academic disciplines. Although the ability to express emotion through the arts is regarded by some as the essence of the arts, it goes hand in hand with the power of the arts to expand mental processes. When students engage in the arts, they can experience the joy, exhilaration, and thrill of creative accomplishment as creators or members of an audience. Those experiences, which involve emotions, reveal connections, and spark insights, expand students' knowledge and create a lifelong love and appreciation for the arts.

6. **World Arts and Cultures**

A broad base of knowledge for teachers of the arts should include knowledge of various world cultures, religious and ceremonial arts, and the American arts, such as musical theatre, mural painting, modern dance, and jazz. Through these rich experiences teachers can view the arts from many different personal or cultural lenses, and the curriculum can reflect the many sources from which American culture has derived its powerful vigor.

7. **Collaboration and Articulation**

At any grade level standards-based arts programs succeed when collaboration takes place. Such collaboration begins with the planning process, involving classroom teachers; arts specialists in dance, music, theatre, and the visual arts; and artists from the community who may participate in classroom instruction. They articulate the program together with the others responsible for developing and confirming the curriculum and resources:

school and school district administrators; curriculum specialists at the district and, perhaps, county levels; faculty from institutions of higher education; arts resource persons from the community; teachers at other grade levels or in other departments; and school librarians, who can help identify appropriate literature and technology resources. The same cooperation and articulation should follow through to the implementation of the program.

8. Student Assessment

Student learning in each of the arts can be assessed. Professional development that includes efforts to understand the purpose and types of assessment and the application of assessments to each of the arts, together with opportunities to develop and implement assessment strategies embedded in student learning, strengthens curriculum and instruction. The design and scoring of assessments should include grounding the lessons in the visual and performing arts content standards and developing and using scoring rubrics reflecting students' application of their knowledge and skills in the five strands of each arts discipline. Teachers skilled in performance assessment at the classroom level should also collaborate with others at the school and school district levels to design assessments for accountability (see Chapter 5).

9. Uses of New Media and Electronic Technology

Teachers can reach all students best when the teachers keep up-to-date on the uses of new media and electronic technology in the arts. They should know how to use new media and electronic technology as a resource, for recording and delivery, and as a tool. When teachers have frequent opportunities to learn about and use a variety of technologies, they become comfortable with the media, are willing to experiment, and can select resources appropriate to meet various learning styles.

Criteria for Evaluating Instructional Materials: Kindergarten Through Grade Eight

Criteria for Evaluating Instructional Materials: Kindergarten Through Grade Eight

This chapter provides criteria for evaluating the alignment of instructional materials with the *Visual and Performing Arts Content Standards for California Public Schools.*[1] The content standards, which were adopted by the California State Board of Education in January 2001, describe what students should know and be able to do at each grade level. This updated *Visual and Performing Arts Framework* was adopted by the State Board of Education in January 2004. It incorporates the standards and instructional guidelines that together define the essential skills and knowledge in visual and performing arts that will enable all California students to enjoy a world-class education.

The instructional materials must provide guidance for the teacher to present the content standards and curriculum and teach the skills required at each grade level. These skills are to be learned through, and applied to, the content standards. Special attention should also be paid to the appendixes in the framework, which address important arts issues.

The following criteria will guide the development and govern the adoption cycle of instructional materials for kindergarten through grade eight beginning in 2006. They do not, however, require or recommend a particular pedagogical approach.

The five categories of the criteria are listed as follows:

1. **Visual and Performing Arts Content/Alignment with Standards:** The content specified in the *Visual and Performing Arts Content Standards for California Public Schools* (see Chapter 3)

2. **Program Organization:** The sequence and organization of the visual and performing arts program

3. **Assessment:** The strategies presented in the instructional materials for measuring what students know and are able to do

---

[1] *Visual and Performing Arts Content Standards for California Public Schools: Prekindergarten Through Grade Twelve.* Sacramento: California Department of Education, 2001.

189

Chapter 7
Criteria
for Evaluating
Instructional
Materials:
Kindergarten
Through
Grade Eight

4. **Universal Access:** The information and ideas that address the needs of every student, including those with diverse learning styles and abilities

5. **Instructional Planning and Support:** The information and materials, typically including a separate edition specifically designed for use by teachers, to assist teachers in implementing visual and performing arts programs

Because instructional materials in the visual and performing arts must support teaching aligned with the content standards, those failing to meet the criteria in category 1 will be considered unsatisfactory for adoption. Categories 2 through 5 must be considered as a whole, each set of materials being judged as a group. And the materials must also satisfy the requirements of categories 2 through 5 to be considered suitable for adoption.

Instructional materials should center on developing fully the content described in the standards. For efficient presentation extraneous content must be insignificant and not contrary to the standards. It must also not detract from the ability of teachers to teach readily and students to learn thoroughly the content specified in the standards.

Category 1
Visual and Performing Arts Content/Alignment with Standards

Instructional materials must support the teaching and learning of the content and skills required by a discipline at a grade level described in the standards. The numerical order of the criteria within each category does not imply the relative importance of the criteria.

To be considered suitable for adoption, instructional materials in the visual and performing arts must provide:

1. A full program that includes all the standards in one or more disciplines at one or more grade levels (There should be no reference to national standards or benchmarks or to any standards other than those contained in the *Visual and Performing Arts Content Standards for California Public Schools.*)

2. A list of evidence, with page numbers or other appropriate references, that demonstrates alignment with the standards (as detailed, discussed, and prioritized in Chapter 3 of the framework)

3. Topics or concepts, lessons, activities, examples, or illustrations, as appropriate, to support the content standards explicitly stated for the grade level(s) in the designated discipline(s) submitted

190

Chapter 7
Criteria
for Evaluating
Instructional
Materials:
Kindergarten
Through
Grade Eight

4. Accurate content, with examples based on current and confirmed research to support the teaching of the visual and performing arts

5. Opportunities for students to increase their knowledge of the visual and performing arts through their study of the historical development of artistic concepts and the lives, contributions, and innovations of certain artists, with all activities centered on the students understanding the standards

6. Opportunities for students to study the connections between the visual and performing arts disciplines to support an understanding of the designated content standards for dance, music, theatre, and the visual arts at various grade levels

7. Content presented in interesting and engaging ways to students

8. Terms and academic vocabulary appropriately used and accurately defined

9. Clear procedures and explanations of underlying concepts, principles, and theories integral to and supportive of the teaching and learning of art forms so that performance skills are learned in the context of specific content standards

10. Guidelines for formal and informal presentations of student work and other artwork focused on demonstrating the artistic elements and principles in the content area, thereby aiding meaningful learning

11. Examples for student work using readily available materials

12. Recommendations for reading and writing about the arts that are aligned with the appropriate grade-level English–language arts standards

13. Graphics (pictures, maps, charts) that are accurate, are well annotated or labeled, and enhance students' focus and understanding of the content

In addition, providers of instructional materials in the visual and performing arts are encouraged to:

- Reinforce, when appropriate, the grade-level-designated content standards for mathematics, science, history–social science, or English–language arts to explain relationships and solve problems

- Identify the key standards for each arts discipline when addressed

- Examine the contributions of the arts to the larger culture and their effects on society

191

Chapter 7
Criteria
for Evaluating
Instructional
Materials:
Kindergarten
Through
Grade Eight

- Discuss the contributions of contemporary media artwork, processes, and concepts and their effects on the arts disciplines
- Make use of electronic resources that add richness and depth of understanding to the standards being taught

Category 2
Program Organization

The organization of the visual and performing arts program structures sequentially what students should learn each year and allows teachers to convey the content efficiently and effectively, thereby providing students with opportunities to achieve the knowledge and skills described in the standards. The content also reflects the variety of instructional models, staffing, and facilities at a given school site.

To be considered suitable for adoption, instructional materials in the visual and performing arts must provide:

1. Introduction of new concepts at a reasonable pace and with depth of coverage, with the explicit aim of preparing students to master content at each grade level so that they can advance to the next level

2. A variety of experiences, problems, applications, and independent practices that organize the appropriate grade-level content in a logical, systematic way so that prerequisite skills and knowledge can be developed before the introduction of the more complex concepts, principles, and theories that depend on them

3. A well-organized structure providing students with opportunities to understand artistic concepts, principles, and theories and building on a foundation of facts, skills, and inquiry

4. A logical, coherent, and sequential organizational structure that facilitates efficient and effective teaching and learning in a lesson, unit, and year aligned with the standards

5. Clearly stated student outcomes and goals that are measurable and are based on the content standards

6. An overview of the content in each chapter or unit that outlines the visual and performing arts concepts and skills to be developed

7. Guidelines for a safe environment or facility appropriate to the level of physical performance and training difficulty called for in the arts curriculum

8. Tables of contents, indexes, glossaries, electronic-based resources, support materials, content summaries, and assessment guides designed to help teachers, parents or guardians, and students navigate the program

Chapter 7
Criteria
for Evaluating
Instructional
Materials:
Kindergarten
Through
Grade Eight

In addition, providers of instructional materials in the visual and performing arts are encouraged to include:

- Guidelines for the implementation of the instructional content within disciplines that reflect general or specialized facilities, various staff expertise, or a range of school resources
- A standards-based curriculum that includes contemporary media technologies or uniquely organized resources that support universal access to information and enhance teaching and learning in the arts
- Delivery of instructional program or units through alternative formats or methods, including but not limited to videos, interactive media, CD-ROMs, DVDs, and online resources, to facilitate ease of duplication and distribution or provide support for universal access

Category 3
Assessment

Instructional materials should contain multiple measures to assess what students know and can do in the visual and performing arts. The measures should reveal students' knowledge of the concepts, principles, theories, and skills related to those arts and students' ability to apply that knowledge to understanding advanced versions of those concepts, principles, and theories. Assessment tools that are part of the instructional material should provide evidence of students' progress in meeting the content standards and useful information for planning and modifying instruction to help all students meet or exceed those standards.

To be considered suitable for adoption, instructional materials in the visual and performing arts must provide:

1. Strategies and tools reflecting the assessment guidelines presented in Chapter 5 (entry-level assessment, progress monitoring, summative evaluation)

2. Multiple measures of individual student progress at regular intervals to evaluate grade-level mastery of the standards

3. Guiding questions to monitor student understanding of the arts

In addition, providers of instructional materials in the visual and performing arts are encouraged to include:

- Suggestions for methods by which a student's work can be compared over time (e.g., portfolios, presentations, performances, journals, CDs)
- Electronic tools providing data for diagnostic purposes and user-friendly features, such as help windows, navigation bars, and font and color conformity across platforms, that are easy to install

Chapter 7
Criteria
for Evaluating
Instructional
Materials:
Kindergarten
Through
Grade Eight

Category 4
Universal Access

Instructional materials should provide access to the standards-based curriculum for all students, including those with diverse learning styles and abilities. In addition, programs must conform to the policies of the State Board of Education and other applicable state and federal guidelines pertaining to diverse populations and special education.

To be considered suitable for adoption, instructional materials in the visual and performing arts must provide:

1. Suggestions for adapting curriculum and instruction to meet students' diverse learning styles and abilities according to current and confirmed research

2. Strategies to help students who are below grade level in the visual and performing arts standards

3. Strategies to help students reading below grade level understand the visual and performing arts content

4. Suggestions that allow advanced learners to study standards-based content in greater depth

In addition, providers of instructional materials in the visual and performing arts are encouraged to include:

- Lesson materials optimizing clear presentation and focus on students
- Electronic tools aligned with industry standards for universal access (including text and audio enhancement) and multiple levels of difficulty that can be adjusted by the teacher or student

Category 5
Instructional Planning and Support

Teacher-support materials built into the instructional materials should specify suggestions and illustrative examples of how teachers can implement a standards-based visual and performing arts program. That assistance should be designed to help the teacher implement the program to ensure that all students have opportunities to learn the essential knowledge and skills called for by the standards. Because the criteria do not recommend or require a particular pedagogical approach, the materials should contain recommendations to teachers regarding those approaches that best fit instructional goals. Accordingly, the materials should offer a variety of instructional approaches that might include but are not limited to direct instruction, reading, writing, demonstrations, creation of artwork, and Internet use and inquiry.

194

Chapter 7
Criteria
for Evaluating
Instructional
Materials:
Kindergarten
Through
Grade Eight

To be considered suitable for adoption, instructional materials in the visual and performing arts must provide:

1. Explicit, systematic, and accurate procedures and prompts; explanations of background, concepts, and principles; and theories understandable to specialists, credentialed arts teachers, and general classroom teachers

2. Strategies to identify and correct common student misconceptions of the visual and performing arts concepts

3. A variety of effective teaching strategies for flexible implementation

4. Lesson plans that reflect properly sequenced instruction with appropriate procedures understandable to specialists, credentialed arts teachers, and general classroom teachers

5. A number of possible strategies for pacing lessons

6. Suggestions for applying student assessment data to instructional planning within the program

7. Resources reflecting strategies found successful in engaging all students in full participation, varied thinking, and meaning-centered tasks

8. A list of suggested equipment, supplies, and facilities supporting implementation of a standards-based program

9. Guidelines to ensure classroom safety and effective use and care of required equipment, materials, and supplies called for by the program during instruction and demonstrations

10. Suggestions for organizing and storing resources in the classroom

11. Economical equipment and supplies together with recommendations for their use (included with the materials) or recommendations for using readily available alternative materials and equipment

12. The program packaged for sale containing all components, including reproducible masters, needed for helping students meet the state requirements

13. A plan for professional development and continuing technical support for users of the materials in implementing the program

14. Technical support and suggestions for the appropriate use of instruments, tools, and equipment as well as audiovisual, multimedia, and information technology resources associated with the program

In addition, providers of instructional materials in the visual and performing arts are encouraged to include:

- Suggestions for using community resources to support the program
- References and resources providing teachers with further information on the visual and performing arts content
- Suggestions to students for exploring the content in the standards at great depth

195

Chapter 7
Criteria
for Evaluating
Instructional
Materials:
Kindergarten
Through
Grade Eight

- Support materials that reinforce, model, and demonstrate effective teaching strategies for teacher use (e.g., video of demonstration lessons, simulations, online resources)
- Homework assignments and periodic letters to the home encouraging student learning and presented so that parents or guardians can easily support their child's academic success.
- Suggestions for informing parents or guardians and the community about the visual and performing arts program
- Electronic tools, including lesson-plan builders, teacher presentations, and technical and implementation support
- Electronic resources promoting interaction of teachers and students and critical thinking, such as presentations with designated points for discussion, interactive simulations, role playing, and multiuse systems

Alternative Delivery Systems

New media and electronic technology are shaping artistic expression by introducing new systems, materials, and processes. More than simply replicating text-based materials in an electronic format, use of the new media involves expressing ideas and creating artwork in unique ways that are not possible without the use of technology. For example, it allows for the replication and changing of images, and the use of those images becomes a new medium of expression. This new and evolving area within the arts serves as a vehicle for creating and communicating aesthetic ideas, enhancing access to artistic media and information, and extending opportunities for instruction, critiques, reflections, and assessments. New media and electronic technology are changing arts education by encouraging teachers and students to employ these new modes of expression and materials in creating artwork.

To be considered suitable for adoption, instructional materials incorporating new media and electronic technology must provide:

1. A standards-based curriculum that includes contemporary media technologies or uniquely organized resources supporting universal access to information and enhancing teaching and learning in the arts
2. Delivery of an instructional program or units through alternative formats or methods, including but not limited to videos, interactive media, CD-ROMs, DVDs, and online resources
3. Technical support and suggestions for the appropriate use of the instruments, tools, and equipment as well as the audiovisual, multimedia, and information technology resources associated with the program
4. Electronic resources promoting interaction of teachers and students and critical thinking, such as presentations featuring role playing or multiuse systems
5. Electronic resources that are cross-platform (e.g., using both Windows and Macintosh operating systems) and use available media systems

Appendixes

Appendix A
Education Code Sections Governing Arts Education Programs

Rationale for Arts Education

Education Code	Description
CHAPTER 5 Arts Education SECTION 8810 Inclusion of arts in the school curriculum	The Legislature finds and declares that there is a need to include the arts in the school curriculum as a means of improving the quality of education offered in California's public schools and reinforcing basic skills, knowledge, and understanding. The Legislature further finds and declares that the use of community arts resources, including professional artists, is one of several means of expanding teacher skills and knowledge in the uses of art, and contributes to the development of a comprehensive curriculum.
CHAPTER 7 California State Summer School for the Arts SECTION 8950 Legislative findings, declarations, and intent for the California State Summer School for the Arts	California State Summer School for the Arts: The Legislature finds and declares that the arts and entertainment industries constitute the third-largest business sector in the state, and that it is within the interests of the people of the state to preserve the artistic and economic benefits which are derived from these major industries through the establishment of a multidisciplinary arts training program which will enable artistically gifted and talented students to receive intensive training in the arts.

Areas of Study

Education Code	Description
CHAPTER 2 Required Courses of Study Article 2 SECTION 51210 Areas of study, grades 1–6	The adopted course of study for grades 1 to 6, inclusive, shall include instruction, beginning in grade 1 and continuing through grade 6, in the following areas of study: . . . (e) Visual and performing arts, including instruction in the subjects of dance, music, theatre, and visual arts, aimed at the development of aesthetic appreciation and the skills of creative expression. *(Amended by Stats. 2001, eff. Oct. 11, 2001.)*
CHAPTER 2 Required Courses of Study Article 3 SECTION 51220 Areas of study, grades 7–12	The adopted course of study for grades 7 to 12, inclusive, shall offer courses in the following areas of study: . . . (g) Visual and performing arts, including dance, music, theatre, and visual arts, with emphasis upon development of aesthetic appreciation and the skills of creative expression. *(Amended by Stats. 2001, eff. Oct. 11, 2001.)*

Graduation Requirements

Education Code	Description
CHAPTER 2 Required Courses of Study Article 3 SECTION 51225.3 Requirements for graduation, commencing with 1988-89 school year	(a) Commencing with the 1988-89 school year, no pupil shall receive a diploma of graduation from high school who, while in grades 9 to 12, inclusive, has not completed all of the following: . . . (E) One course in visual or performing arts or foreign language.

Curriculum; Content Standards

Education Code	Description
CHAPTER 5 California Assessment of Academic Achievement Article 2 Program Provisions SECTION 60605.1 Visual and performing arts curriculum; content standards	(a) No later than June 1, 2001, the State Board of Education shall adopt content standards, pursuant to recommendations developed by the Superintendent of Public Instruction, in the curriculum area of visual and performing arts. (b) The content standards are intended to provide a framework for programs that a school may offer in the instruction of visual or performing arts. Nothing in this section shall be construed to require a school to follow the content standards. (c) Nothing in this section shall be construed as mandating an assessment of pupils in visual or performing arts.

Prohibited Instruction

Education Code	Description
CHAPTER 4 Prohibited Instruction Article 2 SECTION 51511 Religious matters properly included in courses of study	Nothing in this code shall be construed to prevent, or exclude from the public schools, references to religion or references to or the use of religious literature, dance, music, theatre, and visual arts or other things having a religious significance when such references or uses do not constitute instruction in religious principles or aid to any religious sect, church, creed, or sectarian purpose and when such references or uses are incidental to or illustrative of matters properly included in the course of study. (*Operative April 30, 1977. Amended by Stats. 2001, eff. Oct. 11, 2001.*)

Art and Craft Materials

Education Code	Description
CHAPTER 1 School Safety: Public and Private Institutions Article 6 SECTION 32060 Legislative findings, declarations, and intent Toxic art supplies in schools	(a) The Legislature finds and declares that art supplies which contain toxic substances or which are potential human carcinogens pose a significant danger to the health and safety of school children. The Legislature also finds and declares that school children are not sufficiently protected by present health laws in so far as materials which may be seriously harmful are not so labeled and therefore children are not properly warned as to the dangers inherent in the use of those materials. (b) The Legislature intends by this article to ensure that elementary school children are protected by prohibiting the sale of these toxic substances to schools, school districts, and private schools for use in kindergarten and grades 1 to 6, inclusive, and that the toxic substances may be purchased by schools, school districts, and private schools for students in grades 7-12, inclusive, only if the materials are properly labeled, as described in Section 32064. *(Operative June 1, 1987)*
CHAPTER 1 School Safety: Public and Private Institutions Article 6 SECTION 32061 Definition of "art or craft material"	"Art or craft material" means any raw or processed material or manufactured product marketed or being represented by the manufacturer or repackager as being suitable for use in the demonstration or the creation of any work of visual or graphic art of any medium. These media may include, but shall not be limited to, paintings, drawings, prints, sculpture, ceramics, enamels, jewelry, stained glass, plastic sculpture, photographs, and leather and textile goods. *(Operative June 1, 1987)*
CHAPTER 1 School Safety: Public and Private Institutions Article 6 Toxic Art Supplies in Schools SECTION 32064 Order or purchase of art or craft materials containing toxic substance or toxic substance causing chronic illness; labeling standards; exemption of products; presumption	(a) For the 1987-88 academic year and for each academic year thereafter, no art or craft material that is deemed by the State Department of Health Services to contain a toxic substance, as defined by the California Hazardous Substance Act, Chapter 4 (commencing with Section 108100) of Part 3 of Division 104 of the Health and Safety Code, or a toxic substance causing chronic illness, as defined in this article, shall be ordered or purchased by any school, school district, or governing authority of a private school in California for use by students in kindergarten and grades 1 to 6, inclusive. (b) Commencing June 1, 1987, any substance that is defined in subdivision (a) as a toxic substance causing chronic illness shall not be purchased or ordered by a school, school district, or governing authority of a private school for use by students in grades 7 to 12, inclusive, unless it meets the labeling standards specified in Section 32065. (c) If the State Department of Health Services finds that, because the chronically toxic, carcinogenic, or radioactive substances contained in an art or craft product cannot be ingested, inhaled, or otherwise absorbed into the body during any reasonably foreseeable use of the product in a way that

Education Code	**Description**
	could pose a potential health risk, the department may exempt the product from these requirements to the extent it determines to be consistent with adequate protection of the public health and safety.
	(d) For the purposes of this article, an art or craft material shall be presumed to contain an ingredient that is a toxic substance causing chronic illness if the ingredient, whether an intentional ingredient or an impurity, is 1 percent or more by weight of the mixture or product, or if the State Department of Health Services determines that the toxic or carcinogenic properties of the art or craft material are such that labeling is necessary for the adequate protection of the public health and safety.
CHAPTER 1 School Safety: Public and Private Institutions Article 6 SECTION 32065 Warning labels; standards; disclosure of information by manufacturer to department	(b) The warning label shall contain information on the health-related dangers of the art or craft materials

Implementation of Curriculum; Extracurricular Activities

Education Code	**Description**
CHAPTER 2 Governing Boards Article 13 Excursions and Field Trips SECTION 35330 Excursions and field trips	The governing board of any school district or the county superintendent of schools of any county may: (a) Conduct field trips or excursions in connection with courses of instruction or school-related social, educational, cultural, athletic, or school band activities to and from places in the state, any other state, the District of Columbia, or a foreign country for pupils enrolled in elementary or secondary schools. A field trip or excursion to and from a foreign country may be permitted to familiarize students with the language, history, geography, natural sciences, and other studies relative to the district's course of study for such pupils. (b) Engage such instructors, supervisors, and other personnel as desire to contribute their services over and above the normal period for which they are employed by the district, if necessary, and provide equipment and supplies for such field trip or excursion.

Education Code	Description

(c) Transport by use of district equipment, contract to provide transportation, or arrange transportation by the use of other equipment, of pupils, instructors, supervisors, or other personnel to and from places in the state, any other state, the District of Columbia, or a foreign country where such excursions and field trips are being conducted; provided that, when district equipment is used, the governing board shall secure liability insurance, and if travel is to and from a foreign country, such liability insurance shall be secured from a carrier licensed to transact insurance business in such foreign country.

(d) Provide supervision of pupils involved in field trips or excursions by certificated employees of the district.

No pupil shall be prevented from making the field trip or excursion because of lack of sufficient funds. To this end, the governing board shall coordinate efforts of community service groups to supply funds for pupils in need of them.

No group shall be authorized to take a field trip or excursion authorized by this section if any pupil who is a member of such an identifiable group will be excluded from participation in the field trip or excursion because of lack of sufficient funds.

No expenses of pupils participating in a field trip or excursion to any other state, the District of Columbia, or a foreign country authorized by this section shall be paid with school district funds. Expenses of instructors, chaperones, and other personnel participating in a field trip or excursion authorized by this section may be paid from school district funds, and the school district may pay from school district funds all incidental expenses for the use of school district equipment during a field trip or excursion authorized by this section.

The attendance or participation of a pupil in a field trip or excursion authorized by this section shall be considered attendance for the purpose of crediting attendance for apportionments from the State School Fund in the fiscal year. Credited attendance resulting from such field trip or excursion shall be limited to the amount of attendance which would have accrued had the students not been engaged in the field trip or excursion.

Credited attendance shall not exceed 10 school days except in the case of pupils participating in a field trip or excursion in connection with courses of instruction, or school-related educational activities, and which are not social, cultural, athletic, or school band activities. *(Operative April 30, 1977)*

Education Code	Description
Elementary and Secondary Education Local Administration CHAPTER 4 Miscellaneous Provisions Article 1 SECTION 38120 Use of school band equipment on excursions to foreign countries	The governing board of any school district may lend school band instruments, music, uniforms, and other regalia to persons who are or have been, during the prior school year, members of the school band for use by them on excursions to foreign countries whether or not such an excursion is sanctioned by the governing board. The governing board may require the borrower to make a deposit or take other measures to insure that the items borrowed will be returned in usable condition. *(Operative Jan. 1, 1998)*

Definitions of the Arts

Education Code	Description
CHAPTER 5 Arts Education SECTION 8811(a) Definition of arts for use by K–12 public schools	"Arts" includes the four disciplines of dance, drama and theatre, music, and visual arts as set forth in the state's adopted curriculum framework for visual and performing arts as published by the State Department of Education in the *Visual and Performing Arts Framework for California Public Schools, Kindergarten Through Grade Twelve,* and may also include community support for the various other art forms, including folk art, film, video, the writing of plays, poetry, and scripts.
CHAPTER 7 SECTION 8951 Arts defined for use by the California State Summer School	As used in this chapter, "arts" includes, but is not limited to, all of the following: dance; theatre; music; folk art; creative writing; visual arts, including painting, sculpture, photography, and craft arts; design, including graphic arts, computer graphics, and costume design; film; and video. *(Amended by Stats. 2001, eff. Oct. 11, 2001.)*

Appendix B

Recommendations for Clarification of the New Visual and Performing Arts Requirement for Freshman Admission to the University of California and the California State University

All of the following information can be found on the University of California, Office of the President (UCOP), Web site, *http://www.ucop.edu.*

Approved by the University of California Board of Admissions and Relations with Schools (BOARS), February–July 2002.

Submitted by: Margaret C. Marshall, Chair, University Statewide Arts Advisory Committee (USWAA); Faculty, Visual and Performing Arts, and Director, Division of Academic Affairs, UCOP; Faculty, Department of Theatre and Dance, UC San Diego.

(f) Visual and Performing Arts

One unit (equivalent to one yearlong course or two semester courses) is required in any of the following categories: dance, drama/theater, music, or visual arts.

Intent. The intent of instruction is to provide a meaningful experience and breadth of knowledge of the arts so that students may apply their knowledge and experience to the creation of art and/or are better able to understand and appreciate artistic expression on the basis of that experience and knowledge.

The intent of approved visual and performing arts (VPA) courses must be directed at acquiring concepts, knowledge, and skills in the arts disciplines rather than using artistic activities to fulfill nonartistic course objectives.

Prerequisites. Acceptable courses need *not* require any prerequisite courses.

Cocurricular Work. Work outside of class must be required (e.g., portfolio/performance preparation, reading, writing, research projects, and/or critical listening/viewing).

Course Standards. Courses should provide students with an experience in the arts that implements the intent of the California State Board of Education-approved visual and performing arts content standards. The curriculum must be designed to include the VPA content standards at, at least, the proficiency level in each of the five component strands. Each VPA course shall sufficiently address the state content standards under all five component strands, which are as follows:

1. *Artistic Perception:* Processing, analyzing, and responding to sensory information through the language and skills unique to a given art

2. *Creative Expression:* Creating, performing, and participating in a given art

3. *Historical and Cultural Context:* Understanding historical contributions and cultural dimensions of a given art

4. *Aesthetic Valuing:* Responding to, analyzing, and making critical assessments about works of a given art form

5. *Connections, Relationships, Applications:* Connecting and applying what is learned in a given art form to learning in other art forms, subject areas, and careers

For a more detailed description of the VPA content standards, go to *http://www.cde.ca.gov/re/pn/fd/documents/visperfmarts-stnd-comp.pdf.*

Acceptable and Unacceptable Courses. Courses that are primarily recreational or athletic or are designed for body conditioning or social entertainment are *not* acceptable visual or performing arts courses. Commercial courses or courses specifically designed for training for a profession in these areas are also not acceptable. Specific examples of acceptable and unacceptable courses are as follows:

• **Dance.** *Examples of acceptable courses include* ballet, modern dance, jazz and ethnic dance, choreography and improvisation, dance history, and dance production/performance. *Examples of unacceptable courses include* aerobics, drill team, cheerleading, recreational dance, and ballroom dance.

• **Drama/Theater.** *Examples of acceptable courses include* acting, directing, oral interpretation, dramatic production, dramaturgy/history/theory, and stage/lighting/costume design. *Examples of unacceptable courses include* speech, debate, or courses in other disciplines that require students to perform occasional skits.

• **Music.** *Examples of acceptable courses include* band (concert, symphonic, jazz), orchestra, choir (e.g., concert, jazz, soul, madrigal), music history/appreciation, and music theory/composition. *Examples of unacceptable courses include* a musical group that performs primarily for sporting events, parades, competitive field events, and/or community/civic activities.

- **Visual Arts.** *Examples of acceptable courses include* painting, drawing, sculpture, art photography, printmaking, video/film production as an art form, contemporary media, ceramics, and art history. *Examples of unacceptable courses include* craft courses, mechanical drafting, Web page development, yearbook, and photography offered as photojournalism (e.g., as a component of a yearbook or school newspaper publication).

For further clarification of the four categories, see the following policy clarifications:

Policy Clarifications

- **Performance, Production, and Studio Courses.** Courses emphasizing performance and/or production (e.g., drama, dance, music, visual arts, and video production) must include appropriate critical/theoretical and historical/cultural content, as referenced in California's visual and performing arts content standards. Such courses should emphasize creative expression, not rote memorization and/or technical skills.

- **Appreciation, History, and Theory Courses.** Appreciation, history, and theory courses should focus on the ability to make aesthetic judgments about works of art and performances but must also include all component strands of the state VPA content standards, including creative expression.

- **Design Courses.** Visual and performing arts courses in design are expected to provide substantial time for students to understand, learn, and experience the elements of art and principles of design that underlie the medium/media addressed. Design courses must also include all five component strands of the VPA content standards.

- **Technology Courses.** Visual and performing arts courses that utilize technology must focus primarily on arts content. If the technology (i.e., software, equipment) is used as a tool of artistic expression, as a paintbrush would be used in a painting course, and all other component strands are met, then such courses are acceptable. If the technology/software is so complex that the primary concern becomes learning the technology before artistic application is possible, then the course will not be approved to meet the VPA requirement.

Community College and University Transferable Courses. The University of California will accept only three-semester-unit (four-quarter-unit), UC-transferable community college/university courses that clearly fall within one of the four disciplines of the arts (dance, music, theatre, or visual arts).

Honors Courses. Advanced placement (AP) and international baccalaureate (IB) courses are acceptable for UC honors credit. Three-semester-unit (four-quarter-unit), UC-transferable community college and university courses that clearly fall within one of the four disciplines of the arts are likewise acceptable for honors credit. A list of community college and CSU-transferable courses can be found at *http://www.assist.org.* Other honors courses are acceptable if they meet the criteria described in the "Honors Level Courses" section of the *Guide to A–G Requirements.*

Private Study. Private or community-based study in the arts will not qualify for approval to meet the VPA requirement. However, at the discretion of the teacher and consistent with school policy, private study in the arts, which includes standards-based comprehensive study in all five component strands, may serve as an adequate prerequisite for placement into advanced and/or honors-level VPA courses. (See the VPA honors section for further criteria guidelines.)

Independent Study. Following school district-approved guidelines, school-sponsored independent study in the arts may fulfill UC/CSU entrance requirements if it is appropriately monitored by a faculty member, matches a concurrent UC/CSU-approved high school course, and meets the f-requirement guidelines set forth in this document.

G-Elective Courses. Introductory VPA courses may not be used to meet the g-elective requirement. Advanced courses in the visual and performing arts may be considered to meet the g-elective requirement but must also meet the criteria described in the "College Preparatory Elective Courses" section of the *Guide to A–G Requirements.*

Implementation Phase-in Timeline. The visual and performing arts requirement is now in effect. Students who enter the university beginning in the fall of 2003 must meet the new requirement.

The VPA requirement includes a phase-in process, described as follows:

- Students entering up to the fall of 2005 may present any two semesters of acceptable VPA courses provided that both courses are from a single VPA area (dance, music, theatre, or visual arts).
- Students entering in the fall of 2006 or later must satisfy the VPA requirement by completing an appropriate single course in a yearlong sequence (i.e., the second semester must be the continuation of the first semester). If scheduling challenges demand, students may divide the yearlong course into two different academic years as long as the course curriculum is designed as a yearlong sequence and is approved as such by the University.

- Students may satisfy this requirement by taking an approved community college course. Acceptable community college courses are those approved for the Intersegmental General Education Transfer Curriculum (IGETC), area 3A. Please refer to *http://www.assist.org*.

The following will be incorporated into the "College Preparatory Elective" section of the *Guide to A–G Requirements:*

(g) College Preparatory Elective Courses

Subject-Specific Guidelines

Visual and Performing Arts (VPA): Advanced courses in the visual and performing arts can be considered to meet the g-elective requirement but must still address the five strands of the VPA standards. Advanced courses should enable students to understand and appreciate artistic expression and, where appropriate, talk and write with discrimination about the artistic material studied. Courses devoted to artistic performance and developing creative artistic ability should have prerequisites (either one year of introductory course work or experience approved by the instructor) and should assume proficiency beyond the introductory level. Courses must require on the average the equivalent of a five-period class per week. Work outside of the class must also be required (e.g., portfolio/performance preparation, reading, writing, research projects, and critical listening/ viewing). In 2006 and beyond, advanced VPA courses that are a semester in length will be considered only for the g-elective area, not the f-VPA area, which must be satisfied by completing an appropriate sequential yearlong course.

The following will be incorporated into the "Honors Level Courses" section of the *Guide to A–G Requirements:*

General Criteria Guidelines for VPA Honors Courses

UC-approved honors level courses in the visual and performing arts (VPA) should have as a prerequisite at least two years of college preparatory work in the discipline or comparable (alternative) experience that includes all five component strands of the state-adopted VPA content standards.

Honors courses may be open to students who have not completed the prerequisite college preparatory work but whose preparation in the art form is at a high artistic level and who can demonstrate comprehensive knowledge in all five component strands of the art form. Alternative entrance into the honors level course shall be by audition/demonstration and a standards-based content exam (oral, written, or portfolio/performance).

Honors-level courses should be demonstrably more challenging than regular college preparatory classes and should center on content in the art form that is of artistic and cultural merit and represents a variety of styles, genres, or historical periods. The curriculum must be comparable with the college curriculum and target skills and conceptual development beyond the art form's advanced level of the VPA content standards. The curriculum must also require in-depth written assignments that demonstrate student knowledge across the component strands. Each student must complete a variety of individual assessments with a comprehensive final examination that includes a written component as well as other assessment tools appropriate to the five strands of the art form and are representative of high levels of analysis and self-evaluation.

Honors-level course work in the art form may not require a separate class section in the regular college preparatory curriculum. These courses necessitate a separate written curriculum documenting the additional breadth and depth expected as well as an explanation of the differentiated curriculum. The use of college-level textbooks is encouraged.

All VPA honors course work shall include advanced studies/projects, examples of which are listed for each specific arts discipline (Dance, Music, Theatre and Visual Arts) in the following guidelines:

Discipline-Specific Honors Criteria

In addition to the above general criteria, each separate arts discipline must include the following specific guidelines to qualify for honors credit:

Dance courses at the honors level require students to demonstrate artistic superiority in multiple aspects of dance as an art form. Dance honors studies/projects may include but are not limited to sophisticated choreography, including production collaborations, advanced written and oral research analysis, and advanced kinesthetic mastery and historical knowledge of many genres of dance. Critical self-analysis and peer review of projects may be broadened by technology resources, traditional and innovative documentation, and recording (e.g., notation, virtual reality, and/or simulation).

Music course descriptions will delineate the honors level of achievement expected of the individual student as well as explicit descriptions of honors studies/projects that will be completed. These studies/projects may include but are not limited to solo and/or small ensemble performance; score analysis; musical composition and/or arranging; critical analysis of individual performances by others; and critical self-analysis through portfolio development.

Theatre courses at the honors level require students to demonstrate artistic leadership. Collaborative skills continue to be essential in students' work, but the honors distinction is that the individual takes the responsibility for organizing others to complete a theatrical performance project. The student must first qualify as an outstanding playwright, director, designer, dramaturge, actor, or stage manager and then must also serve as producer of the project or chief of a major area of production. Analysis of the honor student's project is required and must include a post-show critique, written or oral, of the student's leadership skills that is conducted by the teacher and ensemble peers, and a critical self-analysis.

Visual Arts course descriptions will define the high level of achievement expected of the individual student as well as suggested descriptions of honors visual arts projects. The honors-level subjects/projects may include but are not limited to compiling a body of work at the mastery level in a particular arts medium and written research and analysis of a particular genre, style, or historical period. Critical self-analysis is required through portfolio development, solo exhibition of original work, and verification of honors-level achievement relevant to the art form.

Appendix C

Careers in the Visual and Performing Arts

The following lists contain a sampling of careers in the visual and performing arts and places in which artists might be employed.

Dance

PreK to postsecondary educator/consultant

Public/private/magnet school
Private studio
Dance assessment
Community outreach program
Community nonprofit arts organization
Movement for actors and singers

Arts administrator

Dance department in school
Community arts council
College or university
Dance program coordinator, nonprofit
District dance coordinator
Professional group or organization
State/federal government
Community center
Dance conference coordinator

Dancer

Ballet
Film/television/video
Folk/social
Improvisation specialist
Jazz
Modern/contemporary/postmodern
Professional/regional company
Theatre dance
Variety/character productions
Industrials/entertainment industry
Cultural/ethnic specialist

Choreographer

Professional and regional companies
Special events
Film/television/video
Industrials/fashion shows/conventions
Opera
Broadway theatre/children's theatre
Community/civic events
Ballroom

Director/producer

Dance captain
Audition coordinator
Dance company
Film/television/video
Nonprofit dance organization

Owner

Dance studio
Dance company
Dance supply business

Technical production

Business manager
Costume designer
Lighting/sound designer
Manager
Public relations representative
Notation expert
Special movement effects designer
Stage manager for dance company
Video technology expert in dance
Set and prop designer
Music composer for dance

Business/management

Advertising agency
Costume construction/rental
Dance supply store
Costume store
Marketing/promotional
Personal agency
Press agency
Prop/scenic construction/rental
Private dance school owner/manager

Notating

Autographer
Reconstructor
Dance media documenter

Dance (Continued)

Criticism/research

Dance textbook/book writer
Scholar/professor
Dance historian
Consumer researcher
Ethnologist
Historian/researcher
Library media teacher
Writer/editor/critic for magazine
    or newspaper

Medicine/science

Adaptive movement specialist
Dance therapist
Kinesiologist
Personal trainer
Physical therapist
Pilates instructor
Scholar/professor
Injury prevention specialist

Media

Computer programmer
Television consultant
Video consultant
Internet
Animation

Government services

Arts councils, national/state/regional
Cultural arts commissions, national/state/
    regional/local

Recreation

After-school programs
Boys'/girls' clubs
Parks/recreation programs
Private camps
YMCA/YWCA

Designer for dance

Costumes
Lighting
Makeup/hair
Model making
Props
Sets/stage
Sound
Environmental
Exhibits
Graphics
Print media
Special effects

Music

Music education
Early childhood music educator
School music educator
Music supervisor/consultant
Music professor
Administrator, university music school
Studio teacher

Instrumental performance
Armed forces musician
Orchestra musician
Small-ensemble musician
Concert soloist
Dance/rock/jazz band musician
Clinician

Vocal performance
Dance band/nightclub vocalist
Concert/opera chorus
Concert soloist
Opera soloist

Conducting
Choir/orchestra/opera conductor

Composing
School music composer
Art music composer
Commercial jingle composer
Television show composer
Film score composer

Music for worship
Organist
Choir director
Cantor/hazan

Music business
Music dealer salesperson
Music dealer manager
Marketing/advertising specialist
Music/instrument/accessories
   distributor

Instrument making and repair
Instrument maker
Instrument repair technician
Piano tuner

Music publishing
Music editor
Notesetter
Publishing sales representative
Copyright/licensing administrator

Music communications
Publisher/editor of music books/
   periodicals
Music reporter
Public relations specialist

Recording industry
Producer/engineer/pixer
Artist and repertoire (A&R) person
Studio arranger
Music copyist

Television and radio industry
Radio/television commercial musician
Copyright/clearance administrator
Music license administrator
Radio program director
Postproduction/scoring
Music adviser/researcher
Disc jockey/video jockey

Music technology
Multimedia publisher
Editor, sound/video
Designer, technology-based music
   instruction

Music librarianship
Librarian, college/university/conserva-
   tory/public library/orchestra

Music therapist
Hospital/psychiatric facility
Special education facility
Clinic for disabled children
Mental health center
Nursing home
Correctional facility
Private practice

Performing arts medicine
Physician
Physical therapist

Theatre

PreK to postsecondary educator/consultant

Public/private school
Visiting artist
Private studio
Distance-learning instruction
Community theatre
Internet/online instruction
Touring theatre
Theatre technology: lighting/sound/
    sets/costumes/animatronics/
    cinematography/business
    management

Arts administrator

Theatre department in school
Community arts council
College/university
Artistic director
Production manager
Private studio
Marketing/public relations
Professional group/association

Actor

Voice coach
Film/television/video/radio/local/cable/
    network/independent/regional/studio

Live theater

Amusement park/theme park
Dinner theatre
Motivational
Musicals
Training films
Professional
Religious
Resident
Stand-up comedy
Stock
Regional
Touring company
Visiting artist

Playwright

Screenwriter
News writer
Commercial
Visiting artist
Documentary
Dramaturge

Director/producer

Film/radio/television/video
National/local/regional/independent/
    student/cable
Arts events/presentations
Casting
Community/regional theatre
Theatre company
Theatrical productions
Commercial productions
Documentary productions
In-house productions
Training films
Religious films

Owner

Theatre
Theatre/film/television company
Film/television/theatre supply business

Technical production

Costume designer
Camera operator
Lighting/sound designer
Scenographer, costumes/lights/sets
Editor
Sets/scenic construction
Designer, sets/props
Sound boom operator
Special effects designer
Stage manager
Grip/stagehand
Video technology expert
Wardrobe dresser
Pyrotechnics
Model making
Props
Hair design
Makeup
Animal trainer
Cinematographer
Gaffer
Best boy
Caterer
Animator
Computer graphics
Costumes
Lighting
Model making
Props

Sets/stage
Sound
Special effects
Actors agency
Press agency
Publicist
Prop construction
Public relations
Sets store
Publisher
Rentals, costumes/sound/lighting/stage/
    scenic/rigging/props
Lawyer

Criticism/research

Dramaturge
Historian/researcher
Market researcher
Library media teacher
Textbook writer
Writer/editor/critic for magazine/
    newspaper/Web publications
Film critiques for magazines
Book author

Medicine/science

Speech therapist
Drama therapist
Movement therapist
Satellite/cable (global)/specialized
    networks
Scientific laboratory

Media

Computer, lighting/sound/visuals/sets/
    animation/holography
Consultant, television/film/cable/video/
    satellite/radio

Government services

Arts councils, national/state/regional/local
Cultural arts commissions, national/state/
    regional/local

Education consultant/specialist

State/regional/district/private/nonprofit

Recreation

Boys/girls clubs
Parks/recreation programs
Day/overnight private camps
Arts camps
YMCA/YWCA
Nonprofit arts camps/agencies/courses,
    consulting/theatres, touring groups/
    artists

Business/management

Business manager
Graphics/text director/agent
Advertising agency
Costume construction
Wardrobe cutter/milliner/stitcher
Marketing/promotion
Programs/billboards/advertising

Visual Arts

New media
3-D animation
Commercial/computer graphics
Film/television design
Halography
Media design
3-D model making
Multimedia game design
Software design
Cinematography
New media art
Photo journalism

Visual artist
Animator
Architect
Art director
Auto designer
Billboard artist
Biomedical photographer
Biomedical illustrator
Book designer
Calligrapher
Cartoonist
Catalog illustrator
Children's book illustrator
Commercial/computer graphics
New media artist
Glass artist
Print maker
Printer
Photographer
Potter/ceramic artist
Sculptor
Site-specific artist
Installation artist
Performance artist
Stained glass artist
Fiber artist

Technical production
CAD designer
Editor
Instillation designer
Lighting designer
Scenic designer
Set/props designer
Special effects designer
Video technology expert
Wardrobe designer
Topographer
Weaver
Engraver

Lithographer
Model maker
Photo editor
Production potter
Sign painter

Business/management
Public relations representative
Advertising agency
Appraiser
Art investment
Art supply manufacturer
Art supply store
Picture framer
Convention/fair
Corporate/private/freelance collection
    management
Gallery/exhibit space
Marketing/promotion
Museum
Party/event designer
Press agency
Private art school owner/manager
Web site development agency
Multimedia presentation creator

Criticism/research
Art law
Consumer researcher
Ethnologist
Historian/researcher
Library media teacher
Textbook writer
Writer/editor/critic for magazine/
    newspaper

Medicine/science:
Biomedical
Art therapist
Illustrator, medical texts/scientific texts/
    law enforcement/courtroom

Designer
Advertising
Amusement/theme park designer
Art materials/supplies
Automobile designer
Coin designer
Costume/mask designer
Ceramist/potter
Couture artist
Covers

Displays
Environmental
Exhibits
Graphics
Interiors
Jewelry
Landscape
Leather goods
Model maker/designer
Museum exhibitions
Scenic designer
Props
Packaging
Sets/stage
Stamp designer
Textiles
Tools
Toys
Urban
Video interface
Wallpaper
Windows
Fashion designer
Furniture designer
Greeting card artist
Industrial designer, packaging/products

Media

Computer programmer
Television consultant
Commercial/computer graphics
Film/television designer
Cinematographer
Holographer
Media designer
3-D model maker
Multimedia game designer
Multimedia presenter
3-D computer-generated imagery
Interactive designer
Software designer
Web site designer
Video producer
Special effects designer

Illustrator

Biomedical
Technical
Editorial
Botanical
Children's literature
Advertising
Fashion
Forensic
Courtroom
Police
Sports
Calligrapher
Catalog

Government services

Art councils, national/state/regional
Cultural arts commissions, national/state/
    regional/local
Education consultant/specialist

Recreation

Boys/girls clubs
Parks/recreation programs
Private camps
YMCA/YWCA

Appendix D

Continuum for Implementing Arts Education Programs

The Arts Education Program Implementation Continuum is a tool that school districts may use in planning and in improving the visual and performing arts programs that they provide for all students. The continuum and the Continuum Grid help in identifying the elements that are required for the implementation of a quality arts education program. The concept of a continuum acknowledges the many points that exist along the way toward reaching a goal. Using the continuum helps educators in identifying the strengths of a program and the areas that need improvement as districts work toward full implementation of instruction in dance, music, theatre, and the visual arts for all students.

Focus Areas

The continuum is based on the descriptions of effective visual and performing arts programs that appear throughout the *Visual and Performing Arts Framework for California Public Schools, Kindergarten Through Grade Twelve* (1996), which was adopted by the State Board of Education in 1996. The continuum is used by a district arts team to assess the elements of an arts education program in a district. The areas that are assessed are called *focus areas* and are listed along the left side of the continuum. The focus areas are:

1. Standards-based curriculum
2. Instruction and methodology
3. Student assessment
4. Professional development
5. Program administration and personnel
6. Partnerships and collaborations
7. Funding
8. Resources and facilities
9. Program evaluation

Three Levels of Criteria

Criteria have been organized under each of the focus areas on the continuum, and the criteria are further grouped into three levels. These levels are

From *Arts Education Program Toolkit: A Visual and Performing Arts Program Assessment Process.* Sacramento: California Department of Education, 2001.

Foundation, Building, and *Best Practices.* The levels are listed across the top of the continuum.

- A school district that identifies with a majority of the criteria at the Foundation level has the awareness and commitment needed to move toward a fully implemented arts program.
- A school district that identifies with a majority of the criteria at the Building level has established a firm basis for program development and growth. It is ready to plan for and to make incremental progress toward full program implementation for all students.
- A school district that identifies with a majority of the criteria at the Best Practices level has a fully implemented, comprehensive visual and performing arts program for all students that includes dance, music, theatre, and the visual arts.

As you review the criteria for each focus area on the continuum, start at the Foundation level and then proceed across the page to the Building level and to the Best Practices level. The criteria are cumulative and are aligned by key words across the page. For example, in the focus area of standards-based curriculum, the first criteria under the Foundation column (A1) is identified by the key word *Framework.* The key word is repeated across the page in the Building column (B1) and in the Best Practices column (C1).

Directions

The continuum is designed to generate conversation, stimulate research, build consensus, enhance decision-making, and support planning. As each criterion is discussed, issues and questions will arise about the elements of an arts education program that your district values. As you work through the continuum, keep a copy of the *Visual and Performing Arts Framework for California Public Schools, Kindergarten Through Grade Twelve* (1996) on hand for reference and help in clarifying terminology.

Make extra copies of the continuum so you can use it many times. With your district arts team members, work your way across the levels for each focus area, from Foundation to Best Practices, discussing each criterion. Put a check or a score beside each criterion.

For the purposes of assigning a score to a criterion, you may use the following scale:

4 = Fully implemented, exemplary accomplishment

3 = Implemented and operational

2 = Introduced, evidence of progress but not fully operational

1 = Not attempted or at the beginning level of development or implementation

0 = Not applicable

Teams who use the continuum find that for any focus area some criteria may be implemented in each of the three levels. For example, all the criteria at the Foundation level may not have been fully implemented, yet some criteria at the Building and Best Practices levels may be implemented and are starting to have results.

The Continuum Grid, which is available in this section of the toolkit, provides an overview of the level of program implementation. You may check each criterion on the grid under the Foundation, Building, or Best Practices columns or, as with the continuum, go to a deeper level of evaluation and assign a score that uses the 4-to-0 scale discussed above. A review of the grid indicates in which areas the school district is in the process of implementing a comprehensive, standards-based arts education program for all students.

Some school districts are structuring a foundation for program improvement. Some school districts demonstrate all aspects of the building process. Some school districts have established best practices in arts education. In moving toward providing arts education programs for all students in California public schools, models at each level of implementation are essential. Given the number and diversity of school districts in California, the need to network and to share successes is evident.

Arts Education Program Implementation Continuum

1. Standards-based curriculum

CRITERION	FOUNDATION	BUILDING	BEST PRACTICES
Framework	**A1.** A district arts committee does an analysis of the *Visual and Performing Arts Framework for California Public Schools, Kindergarten Through Grade Twelve.*	**B1.** Representatives from all schools in the district develop an in-depth understanding of arts education in all the arts as described in the framework and as defined by the community.	**C1.** The district curriculum provides for comprehensive instruction in each of the arts and includes artistic perception, creative expression, historical and cultural context, aesthetic valuing, and connections and application to other disciplines and to careers.
Standards process	**A2.** A process is underway to draft standards for adoption by the district board of education. The standards take into consideration the state arts content standards and the principles discussed in the framework.	**B2.** The district board adopts visual and performing arts standards and begins an implementation plan.	**C2.** An ongoing review and refinement process is in place for the adopted and implemented standards, based on an examination of student work over time.
Sequential curriculum	**A3.** The arts are recognized by the district and site administrations as a part of the core curriculum. The need for a sequential, written curriculum is identified.	**B3.** A plan for developing a standards-based visual and performing arts curriculum for each discipline at every grade level is developed and is underway for one or more of the arts.	**C3.** A sequential, standards-based curriculum in each of the arts disciplines at every grade level is being implemented as a part of the core curriculum for all students.
Integration	**A4.** There is a district-wide understanding that the arts can be a vital part of an integrated curricular approach.	**B4.** The arts curriculum is under development, and the arts are considered to be discrete disciplines that should be integrated into other curricular areas as appropriate.	**C4.** The curriculum is expanded in all subject areas to allow for the integration and the application of arts-related knowledge and skills in a way that is aligned with the standards.

Source: The format for this continuum was developed from work produced by the Australian Student Traineeship Foundation, the Australian Quality Council, and the Kennedy Center Alliance for Arts Education Network.

Note: For the purposes of assigning a score to a criterion, you may use the following scale: 4 = fully implemented, exemplary accomplishment; 3 = implemented and operational; 2 = introduced, evidence of progress but not fully operational; 1 = not attempted or at the beginning level of development or implementation; 0 = not applicable

Arts Education Program Implementation Continuum (Continued)

2. Instructions and methodology

CRITERION	FOUNDATION	BUILDING	BEST PRACTICES
Students' progress and outcomes	**A5.** There is recognition that instruction in the arts must be based on students' progress toward arts standards.	**B5.** Instructional choices are focused on helping students in making progress toward achieving discipline-specific arts standards.	**C5.** Instruction is consistently reviewed and refined based on an analysis of students' work in relation to a high level of achievement of standards.
Equal access and inclusion	**A6.** There is recognition that all students should have the opportunity to receive instruction in comprehensive standards-based arts education.	**B6.** Model strategies for assisting all students in meeting arts standards are continually designed, implemented, and refined by district teachers.	**C6.** Teachers design and modify their instructional practices to ensure that all students make progress toward achieving the standards.
Variety of methodology	**A7.** There is an understanding of the need to use a variety of teaching methodologies to address students' diverse learning styles.	**B7.** A variety of instructional strategies are effectively used in two or more of the arts disciplines.	**C7.** Instruction in all four arts disciplines includes a variety of effective and innovative methodologies that address diversity in teaching and learning styles.
Quality instruction	**A8:** Generalist teachers and arts specialists are supported in their efforts to deliver standards-based instruction in the arts.	**B8:** Each school employs credentialed arts specialist teachers in two or more of the arts disciplines. Generalist classroom teachers are provided with opportunities to refine and to expand their content knowledge and instructional strategies in the arts.	**C8:** Qualified credentialed arts teachers and classroom teachers are recruited to teach all arts disciplines and are actively supported by the administration to ensure quality instruction at all levels.
Support resources	**A9.** Local community arts resources are identified and recognized as valuable partners in instruction.	**B9.** Arts instruction incorporates the unique resources of artists and of the whole community.	**C9.** Instruction in all four arts disciplines reflects collaboration between teachers and community arts providers, artists, business organizations, and others.

Note: For the purposes of assigning a score to a criterion, you may use the following scale: 4 = fully implemented, exemplary accomplishment; 3 = implemented and operational; 2 = introduced, evidence of progress but not fully operational; 1 = not attempted or at the beginning level of development or implementation; 0 = not applicable

Arts Education Program Implementation Continuum (Continued)

3. Student assessment

CRITERION	FOUNDATION	BUILDING	BEST PRACTICES
Approaches	**A10.** Teachers and administrators recognize that arts assessment is possible and necessary and should be based on students' progress toward achieving standards. Educators review and evaluate a variety of assessment models.	**B10.** A variety of assessment models are being piloted in one or more of the arts disciplines and at various grade levels. A forum for feedback and comparison has been established and will lead to a districtwide assessment policy and plan for all the arts.	**C10.** The district has developed and maintains a current, research-based, comprehensive, standards-based approach to assessing students' work in the arts at every grade level.
Formal assessment	**A11.** A district policy and plan for formally assessing students' work in the arts are being considered. The policy and plan include assigning letter grades and using standardized assessment at elementary, middle, and high school levels.	**B11.** The district policy and plan support professional development for teachers in the use of assessment tools for making a formal assessment in one or more of the arts at each school level.	**C11.** Teachers at each school level use multiple measures that were developed as a part of the district's policy and plan for assessing students' work in the arts.
Information to improve teaching and learning	**A12.** District committees review examples of students' work and performances in the arts at various grade levels to identify optimal teaching strategies.	**B12.** The district uses baseline formal and informal assessments in two or more of the arts disciplines to refine and to implement its arts curriculum and instruction.	**C12.** Teachers and administrators continually review data gathered from assessments of students' work to refocus and to revise standards-based arts curricula in all arts disciplines, kindergarten through grade twelve.
Performance and portfolio	**A13.** The creative products of students' work in the arts are seen as an integral part of the assessment process.	**B13.** Teachers provide students with opportunities to demonstrate their progress toward standards through carefully designed portfolio activities and performance activities in two or more of the arts.	**C13.** Students at all levels in all arts disciplines maintain portfolios of their work and their performances for which consistent scoring guides have been designed.
Embedded strategies	**A14.** District arts committees understand the need for arts assessment strategies that are embedded in standards-based curricula.	**B14.** Embedded student assessment strategies are an instructional component of two or more arts disciplines across grade levels.	**C14.** Teachers at all grade levels in all four arts disciplines embed assessment strategies in their curricula on a regular basis.

Note: For the purposes of assigning a score to a criterion, you may use the following scale: 4 = fully implemented, exemplary accomplishment; 3 = implemented and operational; 2 = introduced, evidence of progress but not fully operational; 1 = not attempted or at the beginning level of development or implementation; 0 = not applicable

Arts Education Program Implementation Continuum (Continued)

4. Professional development

CRITERION	FOUNDATION	BUILDING	BEST PRACTICES
Long-range plan	**A15.** A districtwide needs assessment is being administered to develop a professional development plan in arts education for classroom teachers, artists, arts specialists, and administrators.	**B15.** A defined, long-term professional development plan that is based on assessed needs is created for all four arts disciplines. The plan is being implemented in selected disciplines.	**C15.** A districtwide, long-range, comprehensive professional development plan is well established and ongoing for all four arts disciplines. The plan is reviewed and evaluated annually, and it is integrated into other professional development activities.
Knowledge base	**A16.** The district recognizes the need for a professional development program in arts education that provides training based on an understanding of the framework and standards and that uses a variety of strategies and activities.	**B16.** The districtwide professional development program is based on the framework, arts standards, and standards in other subject areas. The program incorporates strategies to include all educators.	**C16.** Professional development is provided for all kindergarten-through-grade-twelve educators, administrators, teachers, specialists, and artists to ensure the implementation of discrete and integrated instruction in all four arts disciplines.
Professional development resources	**A17.** The district begins identifying resources for professional development in all four arts disciplines.	**B17.** The district provides funds annually for continued internal and external professional development in one or more of the arts disciplines.	**C17.** Funds and release time are provided to ensure personal and professional growth through educators' participation in conferences, workshops, and institutes in all four arts disciplines.
Collaborations	**A18.** Plans for professional development opportunities extend to all persons who participate in arts instruction, such as generalist teachers, art specialist teachers, artists, and parents.	**B18.** Specialist teachers and visiting artists who teach are regarded as members of the school team and are provided with opportunities to share their expertise with the entire staff.	**C18.** Teachers, specialist teachers, and visiting artists who teach have time to work in partnership with each other to share best instructional practices.

Note: For the purposes of assigning a score to a criterion, you may use the following scale: 4 = fully implemented, exemplary accomplishment; 3 = implemented and operational; 2 = introduced, evidence of progress but not fully operational; 1 = not attempted or at the beginning level of development or implementation; 0 = not applicable

Arts Education Program Implementation Continuum (Continued)

5. Program administration and personnel

CRITERION	FOUNDATION	BUILDING	BEST PRACTICES
Policy	**A19.** The school board considers the arts to be an integral part of the curriculum.	**B19.** The school board and all members of the administration serve as advocates for arts education.	**C19.** The school board has adopted and supports a clearly articulated arts education policy.
Staff	**A20.** A district plan is established for staffing a comprehensive arts education program.	**B20.** Personnel are identified and provide arts instruction in the schools in a minimum of two of the arts disciplines.	**C20.** Qualified personnel in all four arts disciplines provide comprehensive, standards-based arts instruction.
Leadership	**A21.** Leadership roles at the district and at the school site are defined for the implementation of a standards-based curriculum, for program development, and for evaluation.	**B21.** An identified district arts coordinator or administrator clearly articulates the goals and the objectives of the arts education program and establishes a collegial relationship with administrative staff, teachers, and personnel.	**C21.** Designated administrators in the arts disciplines provide leadership, a vision of the future, and planning capabilities. They oversee implementation of the arts education program in all district schools

Note: For the purposes of assigning a score to a criterion, you may use the following scale: 4 = fully implemented, exemplary accomplishment; 3 = implemented and operational; 2 = introduced, evidence of progress but not fully operational; 1 = not attempted or at the beginning level of development or implementation; 0 = not applicable

Arts Education Program Implementation Continuum (Continued)

6. Partnerships and collaborations

CRITERION	FOUNDATION	BUILDING	BEST PRACTICES
Outside agencies	**A22.** The district identifies as potential partners in implementing arts education programs local, regional, state, and national resources, including institutions of higher education, arts agencies, and the business community.	**B22.** Working relationships with local, regional, state, and national resources for arts education are established through the coordination of specific personnel.	**C22.** Strong relationships with outside agencies are developed and maintained to optimally implement arts education programs.
Partnerships	**A23.** The district establishes a plan for implementing partnerships to provide arts education experiences.	**B23.** Partnerships are established to provide a variety of resources that will support arts education programs.	**C23.** Partnerships support arts education programs that are coordinated, in-depth, and comprehensive.
School organizations	**A24.** The district and organizations that support schools (e.g., PTAs, foundations, booster clubs, and site councils) are made aware of the needs and the issues of the arts education program.	**B24.** The district and organizations that support the arts in schools actively contribute to the implementation of comprehensive arts programs in all four arts disciplines.	**C24.** A coordinated and articulated relationship exists between the district and the organizations that support schools to meet the ongoing needs of arts education programs.

Note: For the purposes of assigning a score to a criterion, you may use the following scale: 4 = fully implemented, exemplary accomplishment; 3 = implemented and operational; 2 = introduced, evidence of progress but not fully operational; 1 = not attempted or at the beginning level of development or implementation; 0 = not applicable

Arts Education Program Implementation Continuum (Continued)

7. Funding

CRITERION	FOUNDATION	BUILDING	BEST PRACTICES
Budget	**A25.** The need for an effective visual and performing arts budget is recognized.	**B25.** Appropriate funds are allocated to implement a basic arts education program in two or more arts disciplines at each school site.	**C25.** An annual budget funds a comprehensive, sequential visual and performing arts program in all four arts disciplines at each school site.
Stability	**A26.** An assessment of funding needs has been conducted to use as the basis for making budget decisions.	**B26.** Based on an assessment of funding needs, district funds and school site funds are provided to support the arts program in two or more arts disciplines.	**C26.** The assessment of funding needs is reviewed and revised annually. Funds are provided to fully support the arts programs in each of the arts disciplines and to provide for program growth.
Partnerships	**A27.** Potential funding sources are identified.	**B27.** Partnerships are established with one or more local, regional, state, or national resources for ongoing funding of special projects and grants.	**C27.** Partnerships are developed and maintained to provide a variety of long-term and short-term funding resources.
Oversight	**A28.** Budget oversight mechanisms at the district level and at the school site level are being developed for the distribution and the monitoring of funds for arts programs.	**B28.** Funding resources are monitored at the district level and at the school site level to provide for program implementation in two or more of the arts disciplines	**C28.** Funding resources and budget oversight mechanisms for all four arts disciplines are coordinated at the district level and at the school site level.

Note: For the purposes of assigning a score to a criterion, you may use the following scale: 4 = fully implemented, exemplary accomplishment; 3 = implemented and operational; 2 = introduced, evidence of progress but not fully operational; 1 = not attempted or at the beginning level of development or implementation; 0 = not applicable

Arts Education Program Implementation Continuum (Continued)

8. Resources and facilities

CRITERION	FOUNDATION	BUILDING	BEST PRACTICES
Facilities, storage, and safety	**A29.** Facilities, storage space, and student safety have been identified as essential to the success of the arts program.	**B29.** School facilities, storage space, and equipment are provided and maintained for two or more arts disciplines.	**C29.** All school sites have facilities and storage space that are specifically designed and maintained to guarantee full implementation of an arts education program in a safe environment. Such facilities include dedicated space for arts instruction in all four arts disciplines (e.g., wooden floors for dance, risers for choirs, stages for theatre, and vented kilns for the visual arts).
Equipment and materials	**A30.** The equipment and materials that are needed to support a basic arts program have been identified and prioritized.	**B30.** Arts-related equipment and materials are provided to all school sites to support instruction in most of the four arts disciplines.	**C30.** High-quality, arts-related equipment and materials are provided at all school sites for all four art forms and are systematically inventoried for replacement, repair, and upgrading.
Outside resources	**A31.** Local, regional, state, and national resources for arts-related facilities, maintenance service, and technical services have been investigated.	**B31.** A strategic plan is in place that connects administrators, teachers, and students to resources and arts facilities in the community, region, state, and nation.	**C31.** All schools in the district use local, regional, state, and national resources and facilities to create an exemplary arts program.

9. Program evaluation

CRITERION	FOUNDATION	BUILDING	BEST PRACTICES
Evaluation tools	**A32.** Evaluation is identified as a necessary component of arts education program development and improvement.	**B32.** Students, staff, and community members participate in a variety of internal and external evaluations that provide qualitative and quantitative data for program implementation and improvement.	**C32.** Evaluation data drive long-term planning efforts to refine and to expand a comprehensive arts education program

Note: For the purposes of assigning a score to a criterion, you may use the following scale: 4 = fully implemented, exemplary accomplishment; 3 = implemented and operational; 2 = introduced, evidence of progress but not fully operational; 1 = not attempted or at the beginning level of development or implementation; 0 = not applicable

The Continuum Grid

School district: _____

Instructions: Make extra copies of the grid so you can use it many times. Work from left to right across the matrix from the Foundation column to the Best Practices column. Place a check beside each item or assign a score to the item by using the scale at the right:

4 = Fully implemented, exemplary accomplishment
3 = Implemented and operational
2 = Introduced, evidence of progress but not fully operational
1 = Not attempted or at the beginning level of development or implementation
0 = Not applicable

	FOUNDATION						BUILDING						BEST PRACTICES				
	4	3	2	1	0		4	3	2	1	0		4	3	2	1	0
1. Standards-based curriculum																	
Framework																	
Standards process																	
Sequential curriculum																	
Integration																	
2. Instruction and methodology																	
Student's progress and outcomes																	
Equal access and inclusion																	
Variety of methodology																	
Quality instruction																	
Support resources																	
3. Student assessment																	
Approaches																	
Formal assessment																	
Information to improve teaching and learning																	
Performance and portfolio																	
Embedded strategies																	
4. Professional development																	
Long-range plan																	
Knowledge base																	
Professional development resources																	
Collaborations																	
5. Program administration and personnel																	
Policy																	
Staff																	
Leadership																	
6. Partnerships and collaborations																	
Outside agencies																	
Partnerships																	
School organizations																	
7. Funding																	
Budget																	
Stability																	
Partnerships																	
Oversight																	
8. Resources and facilities																	
Facilities, storage, and safety																	
Equipment and materials																	
Outside resources																	
9. Program evaluation																	
Evaluation tools																	

Appendix E
Copyright Law and the Visual and Performing Arts

The responsible use of resources, always an important issue, has particularly strong implications for the visual and performing arts. When working in the arts, students have the opportunity to interact with a variety of media that may include books, art prints, artifacts, videos, electronic media, performances, and plays. Ethical behavior in regard to the use of this information and information technology is one of the nine information literacy standards for student learning outlined in *Information Power.*[1] An indicator of the ethical behavior standard is that students understand the concept of copyright and apply it.

Copyright protects the original expression of ideas and safeguards original works of art, literature, music, films, broadcasts, and computer programs from copying and other uses. Students must be informed about the basic purpose of copyright, including fair-use exceptions, so that they will respect and comply with the law. Copying a work without obtaining permission may appear to be an easy and convenient solution to an immediate problem. However, such unauthorized copying may violate the rights of the author or publisher of the copyrighted work and may be contrary to the academic mission to teach respect for ideas and for the intellectual property of those who express those ideas.

Copyright law continues to evolve. For questions that are not answered in this material, some helpful Web sites cited at the end of this appendix can provide answers to a variety of questions.

The following summary of copyright law includes information developed by Mary Hutchings Reed and Debra Stanek for the American Library Association. Mary Hutchings Reed is a partner in the law firm of Sidley and Austin, Chicago, and counsel to the American Library Association. Debra Stanek is a graduate of the University of Chicago Law School. The summary also includes information provided by Carol Simpson of the University of Texas.

[1] *Information Power: Building Partnerships for Learning.* Chicago: American Library Association, 1998.

I. Fair Use for Teaching and Research

The fair-use doctrine is found in Section 107 of the copyright law (*United States Code, Title 17, Copyrights*). It allows limited reproduction of copyrighted works for educational and research purposes. The relevant portion of the copyright statute provides that the fair use of a copyrighted work, including reproduction "for purposes such as criticism, comment, news reporting, teaching (including multiple copies for classroom use), scholarship, or research," is not an infringement of copyright. The law lists the following factors as the ones to be evaluated in determining whether a particular use of a copyrighted work is a permitted fair use rather than an infringement of the copyright:

- The purpose and character of the use, including whether such use is of a commercial nature or is for a nonprofit educational purpose
- The nature of the copyrighted work
- The amount and substantiality of the portion used in relation to the copyrighted work as a whole
- The effect of the use upon the potential market for or value of the copyrighted work

Although all of these factors will be considered, the last factor is the most important in determining whether a particular use is *fair*. Where a work is available for purchase or license from the copyright owner in the medium or format desired, the copying of all or a significant portion of the work in lieu of purchasing or licensing a sufficient number of *authorized* copies would be presumptively unfair. Where only a small portion of a work is to be copied and the work would not be used if purchase or licensing of a sufficient number of authorized copies were required, the intended use is more likely to be found to be fair. For further information refer to the Web site *http://fairuse.stanford.edu*.

II. Use of Videos

The Copyright Revision Act of 1976 clearly protects such audiovisual works as films and videos. The rights of copyright include the rights of reproduction, adaptation, distribution, public performance, and display. All of these rights are subject, however, to *fair use,* depending on the purpose of the use, the nature of the work, the amount of the work used, and the effect the use has on the market for the copyrighted work.

Libraries purchase a wide range of educational and entertainment videos for in-library use and for lending to patrons. Since ownership of a physical object is different from ownership of the copyright, guidelines are necessary to define what libraries may do with the videos they own without infringing the copyrights they do not own. If a particular use would be an infringement, permission can always be sought from the copyright owner.

In-Classroom Use

In-classroom performance of copyrighted videos is permissible under the following conditions:

- The performance must be presented by instructors (including guest lecturers) or by pupils.
- The performance is connected to face-to-face teaching activities.
- The entire audience is involved in the teaching activity.
- The entire audience is in the same room or same general area.
- The teaching activities are conducted by a nonprofit educational institution.
- The performance takes place in a classroom or similar place devoted to instruction, such as a school library, gym, auditorium, or workshop.
- The video is lawfully made. The person responsible had no reason to believe that the video was unlawfully made.

Loan of Videotapes

- Videos labeled For Home Use Only may be lent to patrons for personal use. They should not knowingly be lent to groups for public performances.
- Copyright notice as it appears on the label of a video should not be obscured.
- If patrons inquire about a planned performance of a video, they should be informed that only private uses are lawful.

Examples from the 1986 American Library Association model policy:

1. A high school drama teacher wants to show a video of the film *The Grapes of Wrath* to her class. The video has a label that says For Home Use Only. As long as the requirements for fair use apply, the class may watch the video.
2. Four classes are studying *The Grapes of Wrath.* May the video be shown in the school auditorium or gym? Yes, as long as the auditorium and gym are used as classrooms for systematic instructional activities.
3. Several students miss the performance. May they watch the video at some other time in the school library? Yes, if the library is actually used for systematic instructional activities, the fair use exception applies. Most school libraries are probably used as such. If not, such a performance may be a fair use if the viewing is in a private place in the library.
4. May an elementary school teacher show a video of the film *Star Wars* to the class on the last day of school? Because a classroom is a place where a substantial number of persons outside of a family and friends are gathered, performances in them are public. Assuming that this

performance is for entertainment rather than systematic instruction, the fair-use exception would not apply. It is unlikely that such a public performance would be a fair use.

Off-Air Videotaping

Programs may be taped at home and used in the classroom as long as all educational guidelines are followed. *Cable in the Classroom* at *http:// www.ciconline.com/* provides monthly schedules of programming that may be recorded with specific guidelines for cable networks and specific programs.

From *Cable in the Classroom:*

Copyrights on television programs are held by the program's producers in order to insure proper compensation for their work. Without compensation, the theory goes, there would be no incentive to produce creative work. However, educational use leads to greater appreciation by the public, so certain allowances have been granted over the years for limited educational use of books, magazines, film, television, and now computer documents without the copyright owner's permission.

There are several areas of copyright law regarding the educational use of television. The best-known doctrine is that of fair use, which is applied to broadcast TV. Fair use allows taping for educational purposes as long as the tapes are shown only once within ten days of taping and are erased after 45 days.

See the copyright clearances schedule at *http://www.ciconline.com/resources/copyright.*

Videotaping of Live Performances

If a performance of a recital, concert, choreography, play, or other material that includes material that is not in the public domain is to be videotaped, copyright permission must be obtained from the publisher.

Before a parent records a performance of a play or musical concert or video for private use, the contract with the company from which the performance rights were purchased should be reviewed to determine whether taping is allowed. Copying or distributing such tapes without permission would be contrary to copyright law. Signed releases must be obtained from any professional dancers or musicians who perform to document their performance.

III. Use of Audio Recordings, Including Music

Audio requirements are similar to those for video. Audio items with public performance rights should be marked in some way for easy identification when used for performances not related to the curriculum. A single recording of student performances may be made for evaluation or rehearsal. Audio recordings of music as a background for multimedia productions should be drawn from a collection of royalty-free music clips. Recording a live performance of music not in the public domain on tape or on a CD without gaining permission is a violation of copyright law.

Digital transmission of sound recordings is a new right reserved for the copyright holder in the Digital Millennium Copyright Act (see Section VII). Keeping a library of music for performance on demand is not appropriate since that would mean copying all of the music. The only backup copies permitted are for computer software.

Example:

Storing recorded music on a server as part of a lesson plan for teachers to download is not permissible under current copyright law. Rather, purchased copies of the recorded music should be made available for teachers to check out.

IV. Use of Computer Software

Purchase Conditions

Most computer software purports to be licensed rather than sold. Frequently, the package containing the software includes information similar to the following:

You should carefully read the following terms and conditions before opening this diskette package. Opening this package indicates your acceptance of these terms and conditions. If you do not agree with them, you should promptly return the package unopened, and your money will be refunded.

or

Read this agreement carefully. Use of this product constitutes your acceptance of the terms and conditions of this agreement.

Although there is at present no case law concerning the validity of such agreements (which are unilaterally imposed by producers), in the absence of authority to the contrary, one should assume that such licenses are in fact binding contracts. Therefore, by opening and using the software, the library or classroom may become contractually bound by the terms of the agreement wholly apart from the rights granted the copyright owner under the copyright laws.

Following such information are the terms and conditions of the license agreement. The terms vary greatly between software producers and sometimes between programs produced by the same producer. Many explicitly prohibit rental or lending; some limit the program to use on one identified computer or to one user's personal use.

In-Library and In-Classroom Use of Software

1. License restrictions, if any, should be observed.
2. If only one program is owned under license, it may ordinarily be used only on one machine at a time.

3. Most licenses do not permit a single program to be loaded into a computer that can be accessed by several different terminals or into several computers for simultaneous use.

4. If the machine is capable of being used by a patron to make a copy of a program, a warning should be posted on the machine, such as "Many Computer Programs Are Protected by Copyright" or "Unauthorized Copying May Be Prohibited by Law."

Example:

An art teacher uses one diskette to load a computer program into several terminals for use by students. Doing so would violate copyright laws as well as most license agreements. It violates the Copyright Act, which authorizes the making of one copy if necessary to use the program, because it creates copies of the program in several terminals. Further, many license agreements prohibit the use of the software on more than one terminal at a time and in networking or any system that enables more than one person to use the software at a time.

V. Use of Print and Other Sources

Books

Books usually have copyright information printed on the reverse of the title page. Any rights granted by the author other than standard fair use will be indicated.

Teaching Materials

A teacher may make a single copy of a chapter from a book, an article, a short story, an essay, or a poem for research or class preparation. When multiple copies are made for instruction, copyright guidelines prohibit the creation of anthologies or compilations, copying from consumables like workbooks, or copying instead of purchasing. Copyright guidelines for photocopying multiple copies limit the use of a poem to 250 words, of complete works of prose to 2,500 words, and of prose excerpts to 1,000 words.

Plays

Copyright issues related to plays are included in guidelines for general print resources. The most common abuse of the copyright of plays is the public performance of a part or all of a play to a public audience. Performance rights must be purchased with the printed scripts, and records of those rights should be kept with the printed scripts.

Poetry

Print guidelines should be followed in using poetry. The most critical issue is the adaptation of poetry in creating lyrics, greeting-card verses, poster slogans, and so forth that may not be curriculum related.

Music

Single or multiple copies of excerpts of musical works may be made for study and for instruction. Music may not be copied for performing, creating anthologies, or avoiding purchase. For sheet music these guidelines allow for emergency copying (provided replacement copies are purchased), excerpts of no more than 10 percent of the whole work, and editing as long as the character of the work is not distorted or lyrics altered or added. Purchased copies of a work may be edited or simplified as long as the nature of the work or lyrics are not changed. For further information and clarification from the Music Library Association, refer to the following:

- *Guidelines for Educational Uses of Music. http://www.musiclibraryassoc.org/ Copyright/guidemus.htm*
- *Copyright for Music Librarians. http://www.lib.jmu.edu/Org/MLA/*

Dance

Copyright law protects a tangible form of expression of an idea or a work, not the idea itself. In copyright law choreography falls in the category of a *dramatic* work, which includes films, videos, plays, screenplays, and scripts. However, to be protected by copyright, choreography must be recorded in a tangible form, such as the following formats:

- Video
- Written-word expression
- Drawing of figures
- Dance notation

Web Sites

Fair use of Web resources parallels the use of print resources. Making limited use of some text and graphics as a part of classroom instruction or in a multimedia presentation is permissible. However, teachers and students should not publish those same materials on the Web or on a local or wide-area network without gaining permission from the copyright holder unless the materials are proven to be in the public domain or have been accessed from a copyright-free source. It is permitted to use original graphics or art or images that have been created by digital cameras.

Images

Images are protected under the print or multimedia guidelines of copyright. Images include photographs, art prints, cartoons, sketches, and logos.

Fair use allows the reproduction of an image, notwithstanding the creator's rights, for purposes such as criticism, satire, comment, news reporting, teaching (includes multiple copies for classroom use), scholarship, and research. In the determination of fair use, the purpose of the copying is considered. However, if a copyright notice appears with an image, the user must include that notice with the image. (Watermarks on images are being used more and more for this purpose.)

When language related to downloading images appears on a site, the user must abide by it. For example, the Smithsonian Institution Office of Imaging, Prints, and Photographic Services states that none of its 15,000 images may be reproduced without written permission. And the American Memory at the Library of Congress (*http://memory.loc.gov/*) states that some materials in its collections may be protected by the U.S. Copyright Law (Title 17, U.S.C.) or by the copyright laws of other nations. If an image is accompanied with a statement such as "The Library of Congress is not aware of any restrictions on these photographs," the images may be used. There are also fee-based image services.

If images are obtained from a free-use image resource, it is permissible to store digital art images on a school or district server for teachers to download as part of instruction. For example, AICT (Art Images for College Teaching) at *http://arthist.cla.umn.edu/aict/html* is a free-use image resource for the education community. However, for artwork accessed from museums and other sources, the museum owns the copyright of the image. Scanning and mounting those images is therefore not a good plan, but linking to those images is a perfectly legal practice.

VI. Permission

When a student or teacher wishes to use someone else's writing or graphics from a Web site, permission must be obtained from the copyright holder unless it is proven to be in the public domain. An e-mail request should be sent to the copyright holder. A sample letter is posted at *http://www.bham.wednet.edu/copyperm.htm*. If permission is requested to perform or duplicate published materials, a written request should be sent to the publisher.

VII. Digital Millennium Copyright Act of 1998 (DMCA)

This copyright act tightens controls over access to and use of copyrighted materials, including digital works. Because many of these changes are currently being asserted or challenged in court, in the next few years more changes will come as the courts interpret and apply new statutes. Among the topics included in the DMCA are provisions concerning the circumvention of copyright protection systems, fair use in a digital environment, and liability for online service providers. For further information on the DMCA, refer to *http://www.loc.gov/copyright/legislation/dmca.pdf*.

Appendix F

Guidelines for the Safe Use of Art and Craft Materials

Art and craft supplies that contain toxic substances, including potential human carcinogens, pose a significant danger to the health and safety of school-children. Because art instruction is part of the standard school curriculum, many children may be exposed to toxic chemicals in the materials used. Asbestos, heavy metals, organic solvents, and other toxic ingredients found in some art and craft materials present risks to the health and safety of the schoolchildren using them. These hazards may be greater for a child who is unaware of the dangers and may misuse the products. The following information is presented to assist school personnel in selecting and using safe art and craft products in the classroom.

General Precautions for All Students

1. *How Exposure Occurs.* Exposure to hazardous substances contained in art supplies occurs through inhalation, ingestion, or skin contact:
   a. Inhaling dusts, powders, vapors, gases, and aerosols may present health hazards. So does inhaling silica or asbestos found in dry earth clays, both of which may cause direct damage to the lungs. And inhaling solvent vapors that are absorbed into the bloodstream may inflict damage on bodily organs.
   b. Ingesting of hazardous substances can occur by eating contaminated food or, more directly, by placing in the mouth the hands or tools used in art projects. This route of exposure is an especially important concern with young children.
   c. Experiencing contact of the skin with hazardous materials may result in local or internal injuries. Caustic substances or solvents may cause local skin damage, and certain solvents can pass through the skin into the bloodstream, resulting in damage to other organs.

2. *Possible Illness from Exposure to Hazardous Materials.* Exposure to toxic materials may result in acute or chronic illness. An acute illness may result from a relatively large exposure over a short period of time. An example would be intoxication-like symptoms following deliberate or inadvertent ingestion of toxic solvents. A chronic illness may result from a relatively small exposure over a long period of time (e.g., degeneration of the nervous system from exposure to lead). Although the symptoms are immediately apparent when an acute illness occurs, they are not necessarily apparent in the case of a chronic illness. Chronic illness may arise at a later time because

of the concentration of substances in the body (e.g., asbestos or lead), accumulated damage to the body, or sensitization to a substance after repeated exposure.

3. *Limiting Exposure.* Considerable protection from exposure to toxic materials can be achieved by promoting good hygiene in the classroom. Storing art and craft supplies safely and labeling them appropriately, keeping dust to a minimum by damp mopping rather than sweeping, and cleaning up thoroughly after use will help prevent exposures. Personal hygiene also plays a role in the prevention of potentially harmful exposures. Students should refrain from eating or drinking while engaged in art projects and should wash their hands thoroughly when finished. Another general safety practice is to ensure proper ventilation in the art classroom so that contaminants may be diluted and eventually removed from the air.

Exposure to hazardous dusts and fumes will be minimized if the instructor premixes dry materials with water (for example, temperas, wheat paste, and so forth) and fires ceramic products when students are away from the kiln area. If an art material has been transferred to an unlabeled container and its identity is unknown, it should be disposed of. (For specific information on the proper disposal of art and craft materials, please contact your local county health department.)

Special Concerns: Kindergarten Through Grade Six

Unique factors are associated with the use of art and craft materials by young children. Those factors may increase health risks and should be considered in evaluating the suitability of products for use in schools. For example, young children should not be expected to follow instructions for the proper use of the materials. They may bring the materials into contact with their skin, eyes, mouth, hair, or clothing and be exposed to inhaling, ingesting, or absorbing potentially toxic compounds. That possibility of being adversely affected by such exposure is compounded by the fact that children are generally less able to tolerate exposure to hazardous substances than are adults because of the children's smaller size, higher metabolic rates, and immature organ immune systems.

In purchasing products for a particular application, the buyer should always consider alternative or substitute products and prefer least-toxic products. The following list describes general types of art materials that are likely to be hazardous and suggests substitutes. Although the law does not prohibit the use of all of these materials, they should be used with discretion, and substitutes should be used whenever possible.

Some art and craft projects involve processes inappropriate for young children. Examples include airbrushing, enameling, photo developing, and soldering. Instructors are encouraged to avoid projects that would involve those processes.

Art and Craft Materials to Avoid and Recommended Substitutes

1. *Avoid:* Products that may generate an inhalation hazard (e.g., clay in dry form, powdered paints, glazes, pigments, wheat paste, and aerosols, such as spray paints and fixatives)

   Substitute: Wet or liquid nonaerosol products (If dry products are used, they should be mixed when young children are not present.)

2. *Avoid:* Hazardous solvent-based products (e.g., rubber cement and its thinner, turpentine and other paint thinners, and solvent-based markers)

   Substitute: Water-based glues, paints, markers

3. *Avoid:* Materials that contain lead or other heavy metals (e.g., some paints, glazes, and enamels)

   Substitute: Products that do not contain heavy metals

4. *Avoid:* Cold-water dyes or commercial dyes

   Substitute: Vegetable dyes (onion skins and so forth)

5. *Avoid:* Instant papier-mâché, which may contain asbestos fibers or lead or other metals from pigments in colored printing inks

   Substitute: Papier-mâché made from black and white newspaper and library or white paste (or flour and water paste)

Safe Products for Grades Seven Through Twelve

Education Code Section 32064 mandates the labeling of any toxic art and craft materials purchased for grades seven through twelve. Section 32065 specifies what the label must list, including a warning to alert users of potential adverse health effects, information on the health-related dangers of the materials, and instructions for safe use. The rationale for labeling assumes that students in grades seven through twelve are capable of reading and understanding hazard labels on art products so that, once aware of the hazard, they can take the necessary precautions to minimize exposure.

Although products bearing toxic warning labels (e.g., Harmful if Swallowed, Use with Adequate Ventilation, Avoid Skin Contact) may be purchased for use by older children, exposure to toxic materials should be limited as much as possible. When such materials are used, care should be taken to ensure that the products are used in accordance with the directions on the label and that all cautions are observed. Although not mandated by law, purchasing products that do not contain toxic ingredients will provide an additional measure of safety in the classroom.

For a list of materials that may not be used in the classroom, refer to the Web site of the Office of Environmental Health Hazard Assessment (OEHHA) at *http://www.oehha.ca.gov/education/art/getart.html.* For information regarding updates of the list, contact the California Department of Education or OEHHA. Legislation requires that the list be updated periodically, and the Department will furnish information about the current status of the updates. The Department cannot, however, deal with issues of toxicity, inclusion or exclusion of products from the list, or interpretation of the field safety guidelines. Its basic responsibility is to print and disseminate the list developed by the OEHHA.

In some instances art and craft materials will not bear labels indicating hazardous ingredients. If a product is not properly labeled, contact the California Department of Health Services, Food and Drug Branch, for information as to whether the materials are in compliance with labeling requirements.

Resources for Information on Toxicity of Products

Information on the toxicity of products and the safe use of art and craft materials may be obtained as follows:

1. Check the list of craft materials on the OEHHA Web site. If a product is included on the list, it presents a chemical health hazard to those using it.

2. For information on the toxicity of chemicals, contact OEHHA, California Environmental Protection Agency, Integrated Risk Assessment Section, 1001 I Street, P.O. Box 4010, Sacramento, CA 95812; telephone (916) 324-2829; *http://www.ochha.ca.gov/education/art/getart.html.*

3. For further information about art materials that may be hazardous to students, contact the American Lung Association of California. This organization maintains a library of reference books, brochures, and slide or tape programs and sponsors seminars and workshops for teachers and others regarding safety issues in the arts.

4. For information on the toxicity of art materials and its certification program of art materials, contact the Art and Creative Materials Institute, 1280 Main Street, Second Floor, P.O. Box 479, Hanson, MA 02341; telephone (781) 293-4100; *http://www.acminet.org.*

Appendix G

Funding for Arts Education Programs

As school districts plan their annual budgets, they should include the arts in strategic and long-range planning to provide consistent funding for their arts education programs. The budgets should cover such items as staff salary, facilities, professional development, equipment and materials, curriculum development, textbooks and other instructional materials, new media and electronic technology, maintenance for equipment, visiting artists, and field trips to museums and performances. (*Note:* A section on facility needs for each of the arts disciplines is included in Chapter 4.)

As districts move toward sustaining an arts program, they may consider a variety of supplemental sources to enhance their allocations to the arts. Those that are most successful in garnering funding for their arts program employ a staff member who researches sources and initiates grant writing. The Internet provides an outstanding way to research possible funding sources, including local funding, state funding, federal funding, corporate funding, foundation funding, donations, and grants. (*Note:* Consult the California Department of Education Web site for current information on funding sources: *http://www.cde.ca.gov/fg/fo/*).

Glossary of Selected Terms

AB form—d. A two-part compositional form having an A theme and a B theme. The binary form consists of two distinct, self-contained sections sharing a character or quality (such as the same tempo).

ABA form—d. A three-part compositional form in which the second section contrasts with the first. The third section restates the first section in condensed, abbreviated, or extended form.

abstract—v. Refers to artwork in which the subject matter is stated in a brief, simplified manner. Little or no attempt is made to represent images realistically, and objects are often simplified or distorted.

abstraction—d. An idea or concept conveyed through movement and removed from its original context. For example, when a gesture to communicate happiness, such as jumping, is enlarged, made polyrhythmic, and repeated on different levels, it becomes abstract or nonliteral. The use of abstraction can encourage originality and make movement interesting and engaging.

accent—d. A strong movement or gesture.

accompaniment—m. Vocal or instrumental parts accompanying a melody.

acting—t. The process by which a person uses the entire self—body, mind, voice, and emotions—to interpret and perform the role of an imagined or assumed character.

acting areas—t. See *center stage, downstage, stage left and right,* and *upstage.*

action—t. The core of a theatre piece; the sense of forward movement created by the sequence of events and physical and psychological motivations of the characters. In film it is the basis of a prominent genre known as the action film.

actor—t. A person, male or female, who performs a role in a play or other entertainment.

actor's position—t. The orientation of the actor to the audience (e.g., full back, full front, right profile, left profile).

additive—v. Refers to the process of joining parts together to create a *sculpture.*

aerial perspective—v. Aerial or atmospheric perspective is achieved by using bluer, lighter, and duller hues for distant objects in a two-dimensional work of art.

aerophone—m. A musical instrument, such as a trumpet or flute, in which sound is generated by a vibrating column of air.

Note: An abbreviation appearing after a term designates which of the visual and performing arts the term refers to: *d:* dance, *m:* music, *t:* theatre, *v:* visual arts

aesthetic criteria—d. Standards applied in making judgments about the artistic merit of a work.

aesthetics—v. A branch of philosophy dealing with the study of art and theories about the nature and components of aesthetic experience.

alignment—d. The relationship of the skeleton to the line of gravity and base of support.

analog—v. Information or data stored in the form of the original signal, such as voltages, rotations, or magnetic force. For example, an analog watch has hands, in contrast to a digital watch, which uses a liquid crystal display.

analogous—v. Refers to closely related colors; a color scheme that combines several hues that fall next to each other on the color wheel.

antagonist—t. An adversarial person or situation or the protagonist's inner conflict.

apron—t. The stage area in front of the main curtain that extends toward the audience.

arbitrary colors—v. Colors selected and used without reference to those found in reality.

architectonic—v. Having an organized and unified structure that suggests an architectural design.

arena stage—t. A stage positioned in the center of the audience.

art criticism—v. An organized system for looking at the visual arts; a process of appraising what students should know and be able to do.

art elements—v. See *elements of art.*

art materials—v. Resources used in the creation and study of the visual arts (e.g., paint, canvas, fiber, charcoal, crayons, wood, clay, film, metal).

articulation—m. The manner in which notes are performed, such as staccato or legato.

articulation—t. The clear and precise pronunciation of words.

arts teacher—A teacher credentialed in California who has expertise in the arts. Music and visual arts teachers are credentialed in their respective fields. Dance teachers are credentialed in physical education through course work in dance, and theatre teachers are credentialed in English through course work in theatre.

assemblage—v. A three-dimensional composition in which a collection of objects is unified in a sculptural work.

assessment of applied academic skills—*Education Code* Section 60603(b) defines this term as "a form of assessment that requires pupils to demonstrate their knowledge of and ability to apply academic knowledge and skills in order to solve problems and communicate. It may include but is not limited to writing an essay response to a question, conducting an experiment, or constructing a diagram or model. An assessment of applied academic skills may not include assessments of personal behavioral standards or skills, including but not limited to honesty, sociability, ethics, or self-esteem."

Assessment in the arts may be accomplished through performance, critique, or analysis.

asymmetry—v. Intentionally unbalanced parts on opposite sides of a perceived boundary giving the appearance of equal visual weight.

atmospheric perspective—v. See *aerial perspective.*

atonal—m. A type of music in which tones and chords are not related to a central keynote.

augmented interval—m. A major or perfect interval raised by a half step.

axial movement—d. Movement anchored to one spot by a body part. Only the available space in any direction is used while the initial body contact is maintained. Organized around the axis of the body, this movement is not designed for travel from one location to another. It is also known as nonlocomotor movement (e.g., stretching, bending, turning in place, gesturing).

background—v. The part of the picture plane that seems to be farthest from the viewer.

balance—d. A state of equilibrium. It refers to the even distribution of weight or the spatial arrangement of bodies. Designs may be balanced on both sides of center (symmetrical) or off center (asymmetrical).

balance—v. The arrangement of visual arts elements are arranged to create a feeling of equilibrium in a work of art. The three types of balance are symmetry, asymmetry, and radial.

ballet—d. A classical Western dance form that originated in the Renaissance courts of Europe.

beat—m. A unit of measure of rhythmic time.

Benesh notation—d. A system for analyzing and recording human movement by using a musical staff. It is named after a French dance notator.

blocking—t. The planning and working out of the movements of actors on stage.

body positions—t. See *actor's position.*

canon—d. A passage, movement sequence, or piece of music in which the parts, overlapping one another, are done in succession.

canon—m. A musical form in which a melody is imitated exactly in one or more parts. It is similar to a *round.*

catharsis—t. The purification or purging of the emotions (as pity and fear) caused while viewing a tragedy.

center stage—t. The center of the acting area.

character—t. The personality or part an actor re-creates.

characterization—t. The development and portrayal of a personality through thought, action, dialogue, costuming, and makeup.

chord—m. Three or more tones sounded simultaneously.

chordaphone—m. A musical instrument in which sound is created by the stretching of strings between two points.

choreography—d. The art of composing dances, including shaping movement, structuring phrases, and revising and refining dances.

classroom teacher—A credentialed California teacher assigned to a self-contained classroom, kindergarten through grade six.

clef, bass, or treble—m. A symbol written at the beginning of a musical staff indicating which notes are represented by which lines and spaces.

climax—t. The point of highest dramatic tension or major turning point in the action.

coaching in dance—d. The inclusion of dance choreography, dance instruction, or dance composition consultancy in athletic sports (e.g., gymnastics, team dance, ice skating).

cold reading—t. The reading of a script by an actor who did not review it previously.

collaboration—t. The act of working in a joint intellectual effort.

collage—v. An artistic composition made of various materials (e.g., paper, cloth, wood) and glued onto a surface.

color—v. The visual connections depending on the reflection or absorption of light from a given surface. The three characteristics of color are hue, value, and intensity.

color relationships—v. The connections of colors on the color wheel. Also called color schemes or harmonies. Basic color schemes include monochromatic, analogous, and complementary.

color theory—v. The science of color relationships and properties (hue, intensity, and value).

comedy—t. A play that is humorous in its treatment of theme and, generally, has a happy ending in which the protagonist is victorious. It was a major genre in early film, as in the silent comedy.

commedia dell'arte—t. A professional form of theatrical improvisation developed in Italy in the 1500s and featuring stock characters and standardized plots.

complementary colors—v. Colors that oppose one another on the color wheel (e.g., red and green, blue and orange, yellow and violet).

complication—t. See *rising action.*

composition—d. The presence of unity, continuity (transitions), and variety (contrasts and repetition) in choreography.

composition—m. The creation of original music by organizing sound. It is usually written for others to perform.

composition—v. The organization of the elements of art and principles of design.

compound meter—m. A type of meter in which the beat is divided into threes or sixes.

concerto—m. A composition for orchestra and soloist.

conflict—t. The opposition of persons or forces giving rise to dramatic action in a play.

constructed response—v. An assessment tool requiring students to respond to a prompt by performing a given task.

contact improvisation—d. Movement using the force created by combining body contact and spontaneous response and recovery.

content—v. The messages, ideas, or emotions expressed in a work of art.

content standards—*Education Code* Section 60603(d) defines this term as "the specific academic knowledge, skills, and abilities that all public schools in this state are expected to teach and all pupils expected to learn in each of the core curriculum areas at each grade level tested."

context—t. The interrelated conditions in which a play exists or occurs.

contour drawing—v. The drawing of an object as though the drawing tool were moving along the edges and ridges of the form.

contrast—d. Setting elements side by side to emphasize their differences. Two contrasting movements might differ in energy, space (e.g., size, direction, level), design (e.g., symmetrical or asymmetrical, open or close), timing (e.g., fast or slow, even or uneven), or two or more different themes or patterns.

contrast—v. The difference between two or more elements (e.g., value, color, texture) in a composition; juxtaposition of dissimilar elements in a work of art; also the degree of difference between the lightest and darkest parts of a picture.

conventions of theatre—t. See *theatrical conventions.*

cool colors—v. Colors suggesting coolness: blue, green, and violet.

costume—t. Any clothing worn by an actor on stage during a performance.

counterbalance—d. A weight that balances another weight. The term usually refers to one or more dancers combining their weight in stillness or in motion to achieve an independent movement or design. A limb moving in one direction must be given a counterweight.

creative drama—t. An improvisational, process-centered form of theatre in which participants are guided by a leader to imagine, enact, and reflect on human experiences.

creative movement—d. Dance based on improvisation; the free exploration of movement, usually stimulated by an emotional or narrative theme (e.g., anger, war) or the exploration of an element of movement—time, force, or space (e.g., finding ways of moving on various levels or with varying amounts or qualities of force or energy).

crisis—t. In the plot of a play, a decisive point on which the outcome of the remaining actions depends.

critique—t. Opinion and comment based on predetermined criteria to be used for self-evaluation or the evaluation of the actors or the production itself.

cue—t. A verbal or physical signal indicating that something else, such as a line of dialogue or an entrance, is to occur.

curriculum—An organized course of study that follows standards-based guidelines for sequencing learning across the K–12 continuum and is specific enough to guide short-term and long-term instructional goals. The curriculum assists teachers in their day-to-day instructional choices and provides students with the essential knowledge and skills needed to progress toward future goals.

curvature—v. The act of curving or bending; one of the characteristics of line.

curvilinear—v. Formed or enclosed by curved lines.

cyclorama—t. A large cloth hanging across the back of a stage that is used for special lighting effects.

dance—d. (1) A unified work similar to a poem, a piece of music, a play, or a painting. Its structure has a beginning, middle, and end unified by a purpose or set of movement themes into a recognized form. Often, it is rhythmic or is accompanied by music. (2) The field of study including the functions of dance in society past and present, methods of choreography and performance, kinesiology, dance therapy, dance education, dance medicine, and other related studies.

dance content—d. Bodily movement as the medium of dance as sound is the medium of music. The elements of dance are space, time, and force or energy.

dance study—d. A short work of dance investigating a specific idea or concept and presenting a selection of movement ideas. It may be improvised or composed.

denouement design—t. The final resolution of the conflict in a plot.

descant—m. A melodic line or counterpoint accompanying an existing melody.

design—t. The creative process of developing and executing aesthetic or functional elements in a production, such as costumes, lighting, sets, and makeup.

design—v. The plan, conception, or organization of a work of art; the arrangement of independent parts (the elements of art) to form a coordinated whole.

dialogue—t. The conversation between actors on stage, in film, and in television or videos.

diatonic scale—m. The notes found within a major or minor scale.

diction—t. The pronunciation and choice of words and the manner in which a person expresses himself or herself.

digital—v. Refers to the recording, converting, or storing of information signals in on-or-off pulses or the binary code (ones and zeros) as opposed to the analog form.

diminished interval—m. A minor or perfect interval lowered by a half step.

directing—t. (1) The art and technique of bringing the elements of theatre, film, television, and video together. (2) The process by which an individual or individuals take responsibility for the creative look, style, and action of a play, film, video, or media piece. In film theory the *auteur* (director as artist) is the creative center of the work.

director—t. The person who oversees the entire process of staging a theatrical or media production.

distortion—v. The condition of being twisted or bent out of shape. In art distortion is often used as an expressive technique.

dominance—v. The emphasis of one aspect over all other aspects of a design.

dominant—v. The most prominent principle or the most obvious in influence or position.

downstage—t. The stage area toward the audience.

dramatic play—t. Children's creation of scenes when they pretend.

dramatic structure—t. The special literary style in which plays and screenplays are written.

dramaturge—t. A person who provides specific, in-depth knowledge and literary resources to the director, producer, theatre company, or audience.

dress rehearsals—t. The final few rehearsals prior to opening night in which the performance is run with full technical elements. Full costumes and makeup are worn by the actors.

duple meter—m. A time signature with groups of two beats to the measure.

dynamic markings—m. Symbols indicating varying degrees of volume: *pp* (*pianissimo*), very soft; *p* (*piano*), soft; *mp* (*mezzo piano*), medium soft; *mf* (*mezzo forte*), medium loud; *f* (*forte*), loud; and *ff* (*fortissimo*), very loud.

dynamics—d. The energy of movement expressed in varying intensity, accent, and quality.

dynamics—m. Varying degrees of volume in the performance of music.

earth tones—v. Various rich, dark colors containing some brown.

editing—t. Assembling the various pieces of a production. In film and video the editor is responsible for the rhythm and the narrative or thematic development of the piece.

electronic media—An art-making process based primarily on the use of electronic technology to create such artwork as videos, digital animation, films, computer graphics, digital photography, multimedia, and interactive media.

electronic resources (e-resources)—Materials and systems facilitating the retrieval, delivery, or exchange of information. E-resources may include live, recorded, or virtual information or experiences. Formats and systems may include CD-ROMs, DVDs, streamed videos, videotapes, software programs, audio CDs, interactive multimedia and Internet sites, Internet events, and virtual experiences.

electronic technology—Equipment, tools, or systems used to facilitate the learning, teaching, or production of art, music, or performances.

elements of art—v. Sensory components used to create works of art: line, color, shape or form, texture, value, and space.

elements of dance—d. Sensory components used to create and talk about dance: *force, space,* and *time.* (See the individual entries in this glossary.)

elements of music—m. Form, harmony, melody, and rhythm as well as the expressive elements of dynamics, tempo, and timbre (tone color).

elements of theatre—t. The individual components used to create and talk about works of theatre: character, dialogue, music, plot, and theme.

Elizabethan theatre—t. English theatre existing during the reign of Queen Elizabeth I (1533–1603) and often extending to the closing of the theatres in 1642.

embellishments—m. Notes added to ornament a melody or rhythmic pattern.

emphasis—v. Special stress given to an element to make it stand out.

ensemble—t. A group of theatrical artists working together to create a production.

epic theatre—t. A theatrical movement of the early 1920s and 1930s characterized by the use of such artificial devices as cartoons, posters, and film sequences. It distanced the audience from theatrical illusion and allowed the audience to focus on the play's message.

ethnic dance—d. A dance genre or form representing the characteristics of a specific culture of a country. Regional detail should be identified.

exposition—t. Detailed information revealing the facts of a plot.

expressive content—v. The expression of ideas and moods.

farce—t. A comedy with exaggerated characterizations, abundant physical or visual humor, and, often, an improbable plot. It was the source of early slapstick film comedy.

figurative—v. (1) Pertaining to the representation of form or figure in art. (2) Pertaining to the human figure. For example, many of the religious paintings by Peter Paul Rubens in the early seventeenth century focused on the human figure, as did the paintings of Edgar Degas in the nineteenth century and those by Alice Neel in the twentieth century.

focal point—v. The place in a work of art on which attention becomes centered.

folk or traditional dance—d. A dance associated with a national origin. Today, such dances are usually performed for recreation or at social gatherings or professional venues as the surviving portion of a tradition.

force or energy—d. This element is characterized by the release of potential energy into kinetic energy. It utilizes body weight, reveals the effects of gravity on the body, is projected into space, and affects emotional and spatial relationships and intentions. The most recognized qualities of movement (i.e., ways in which to release energy) are sustained, percussive, suspended, swinging, and collapsing.

foreground—v. Part of a two-dimensional artwork appearing to be nearer to the viewer or in the front. The middle ground and the background are the parts of the picture that appear to be farther and farthest away.

form—d. The organization or plan for patterning movement; the overall structural organization of a dance or music composition (e.g., ĀB, ĀBĀ, call and response, rondo, theme and variation, canon, and the interrelationships of movements within the overall structure).

form—m. The organization and structure of a composition and the interrelationships of musical events within the overall structure.

form—t. The overall structure or shape of a work that frequently follows an established design. A form may refer to a literary type (e.g., narrative form, short story form, dramatic form) or to patterns of line, meter, and rhymes (e.g., stanza form, verse form).

form—v. A three-dimensional volume or the illusion of three dimensions (related to shape, which is two-dimensional); the particular characteristics of the visual elements of a work of art (as distinguished from its subject matter or content).

formal theatre—t. Theatre that focuses on public performance in front of an audience and in which the final production is most important.

fugue—m. A composition in which three or more voices enter one after the other and imitate the main melody in various ways according to a set pattern.

function—v. The purpose and use of a work of art.

genre—d. A class or category of artistic endeavor having a particular form, content, or technique (e.g., ballet, modern, tap, jazz, Indonesian, East Indian, Bugaku). Each kind of dance is characterized by a recognizable technique, system, vocabulary of movement, composition, form, and way of performing.

genre—m. A type or kind of musical work, such as opera, jazz, mariachi.

genre—t. A category of plays characterized by a particular style, form, and content (e.g., tragedy, comedy, tragicomedy, melodrama, farce). In electronic media, *genre* refers to categories of films, videos, and other media that share narrative and stylistic characteristics, such as the Western or gangster film and slapstick comedy.

genre—v. The representation of people, subjects, and scenes from everyday life.

geometric—v. Refers to shapes with uniformly straight or curved edges or surfaces.

gesture—d. The movement of a body part or combination of parts, with emphasis on the expressive aspects of the movement. Gesture includes all movements of the body not supporting weight.

gesture—t. An expressive movement of the body or limbs.

gesture drawing—v. The drawing of lines quickly and loosely to show a subject moving.

Greek theatre—t. Theatrical events in Ancient Greece honoring the god Dionysus and including play competitions and a chorus of masked actors.

harmonic progression—m. A succession of individual chords or harmonies forming larger units of phrases, sections, or compositions.

harmony—m. The simultaneous sounding of two or more tones.

harmony—v. The principle of design that combines elements in a work of art to emphasize the similarities of separate but related parts.

hue—v. The attribute of colors that permits them to be classed as red, yellow, green, and so on.

idiophone—m. A musical instrument producing sound by shaking or scraping.

improvisation—d. Movement created spontaneously, ranging from free-form to highly structured, always including an impromptu element of chance.

improvisation—m. Spontaneous creation of music.

improvisation—t. A spontaneous style in which scenes are created without advance rehearsing or scripting.

informal theatre—t. A performance focusing on small presentations, such as one taking place in a classroom. Usually, it is not intended for public viewing.

information—v. Data, facts, documentation message (storytelling, recounting history), and commentary. It may provoke thought or feeling (emotional impact, laughter, fright, spirituality).

installation art—v. The hanging of ordinary objects on museum walls or the combining of found objects to create something completely new.

instruction—The activities, materials, and strategies used to implement a standards-based curriculum supporting students' learning in the arts.

intensity—v. The brightness of a color. Also called chroma or saturation. Full intensity occurs only when the color is pure and unmixed. Color intensity can be changed by adding a complementary color.

isolation—d. Movement made with one part or a small part of the body (e.g., rolling the head, shrugging the shoulders, rotating the hips).

interval—m. The distance in pitch between two tones.

jazz dance—d. Dance marked by movement isolations and complex, propulsive polyrhythms. An outgrowth of African American ragtime, jazz, spirituals, blues, work songs, and so forth, it is an original American dance style. It was also influenced by East Indian, Gypsy, Spanish, Caribbean, and South American gestures and rhythms. Jazz dance was further developed by choreographers Lester Wilson, Jack Cole, and Bob Fosse.

Kabuki—t. One of the traditional forms of Japanese theatre originating in the 1600s and combining stylized acting, costumes, makeup, and musical accompaniment.

kinesthetic awareness—d. Conscious perception of movement.

kinesthetic principles—d. Principles of physics governing motion, flow, and weight in time and space. They include the law of gravity, balance, and centrifugal force.

Labanotation—d. A system for analyzing and recording human movement invented by Rudolf von Laban (1879–1958).

level—t. The height of an actor's head as determined by his or her body position (e.g., sitting, lying, standing, elevated by artificial means).

levels of difficulty—m. The levels of difficulty for the music content standards are as follows:

Level 1: very easy; easy keys, meters, and rhythms; limited ranges.

Level 2: easy; may include changes of tempo, key, or meter; modest ranges.

Level 3: moderately easy; contains moderate technical demands, expanded ranges, and varied interpretive requirements.

Level 4: moderately difficult; requires well-developed technical skills, attention to phrasing and interpretation, and the ability to perform various meters and rhythms in a variety of keys.

Level 5: difficult; requires advanced technical and interpretive skills; contains key signatures with numerous sharps or flats, usual meters, complex rhythms, and subtle dynamic requirements.

Level 6: very difficult; suitable for musically mature students of exceptional competence.

line—v. A point moving in space. It can vary in width, length, curvature, color, or direction.

linear perspective—v. A graphic system used by artists to create the illusion of depth and volume on a flat surface. The lines of buildings and other objects in a picture are slanted, making them appear to extend back into space.

line direction—v. The horizontal, vertical, or diagonal direction of a line.

line quality—v. The unique character of a drawn line as it changes in lightness or darkness, direction, curvature, or width.

locomotor—d. Movement progressing through space from one spot to another. Basic locomotor movements include walking, running, galloping, jumping, hopping, skipping, sliding, leaping.

major key—m. Tonally, a key based on a major scale containing the step pattern whole, whole, half, whole, whole, whole, half or using the solfege tones of *do, re, mi, fa, so, la, ti, do.*

makeup—t. Cosmetics and, sometimes, hairstyles worn by an actor on stage to emphasize facial features, historical periods, characterizations, and so forth.

maquette—v. A small preliminary model (as of a sculpture or a building).

masks—t. Coverings worn over the face or part of the face by an actor to emphasize or neutralize facial characteristics.

mass—v. The outside size and bulk of a form, such as a building or sculpture; the visual weight of an object.

media—v. Plural of *medium*, referring to (1) materials used to make art; and (2) particular categories of art (e.g., painting, sculpture, film).

media—v. The materials, methods, systems, or vehicles used to communicate ideas, information, a message, or a feeling. Contexts include such materials as paint, clay, and videotape; such methods as print, electronic, and digital signals; such systems as cable and the Internet; and such vehicles as billboards, broadcasts, and photographs.

media literacy—v. The ability to read, analyze, evaluate, gain access to, and produce media, particularly media in an electronic form.

medium—v. A material used to create an artwork.

melodic and rhythmic form—m. The organization and structure of a composition and the interrelationships of musical events within the overall structure.

melodrama—t. A dramatic form popular in the 1700s and 1800s and characterized by an emphasis on plot and physical action, stereotypical characters, cliff-hanging events, heart-tugging emotional appeals, the celebration of virtue, and a strongly moralistic tone. Early American film borrowed heavily from melodramatic theatre.

melody—m. An organized sequence of single notes.

membranophone—m. A musical instrument in which sound is produced through the vibrations of a membrane.

meter—m. The grouping of beats by which a piece of music is measured.

middle ground—v. The area in a two-dimensional work of art between the foreground and the background.

MIDI—m. See *Musical Instrument Digital Interface.*

mime—t. An ancient art form based on pantomime in which conventionalized gestures are used to express ideas rather than to represent actions; also, a performer of mime.

minor key—m. Tonally, a key based on a minor scale containing the step pattern whole, half, whole, whole, half, whole, whole or using the solfege tones of *la, ti, do, re, me, fa, so, la.*

minstrel show—t. Musical theatre that usually consisted of traditional African American music and dance performed by white actors wearing blackface and characterized by exploitive racial stereotypes.

mixed media—v. A work of art for which more than one type of art material is used to create the finished piece.

mixed meter—m. A mixture of duple and triple meters.

mode—m. A type of scale having a particular arrangement of intervals (e.g., Aeolian, Dorian, Ionian, Locrian, Lydian, Mixolydian, Phrygian).

modern dance—d. A type of dance that values expressive and original or authentic movement. It is a twentieth-century idiom first explored throughout Europe by the American Isadora Duncan and in Germany by Mary Wigman and Rudolf von Laban. Significant innovators in the United States were Ruth St. Denis, Ted Shawn, Martha Graham, Doris Humphrey, and Charles Weidman, who are considered the pioneers of modern dance.

monochromatic—v. Refers to a color scheme involving the use of only one hue that can vary in value or intensity.

monologue—t. A long speech given by a single character.

mood—v. The state of mind or feeling communicated in a work of art, frequently through color.

motif—d. A distinctive and recurring gesture used to impart a theme or unifying idea.

motif—v. A unit repeated over and over in a pattern. The repeated motif often creates a sense of rhythm to create the pattern.

motivation—t. A character's reason for his or her actions or words in a play, film, television, program, or video.

movement—v. The principle of design dealing with the creation of action. It is a way, implied or actual, of causing the eye of the viewer to travel within and across the boundary of a work of art.

movement problem—d. A specific focus or task that serves as a point of departure for exploring and composing, usually with particular criteria.

multimedia—v. Artwork involving the use of text, images (static or moving), and sound in a single presentation. May refer also to artwork created by the use of more than one traditional medium.

Musical Instrument Digital Interface (MIDI)—m. A standardized language of digital bits enabling different electronic devices to communicate and work together (e.g., a computer and keyboard).

musicality—d. Attention and sensitivity given to the musical elements of dance while it is being created or performed.

musical theatre—t. A type of entertainment featuring music, songs, and, usually, dance. It may also refer to a genre of film based on music, song, and dance.

narrative—t. Story development that has a beginning, middle, and end.

negative—v. Refers to the shape or space that exists or represents an area unoccupied by an object.

neoclassical dance—d. A choreographic combination of classical and modern dance styles.

neutrals—v. Black, white, and gray. When added to colors, they change the color's value.

Noh—t. One of the traditional forms of Japanese theatre in which masked male actors use highly stylized dance and poetry to tell stories.

nonobjective—v. Having no recognizable object as an image; also called *nonrepresentational.*

notation—d. Various systems of writing and recording dance movements. Benesh notation and Labanotation are those most frequently used. Late twentieth-century technology has made the use of the videotape an indispensable method of recording dance.

notation—m. Written music indicating pitch and rhythm for performance.

nuance—d. A subtle difference in style of meaning; the subtle or slight movements that identify the distinct characteristics of a particular performer or the dances of a particular choreographer or period.

objective—t. A character's goal or intention.

observational drawing skills—v. Skills learned while observing firsthand an object, figure, or place.

one-point perspective—v. A means of illustrating three-dimensional objects on a two-dimensional surface. Lines appear to go away from the viewer and meet at a single point, known as the vanishing point, on the horizon.

opera—m. A drama set to music for voices and orchestra and presented with costumes and sets.

operetta—t. A theatrical production with elements of opera but lighter and more popular in subject and style.

oratorio—m. A dramatic musical composition usually set to a religious text and performed by solo voices, chorus, and orchestra without action, special costumes, or scenery.

organic—v. Refers to shapes or forms with irregular edges or to surfaces or objects resembling things in nature.

ostinato—m. A rhythmic or melodic accompaniment figure repeated persistently at the same pitch throughout a composition.

pacing—t. The tempo of an entire theatrical performance.

pageant—t. An elaborate street presentation or a series of tableaux across a stage.

paint program—v. Software emulating and expanding traditional two-dimensional art-making media and processes, such as drawing, painting, watercolor, pastel, and charcoal.

pantomime—t. Acting without words through facial expression, gesture, and movement.

partnering—d. Skills that require cooperation, coordination, and dependence with a partner, including imitation, lead and follow, echo, mirroring, and call and response as well as traditional male-female classical duets.

pathway—d. A line along which a person or a part of the person, such as an arm or head, moves. *Examples:* "Her arm took a circular path." "He traveled along a zigzag pathway."

pattern—v. Lines, shapes, and colors repeated in a variety of predictable combinations.

pentatonic scale—m. A scale having five tones to the octave and containing no half steps: *do, re, mi, so, la.*

performance art—v. A type of art in which events are planned and enacted before an audience for aesthetic reasons.

performance standards—*Education Code* Section 60603(h) defines this term as "standards that define various levels of competence at each grade level in each of the curriculum areas for which content standards are established. Performance standards gauge the degree to which a pupil has met the content standards and the degree to which a school or school district has met the content standards."

perspective—v. A system for representing on a two-dimensional surface three-dimensional objects viewed in spatial recession.

phrase—d. A partial dance idea composed of a series of connecting movements and similar to a sentence in written form.

phrase—m. A musical idea comparable to a sentence or a clause in language.

phrasing—d. The way in which the parts of a dance are organized.

pitch—m. The location of a note as to whether it is high or low.

pitch—t. The highness or lowness of the voice.

pitch bend—m. Sliding from one note to another by shifting the pitch gradually.

play—t. The stage representation of an action or a story; a dramatic composition.

playwright—t. A person who writes plays.

plot—t. That which happens in a story: the beginning, which involves the setting, the characters, and the problem they are facing; the middle, which tells how the characters work to solve the problem; and the ending, in which the problem is resolved.

point of view—v. The angle from which the viewer sees objects or a scene.

portamento—m. Gradually changing pitch up or down between two scale tones. Also called *slide.*

portfolio—v. A systematic, organized collection of a student's work.

positive—v. A shape or space that is or represents a solid object.

postmodern dance—d. A type of dance that emerged in the 1960s and is generally characterized by a departure from narrative theme and evocative emotion. The use of pedestrian gesture and minimalism is characteristic of this type of dance, which is exemplified in the work of Merce Cunningham, Yvonne Ranier, Trisha Brown, Steve Paxton, and Rudy Perez.

primary colors—v. The painting pigments of red, yellow, and blue. From those pigments all paint colors are created. Magenta, cyan, and yellow are primary hues to create all other hues used in printing and new media.

principles of design—v. The organization of works of art involving the ways in which the elements of art are arranged (e.g., balance, contrast, dominance, emphasis, movement, repetition, rhythm, subordination, unity, variety).

printmaking—v. The transfer of an inked image from one surface (plate or block) to another (usually paper).

process—v. A series of actions, changes, or functions that brings about a result.

production values—t. (1) The critical elements of a production, such as acting, directing, lighting, costuming, sets, and makeup. (2) A confident presentation of one's body and energy to communicate vividly movement and meaning to an audience. It also refers to performance quality.

projection—t. (1) The placement and delivery of the volume, clarity, and distinctness of the voice in communicating to an audience. (2) The use of light waves or electronic characteristics to deliver a film or media production to an audience.

proportion—v. The relationships in size of one part to the whole and of one part to another.

props (properties)—t. Items carried on the stage by an actor or the small items on the set used by the actors.

proscenium—t. The enlarged hole cut through a wall to allow the audience to view the stage; also called the *proscenium arch*. The archway is, in a sense, the frame for the action on the stage.

proscenium stage—t. The stage framed by the proscenium.

protagonist—t. The main character of a play or media production and the character with whom the audience identifies most strongly.

pulse—d. The underlying and consistent beat expressed by movement.

puppetry—t. Almost anything brought to life by human hands to create a performance. Types of puppets include rod, hand, and marionette.

radial—v. Lines, shapes, or colors that emanate from a center.

reader's theatre—t. A performance created by actors reading a script rather than working from memory.

rectilinear—v. Formed or enclosed by straight lines to create a rectangle.

reflection—v. Personal and thoughtful consideration of an artwork; an aesthetic experience; the creative process.

rehearsal—t. A practice session in which the actors and technicians prepare for public performance through repetition.

repetition—d. Reversal of the order of movements or movement phrases within the choreography.

repetition—v. The recurrence of elements of art at regular intervals.

retrograde—d. Reversal of the order of a sequence of choreography.

rhythm—d. The organization or pattern of pulses or beats, metered or unmetered, involving music or sounds made by the human body; the dance pattern produced by the emphasis and duration of notes in music.

rhythm—m. The combinations of long and short, even or uneven sounds that convey a sense of movement in time.

rhythm—v. Intentional, regular repetition of design elements to achieve a specific repetitious effect or pattern.

rising action—t. The middle part of a plot consisting of complications and discoveries that create conflict.

ritual dance—d. A type of dance associated with spiritual ceremonies or rites of passage in a particular culture.

rondo form—m. A musical form in which a section is repeated, with contrasting sections in between (e.g., $\overline{A}\overline{B}\overline{A}\overline{C}\overline{A}$).

round—m. A composition in which the same melody is started at different times and sounded together; also called a *canon*.

rubric—v. A guide for judgment or scoring; a description of expectations.

run-through—t. A rehearsal moving from start to finish without stopping for corrections or notes.

scale—m. The arrangement of notes in a specific order of whole and half steps.

scale—v. Relative size, proportion. Used to determine measurements or dimensions within a design or work of art.

score—m. The organized notation of the instrumental and vocal parts of a composition.

screen—t. A reflective surface onto which a film or video is projected.

screen left or right—t. The left side or right side of the screen from the audience's perspective.

script—t. The written text of a play.

sculpture—v. A three-dimensional work of art, either in the round (to be viewed from all sides) or in bas-relief (low relief, in which figures protrude slightly from the background).

secondary colors—v. Colors that are mixtures of two primary hues: orange, made from red and yellow; green, made from yellow and blue; and violet, made from blue and red.

sense memory—t. Memories of sights, sounds, smells, tastes, and textures. Used to help define a character in a certain situation.

sequence—d. The order in which a series of movements and shapes occurs.

serial music—m. A type of composition based on a technique involving a twelve-tone scale. (See also *twelve-tone scale*.)

set—t. Scenery, backdrops, and props used to create an environment for a performance.

setting—t. The locale of the action of a play.

shade—v. Color with black added to it.

shape—d. The positioning of the body in space: curved, straight, angular, twisted, symmetrical or asymmetrical.

shape—v. A two-dimensional area or plane that may be open or closed, free form or geometric, found in nature or made by humans.

slide—m. Gradually changing pitch up or down between two scale tones. Also called *portamento*.

social dance—d. Dance done in a social setting, usually done with a partner.

solfège—m. A system of designating verbal syllables for the degrees of the scale.

soliloquy—t. A monologue in which an actor reveals his or her inner thoughts.

sonata-allegro form—m. A musical form using the overall design of exposition, development, and recapitulation.

space—d. The immediate, spherical space surrounding the body in all directions. Use of space includes shape, direction, path, range, and level of movement. Space is also the location of a performed dance.

space—v. The emptiness or area between, around, above, below, or within objects. Shapes and forms are defined by the space around and within them.

spatial—d. Of or relating to space or existing in space.

specialist—d, m, t, v. An artist who works in the schools or a credentialed teacher with a special authorization to teach one of the arts.

staff (staves)—m. The horizontal lines on and between which notes are written.

stage—t. The area where actors perform.

stagecraft—t. The knowledge and skills required to create the physical aspects of a production (e.g., scenery, properties, lights, sound).

stage crew—t. The backstage crew responsible for technical work. In small theatre companies the same persons build the set and handle the load-in. Then, during performances, they change the scenery and handle the curtain.

stage left and right—t. The left and right side of the stage from the perspective of an actor facing the audience.

stage manager—t. The director's liaison backstage or in the television or video studio during rehearsal and performance. The stage manager is responsible for the running of each performance.

still life—v. An arrangement or a work of art showing a collection of inanimate objects.

stock characters—t. Established characters, such as young lovers, neighborhood busybodies, sneaky villains, and overprotective fathers, who are immediately recognizable by an audience.

storyboard—t. A graphic outline of the course of action in an improvisation, play, film, or television drama.

structure—d. The way in which a dance is constructed or organized; a supporting framework or the essential parts of a dance.

structure—v. The way in which parts are arranged to form a whole.

style—t. The manner in which a play is performed. The two principal styles are presentational and representational. In the presentational style the actors openly acknowledge the presence of the audience and play to it. In the representational style the actors seem to ignore the presence of the audience. In film, style is the mode of production in which similar uses are made of lighting, sets, set design, costuming, and acting. *Examples:* in film, German Expressionism or New Wave; in theatre, Elizabethan or commedia dell arte.

style—v. A set of characteristics of the art of a culture, period, or school of art; the characteristic expression of an individual artist.

stylized—v. Simplified or exaggerated.

subordination—v. Making an element appear to hold secondary or lesser importance within a design or work of art.

subtext—t. Information, including actions and thoughts, implied by a character but not stated by the character in dialogue.

subtractive—v. Refers to a sculpting method in which the original material is removed (the opposite of *additive*).

suite—m. A musical composition consisting of a succession of short pieces.

symmetrical—v. Refers to an arrangement of parts to produce a mirror image.

symmetry—v. A balance of parts on opposite sides of a perceived boundary.

symphony—m. A long orchestral work divided into three to five movements.

syncopation—m. The placement of rhythmic accents on weak beats or weak portions of beats.

tableau—t. A silent, motionless depiction of a scene created by actors, often from a picture. The plural is *tableaux.*

tap dance—d. A type of dance that concentrates on footwork and rhythm. It grew out of American popular dancing and has significant roots in African American, Irish, and English clogging traditions.

teaching artists—Artists hired by a school district to teach the visual or performing arts to students alongside credentialed teachers; sometimes referred to as artists-in-residence.

technique—d. (1) The physical skills enabling a dancer to execute the steps and movements required in different dances. (2) The style and form of specific training in dance. Different styles or genres of dance often have specific techniques.

technique—v. The method or procedure used to create an artwork.

tempo—d. The specified speed of a dance.

tempo—m. The pace at which music moves according to the speed of the underlying beat.

text—t. The printed words of a script, including dialogue and stage directions.

texture—m. The character of the different layers of horizontal and vertical sounds.

texture—v. The surface quality of materials, either actual (tactile) or implied (visual). Texture is one of the elements of art.

theatre—t. (1) The imitation or representation of life performed for other people; the performance of dramatic literature; drama; the milieu of actors, technicians, and playwrights; the place where dramatic performances take place. (2) Art that is focused on the audience and includes such activities as acting, directing, designing, managing, and performing other technical tasks leading to formal or informal presentations.

theatre of the absurd—t. Theatrical movement of the twentieth century in which playwrights created works representing the universe as unknowable and human existence as meaningless.

theatrical conventions—t. The established techniques, practices, and devices unique to theatrical productions.

theatrical experiences—t. Events, activities, and productions associated with theatre, film and video, and electronic media.

theatrical games—t. Noncompetitive games designed to develop acting skills. They were popularized by Viola Spolin.

theme—t. The central thought, idea, or significance of the action with which a play or story deals.

theme—v. An idea based on a particular subject.

theme and variation—m. A compositional form in which a theme is clearly stated and followed by a number of variations.

theme and variation—v. An idea or dominant feature giving a work of art its character; the subject of a work of art, sometimes having a number of phases or different examples.

three-dimensional—v. Having height, width, and depth. Also referred to as *3-D.*

thrust stage—t. A stage around which the audience is positioned on three sides.

timbre—m. Tone color, or quality of sound.

time—d. An element of dance involving rhythm, phrasing, tempo, accent, and duration. Time can be metered, as in music, or based on body rhythms, such as breath, emotions, and heartbeat.

tint—v. Color lightened by the addition of white.

tonality (key)—m. The tonal center of a composition.

tone—m. Multiple meanings: a sound of distinct pitch, quality, or duration; a musical note; the quality or character of a sound; the characteristic quality or timbre of a particular instrument or voice.

tone—v. Color shaded or darkened by the addition of gray (black plus white).

tone poem—m. An orchestral composition based on an extramusical idea; a tone picture (e.g., *The Pines of Rome,* by Ottorino Respighi).

tragedy—t. A play in which the protagonist (leading character) is ultimately defeated or dies. Examples of tragedies are *Romeo and Juliet* by Shakespeare and *Oedipus Rex* by Sophocles.

transition—d. The bridging point at which a single movement, the end of a phrase, or the end of a larger section of a dance progresses into the next movement, phrase, or sequence.

triple meter—m. Beats grouped into a set of three.

twelve-tone scale—m. A scale containing twelve notes separated from one another by a half step; also known as the chromatic scale.

two-dimensional—v. Having height and width but not depth. Also referred to as *2-D.*

two-point perspective—v. A system to show three-dimensional objects on a two-dimensional surface; the illusion of space and volume through the use of two vanishing points on the horizon line.

unison—d. Dance movement done simultaneously by a group of dancers.

unity—d. A sense of wholeness accomplished when all of the parts work well together.

unity—v. The total visual effect of a composition achieved by the careful blending of the elements of art and the principles of design.

upstage—t. As a noun, the stage area farthest away from the audience; as a verb, to steal the focus of a scene.

urban dance—d. Any contemporary fusion dance form drawn from current social influences (e.g., hip-hop, break dancing, trance dancing).

value—v. Lightness and darkness of a hue or neutral color; the gradations of light and dark in a two-dimensional artwork and on the surface of three-dimensional objects.

value scale—v. A scale showing the range of values from black to white and light to dark.

vanishing point—v. In perspective drawing a point at which receding lines seem to converge. Usually located on the horizon line.

variety—v. A principle of art concerned with combining elements of art in different ways to create interest.

virtual—v. Refers to an image produced by the imagination and not existing in reality. Usually applied to experiences that occur in environments that exist within a computer or on the Internet or to procedures or functions creating the illusion that they are actually present.

visual literacy—v. Includes thinking and communication. Visual thinking is the ability to transform thoughts and information into images. Visual communication takes place when people are able to construct meaning from a visual image.

visual metaphor—v. Images in which characteristics of objects are likened to one another and represented as such. Closely related to concepts about symbolism.

vocal projection—t. See *projection.*

vocal quality—t. The characteristics of a voice (e.g., shrill, nasal, raspy, breathy, booming).

volume—t. The degree of loudness or intensity of a voice.

volume—v. Any three-dimensional quantity bound or enclosed, whether solid or void.

warm colors—v. Colors suggesting warmth: red, yellow, and orange.

wings—t. Off-stage areas out of view on stage left and stage right that may be used for exits, entrances, and set changes.

work—d. A piece of choreography or a dance.

Selected References and Resources

Resources from Key Arts Education Organizations

Resources providing a wealth of information on visual and performing arts education are available on the Web sites of the following key arts education organizations:

California Organizations and Resources

California Alliance for Arts Education (CAAE). *http://www.artsed411.org*

The California Art Education Association (CAEA). *http://www.caea-arteducation.org*

California Arts Council (CAC). *http://www.cac.ca.gov*

The California Arts Project (TCAP). *http://csmp.ucop.edu/tcap*

California Assembly of Local Arts Agencies (CALAA). *http://www.calaa.net*

California Association for Music Education (CMEA). *http://www.calmusiced.com*

California Dance Educators Association (CDEA). *http://www.cdeadans.org*

California Educational Theatre Association (CETA). *http://www.cetaweb.org*

California State PTA. *http://www.capta.org/sections/programs-smarts/index.cfm*

California State Summer School for the Arts. *http://www.csssa.org*

California State University Summer Arts. *http://www.calstate.edu/summerarts*

UC/CSU Admission Requirements. *http://pathstat1.ucop.edu/ag/a-g/index.html*

California Department of Education Resources

Arts Education Program Toolkit: A Visual and Performing Arts Program Assessment Process. http://www.cde.ca.gov/re/pn/rc/

Arts Work: A Call for Arts Education for All California Students: The Report of the Superintendent's Task Force on the Visual and Performing Arts. http://www.cde.ca.gov/re/pn/rc/

California Arts Assessment Network (CAAN). *http://www.teachingarts.org/CAAN*

Local Arts Education Partnership Grant Program. *http://www.cac.ca.gov*

Local Arts Education Partnership Grant Program: The Arts Work Visual and Performing Arts Grant Program. *http://www.cde.ca.gov/pd/ca/vp/visperffunding.asp*

Note: The publication data in this section were supplied by the Curriculum Frameworks and Instructional Resources Division, California Department of Education. Questions about the data should be addressed to that office: telephone (916) 319-0881.

Model Arts Program (MAP) Network. *http://www.teachingarts.org/MAP*

Performance Assessment Professional Development Handbook: *http://ursula@artsed411.org*

TeachingArts.Org. *http://www.teachingarts.org*

Visual and Performing Arts Content Standards for California Public Schools, Prekindergarten Through Grade Twelve. http://www.cde.ca.gov/be/st/ss/index.asp

Visual and Performing Arts Education. *http://www.cde.ca.gov/pd/ca/vp/*

Visual and Performing Arts Framework for California Public Schools, Kindergarten Through Grade Twelve. http://www.cde.ca.gov/ci/vp/cf/

National Organizations and Resources

American Orff-Schulwerk Association. *http://www.aosa.org*

Americans for the Arts. *http://www.americansforthearts.org/*

Annenberg/CPB. *http://www.learner.org*

Arts Education Partnership (AEP). *http://www.aep-arts.org/*

Arts Education Resources: *http://www.artslynx.org/artsed*

Dance Educators Professional Teachers' Association (DEPTA). *http://hsc.csu.edu.au/pta/members/depa.html*

Educational Theatre Association (ETA). *http://www.edta.org*

The Getty's ArtsEdNet. *http://www.getty.edu/artsednet*

Kennedy Center ArtsEdge. *http://artsedge.kennedy-center.org*

Lincoln Center Institute. *http://www.lincolncenter.org*

The Music Educators National Conference (MENC). *http://www.menc.org*

National Art Education Association (NAEA). *http://www.naea-reston.org*

National Assembly of State Arts Agencies. *http://www.nasaa-arts.org*

National Board for Professional Teaching Standards. *http://www.nbpts.org*

National Dance Association (NDA). *http://www.aahperd.org/nda*

National Dance Educators Organization (NDEO). *http://www.ndeo.org*

National Endowment for the Arts (NEA). *http://www.arts.gov*

General Arts References and Resources

Aiming High: High Schools for the Twenty-first Century. Sacramento: California Department of Education, 2002.

The Arts: A Competitive Advantage for California. Prepared by the Policy Economics Group. Sacramento: KMPG Peat Marwick and the California Arts Council, 1994.

Arts Education Program Toolkit: A Visual and Performing Arts Program Assessment Process. Sacramento: California Department of Education, 2001.

Arts Work: A Call for Arts Education for All California Students. Sacramento: California Department of Education, 1997.

Selected References and Resources

Champions of Change: The Impact of the Arts on Learning. Edited by Edward B. Fiske. Washington, D.C.: The President's Committee on the Arts and the Humanities and the Arts Education Partnership, 1999.

Cornett, Claudia E. *The Arts as Meaning Makers: Integrating Literature and the Arts Throughout the Curriculum.* Upper Saddle River, N.J.: Prentice-Hall, 1998.

Csikszentmihalyi, Mihaly, and Rick E. Robinson. *The Art of Seeing: An Interpretation of the Aesthetic Encounter.* Los Angeles: Getty Publications, 1991.

Current Research in Arts Education: An Arts in Education Research Compendium. Sacramento: California Arts Council, 2001.

Dissanayake, Ellen. *What Is Art For?* Seattle: University of Washington Press, 1990.

Eaton, Marcia Muelder. *Basic Issues in Aesthetics.* Long Grove, Ill.: Waveland Press, 1999.

Eisner, Elliot W. "The Arts as a Way of Knowing," *Principal,* Vol. 60, No. 1 (September 1980), 11–14.

Eisner, Elliot W. *Cognition and Curriculum: A Basis for Deciding What to Teach and How to Evaluate.* New York: Longman Group Publishing, 1982.

Eisner, Elliot W. "Does Experience in the Arts Boost Academic Achievement?" *Arts Education Policy Review,* Vol. 100, No. 1 (September/October 1998), 32–38.

Eisner, Elliot W. "Getting Down to Basics in Arts Education," *Journal of Aesthetics Education,* Vol. 33, No. 4 (Winter 1999), 145–59.

Eisner, Elliot W. *The Kind of Schools We Need: Personal Essays.* Portsmouth, N.H.: Heinemann, 1998.

Elementary Art Programs: A Guide for Administrators. Reston, Va.: National Art Education Association, 2004.

"Focus on the Visual and Performing Arts," *Curriculum/Technology Quarterly,* Vol. 10, No. 3 (Spring 2001).

Fowler, Charles. *Can We Rescue the Arts for America's Children: Coming to Our Senses—10 Years Later.* Washington, D.C.: Americans for the Arts, 1988.

Fowler, Charles. *Strong Arts, Strong Schools: The Promising Potential and Short-sighted Disregard of the Arts in American Schooling.* New York: Oxford University Press, 2002.

Gaining the Arts Advantage: Lessons from School Districts That Value Arts Education. Washington, D.C.: The President's Committee on the Arts and the Humanities and the Arts Education Partnership, 1999.

Gardner, Howard. *Art, Mind and Brain: A Cognitive Approach to Creativity.* New York: Basic Books, 1984.

Gardner, Howard. *The Arts and Human Development: A Psychological Study of the Artistic Process.* New York: Basic Books, 1994.

Gardner, Howard. *Creating Minds: An Anatomy of Creativity Seen Through the Lives of Freud, Einstein, Picasso, Stravinsky, Eliot, Graham, and Gandhi.* New York: Basic Books, 1993.

Gardner, Howard. *Frames of Mind: The Theory of Multiple Intelligences* (Tenth edition). New York: Basic Books, 1993.

Gardner, Howard. *Intelligence Reframed: Multiple Intelligences for the Twenty-first Century.* New York: Basic Books, 2000.

Gardner, Howard. *Multiple Intelligences: The Theory in Practice.* New York: Basic Books, 1993.

Green, Maxine. *Releasing the Imagination: Essays on Education, the Arts, and Social Change.* New York: John Wiley & Sons, Inc., 2000.

Guide and Criteria for Program Quality Review—Elementary Grades. Sacramento: California Department of Education, 1998.

Guide and Criteria for Program Quality Review—Middle Grades. Sacramento: California Department of Education, 1998.

Habermeyer, Sharlene. *Good Music, Brighter Children: Simple and Practical Ideas to Help Transform Your Child's Life Through the Power of Music.* Rocklin, Calif.: Prima Publishing, 2000.

Holdren, John. "The Limits of Thematic Instruction," *Common Knowledge: A Newsletter of the Core Knowledge Foundation,* Vol. 7, No. 4 (Fall 1994).

"The Impact of Arts Education on Workforce Preparation." Issue brief, National Governors Association Center for Best Practices, May 1, 2002.

Information Power: Building Partnerships for Learning. Chicago: American Library Association, 1998.

Jackson, Philip W. *John Dewey and the Lessons of Art.* New Haven, Conn.: Yale University Press, 2000.

Jensen, Eric. *Arts with the Brain in Mind.* Alexandria, Va.: Association for Supervision and Curriculum Development, 2001.

Kaagan, Stephen S. *Aesthetic Persuasion: Pressing the Cause of Arts Education in American Schools.* Los Angeles, Calif.: The Getty Center for Education in the Arts, 1990.

Lehman, Paul R. "What Students Should Learn in the Arts," in *Content of the Curriculum.* The 1988 ASCD Yearbook. Alexandria, Va.: Association for Supervision and Curriculum Development, 1988, pp. 109–31.

Nachmanovitch, Stephen. *Free Play: The Power of Improvisation in Life and the Arts.* New York: Putnam Publishing Group, 1991.

National Standards for Arts Education: What Every Young American Should Know and Be Able to Do in the Arts. Developed by the Consortium of the National Arts Education Association (the American Alliance for Theatre and Dance, the Music Educators National Conference, the National Art Education Association, and the National Dance Association) under the guidance of the National Committee for Standards in the Arts. Reston, Va.: Music Educators National Conference, 1994.

Opportunity-to-Learn Standards for Arts Education. Reston, Va.: Consortium of the National Arts Education Association, 1995.

Perspectives on Education Reform: Art Education as Catalyst. Los Angeles: Getty Publications, 1994.

Pistone, Nancy. *Envisioning Arts Assessment: A Process Guide for Assessing Arts Education in School Districts and States.* Washington, D.C.: Council of Chief State School Officers and the Arts Education Partnership, 2002.

Postman, Neil. *Technopoly: The Surrender of Culture to Technology.* New York: Knopf Publishing Group, 1993.

The Power of the Arts to Transform Education: Summary Report. Washington, D.C.: The Arts Education Partnership, the John F. Kennedy Center for the Performing Arts, and the J. Paul Getty Trust, 1993.

Program Evaluation: Visual and Performing Arts. Indicators of Schools of Quality and Program Evaluation Series. Schaumburg, Ill.: National Study of School Evaluation, 1998.

Public Opinion Survey. Sacramento: California Arts Council, 2001.

Remer, Jane. *Changing Schools Through the Arts: How to Build on the Power of an Idea.* New York: Americans for the Arts, 1990.

"Report of the American Council for the Arts." Report presented at the American Council of the Arts Symposium in Atlanta, Georgia, September 18–20, 1992.

The Results of the Arts Work Survey of California Public Schools. Sacramento: California Department of Education, 2001.

Seidel, Steven, and Meredith Eppel. *Arts Survive: A Study of Sustainability in Arts Education Partnerships.* Cambridge, Mass.: Harvard Project Zero, 2001.

Shlain, Leonard. *Art and Physics: Parallel Visions in Space, Time, and Light.* New York: Quill, 1993.

Shore, Bruce M., and others. *Recommended Practices in Gifted Education.* A Critical Analysis in the Education and Psychology of the Gifted Series. New York: Teachers College Press, 1991.

Toward Civilization: A Report on Arts Education. Washington, D.C.: National Endowment for the Arts, 1988.

Visual and Performing Arts Content Standards for California Public Schools, Prekindergarten Through Grade Twelve. Sacramento: California Department of Education, 2001.

Weitz, Judith H. *Coming Up Taller: Arts and Humanities Programs for Children and Youth at Risk.* Upland, Pa.: DIANE Publishing Company, 1997.

What Work Requires of Schools: A Scans Report for America 2000. Upland, Pa.: DIANE Publishing Company, 1991.

Wolf, Dennie Palmer, and Joan Boykoff Baron. "Standards, Curriculum, and Assessment in Arts Education: Envisioning New Possibilities," in *Measuring Up to the Challenge.* Edited by Ruth Mitchell. New York: Americans for the Arts, 1994.

Web Resources

The following uniform resource locators (URLs) were valid at the time this document was prepared:

Americans for the Arts. *http://www.artsusa.org*

Arts Education Partnership. *http://www.aep-arts.org*

Association for Supervision and Curriculum Development. *http://www.ascd.org*

California Alliance for Arts Education. *http://www.artsed411.org*

California Arts Council. *http://www.cac.ca.gov*

The California Arts Project. *http://csmp.ucop.edu/tcap*

California Department of Education, Arts Education. *http://www.cde.ca.gov/ci/vp*

California Department of Education, Frameworks. *http://www.cde.ca.gov/ci/cr/cf/index.asp*

Critical Links: Learning in the Arts and Student Academic and Social Development. Edited by Richard Deasy. Arts Education Partnership. *http://www.aep-arts.org/cllinkspage.htm*

Getty Center for Education in the Arts. *http://www.getty.edu/artsednet*

Kennedy Center Arts Edge. *http://www.artsedge.Kennedy-center.org*

Project Muse Scholarly Journals Online. This site offers fee-based services available through the Johns Hopkins University Press. *http://muse.jhu.edu*

TeachingArts.Org. This is a statewide online arts resource center, developed by the Kern and San Bernardino county offices of education in collaboration with the California Department of Education. *http://www.teachingarts.org*

Assessment References and Resources

Assessing Student Learning: A Practical Guide (CD-ROM). Edited by Kent Seidel. Cincinnati: Alliance for Curriculum Reform, 2000.

Assessing Student Learning: New Rules, New Realities. Edited by Ronald S. Brandt. Arlington, Va.: Educational Research Services, 1998.

Into the Process: A Visual Arts Portfolio Assessment Pilot Project. Carmichael, Calif.: California Art Education Association, 1991.

Lehman, Paul. "Making the National Standards Work for You: Standards and Assessment." Remarks made at the National Assembly of the Music Educators National Conference, Phoenix, Arizona, April 14, 1998.

McTighe, Jay, and Steven Ferrara. *Assessing Learning in the Classroom.* Washington, D.C.: National Education Association, 1998.

Measuring Up to the Challenge: What Standards and Assessment Can Do for Arts Education. Edited by Ruth Mitchell. New York: American Council for the Arts, 1994.

Mitchell, Ruth, and Amy Stempel. "Six Case Studies of Performance Assessment," in *Testing in American Schools: Asking the Right Questions.* Upland, Pa.: DIANE Publishing Company, 1992.

Prelude to Performance Assessment in the Arts, Kindergarten Through Grade Twelve. Sacramento: California Department of Education, 1994.

Standards-Based Performance Assessments in the Arts: Using Scoring Guides and Rubrics. California Assessment Network. Pasadena: California Alliance for Arts Education, 2001.

Wiggins, Grant, and Jay McTighe. *Understanding by Design.* Alexandria, Va.: Association for Supervision and Curriculum Development, 1998.

Wolf, Dennie Palmer. "Opening Up Assessment," *Educational Leadership,* Vol. 45, No. 4 (December 1987/January 1988), 24–29.

Wolf, Dennie Palmer. "Portfolio Assessment: Sampling Student Work," *Educational Leadership,* Vol. 46, No. 7 (April 1989), 35–39.

Wolf, Dennie Palmer, and Nancy Pistone. *Taking Full Measure: Rethinking Assessment Through the Arts.* New York: College Entrance Examination Board, 1991.

Web Resources

California Arts Assessment Network. This network, facilitated through the California Department of Education, develops and pilots assessment instruments for schools and school districts involved in arts assessment. *http://www.teachingarts.org/CAAN*

National Assessment of Educational Progress. "The Nation's Report Card" at this site includes assessment in a number of subject areas, including the visual and performing arts. Sample assessment items are available online. *http://nces.ed.gov/nationsreportcard*

Standing Conference of Arts and Social Sciences (a British organization). *http://www.scass.org.uk*

Western Michigan University. The summary of the student evaluation standards at this site presents classroom-level assessment guidelines. *http://ec.wmich.edu/jointcomm/SES/All_Summary.htm*

Dance References

Alter, Judith B. *Stretch and Strengthen: A Safe, Comprehensive Exercise Program to Balance Your Muscle Strength.* Boston: Houghton Mifflin Company, 1992.

Blom, Lynne Anne; L. Tarin Chaplin; and Alma M. Hawkins. *The Intimate Act of Choreography.* Pittsburgh: University of Pittsburgh Press, 1982.

Cheney, Gay. *Basic Concepts in Modern Dance: A Creative Approach* (Third edition). Pennington, N.J.: Princeton Book Company, 1989.

Ellfeldt, Lois. *A Primer for Choreographers.* Prospect Heights, Ill.: Waveland Press, Inc., 1988.

Frank, Rusty. *Tap! The Greatest Tap Dance Stars and Their Stories, 1900–1955.* New York: DaCapo Press, 1995.

Friedman, Lise. *First Lessons in Ballet*. New York: Workman Publishing Company, 1999.

Ganeri, Anita. *The Young Person's Guide to the Ballet, with Music on CD from the Nutcracker, Swan Lake, and Sleeping Beauty*. London: Harcourt Brace and Company, 1998.

Grau, Andree. *Dance*. Eyewitness Books Series. New York: Dorling Kindersley Publishing, Inc., 2000.

Hanna, Judith Lynne. *Partnering Dance and Education: Intelligent Moves for Changing Times*. Champaign, Ill.: Human Kinetics Publishers, 1999.

Humphrey, Doris. *The Art of Making Dances*. Pennington, N.J.: Princeton Book Company, 1991.

Jonas, Gerald. *Dancing: The Power of Dance Around the World*. New York: Abrams, 1992.

Joyce, Mary, and Patty Haley. *First Steps in Teaching Creative Dance to Children* (Third edition). Burr Ridge, Ill.: McGraw-Hill Higher Education, 1993.

Lane, Christy. *Multicultural Folk Dance Guide*. Champaign, Ill.: Human Kinetics Publishers, 1998.

Lee, Mary Ann; Ann Cannon; and Joni Urry Wilson. *Move! Learn! Dance! A K–6 Teaching Resource Guide*. Salt Lake City, Utah: Children's Dance Theatre, 1996.

Mazo, Joseph. *Prime Movers: The Makers of Modern Dance in America* (Second edition). Hightstown, N.J: Princeton Book Company Publishers, 1999.

McGreevy-Nichols, Susan, and Helene Scheff. *Building Dances: A Guide to Putting Movements Together*. Champaign, Ill.: Human Kinetics Publishers, 1995.

Minton, Sandra. *Choreography: A Basic Approach Using Improvisation* (Second edition). Champaign, Ill.: Human Kinetics Publishers, 1997.

Mitchell, Jack. *Alvin Ailey American Dance Theater: Jack Mitchell Photographs*. Kansas City, Mo.: Andrews McMeel Publishing, 1993.

Schrader, Constance A. *A Sense of Dance: Exploring Your Movement Potential*. Champaign, Ill.: Human Kinetics Publishers, 1997.

Stearns, Marshall, and Jean Stearns. *Jazz Dance: The Story of American Vernacular Dance*. New York: DaCapo Press, 1994.

Stinson, Sue W. *Dance for Young Children: Finding the Magic in Movement*. Reston, Va.: The American Alliance for Health, Physical Education, Recreation, and Dance, 1988.

Strandberg, Julie, and Carolyn Adams. *Dancing Through the Curriculum: A Guide to Dance Videotapes Created and Designed to Enrich the School Curriculum*. Providence, R.I.: Jay Ess Press, 1997.

Thomas, Annabel. *Ballet and Dance*. Tulsa, Okla.: EDC Publishing, 1992.

Weikart, Phyllis. *Movement in a Steady Beat: Activities for Children Ages 3–7*. Ypsilanti, Mich.: High/Scope Press, 1990.

Weikart, Phyllis. *Movement Plus Rhymes, Songs, and Singing Games.* Ypsilanti, Mich.: High/Scope Press, 1998.

Weikart, Phyllis. *Round the Circle: Key Experiences in Movement for Children Ages 3 to 5.* Ypsilanti, Mich.: High/Scope Press, 1987.

Weikart, Phyllis. *Round the Circle: Key Experiences in Movement for Young Children* (Second edition). Ypsilanti, Mich.: High/Scope Press, 2000.

Weikart, Phyllis. *Teaching Folk Dance: Successful Steps.* Ypsilanti, Mich.: High/Scope Press, 1999.

Weikart, Phyllis. *Teaching Movement and Dance: A Sequential Approach to Rhythmic Movement* (Fifth edition). Ypsilanti, Mich.: High/Scope Press, 2003.

Weikart, Phyllis, and Elizabeth Carlton. *Guides to Rhythmically Moving.* Ypsilanti, Mich.: High/Scope Press, 1997.

Music References

Abeles, Harold F.; Charles R. Hoffer; and Robert H. Klotman. *Foundations of Music Education* (Second edition). Belmont, Calif.: Wadsworth Publishing Company, 1994.

Anderson, William M. *Teaching Music with a Multicultural Approach.* Reston, Va.: Music Educators National Conference, 1991.

An Arts Education Research Compendium. Sacramento: California Arts Council, 2001.

Choksy, Lois, and others. *Teaching Music in the Twenty-first Century* (Second edition). Englewood Cliffs, N.J.: Prentice-Hall College Division, 2000.

Davidson, Lyle, and others. *Arts Propel: Handbook for Music.* Cambridge, Mass.: Project Zero and Educational Testing Service, 1992.

Doerksen, David P. *Guide to Evaluating Teachers of Music Performance Groups.* Reston, Va.: MENC–The National Association for Music Education, 1990.

Frazee, Jane, and Kent Kreuter. *Discovering Orff: A Curriculum for Music Teachers.* Valley Forge, Pa.: European American Music Distributors Corp., 1987.

Geerdes, Harold P. *Music Facilities: Building, Equipping, and Renovating.* Reston, Va.: MENC–The National Association for Music Education, 1987.

George, Luvenia A. *Teaching the Music of Six Different Cultures* (Revised edition). Danbury, Conn.: World Music Press, 1987.

Guidelines for Performances of School Music Groups: Expectations and Limitations. Prepared by the Music Educators Conference Committee on Standards. Reston, Va.: MENC–The National Association for Music Education, 1994.

Hansen, Dee. *Handbook for Music Supervision.* Reston, Va.: MENC–The National Association for Music Education, 2002.

Harvard Dictionary of Music (Second edition). Edited by Willi Apel. Cambridge, Mass.: Harvard University Press, Belknap Press, 1992.

Jones, Bessie, and Bess L. Hawes. *Step It Down: Games, Plays, Songs, and Stories from the Afro-American Heritage.* Athens: University of Georgia Press, 1987.

Katz, Susan A., and Judith A. Thomas. *Teaching Creatively by Working the Word: Language, Music, and Movement.* Englewood Cliffs, N.J.: Prentice-Hall, 1992.

Kohut, Daniel L. *Instrumental Music Pedagogy: Teaching Techniques for School Band and Orchestra Directors.* Champaign, Ill.: Stipes Publishing Company, 1996.

Mark, Michael L. *Contemporary Music Education* (Third edition). Belmont, Calif.: Wadsworth Publishing Company, 1996.

Music at the Middle Level: Building Strong Programs. Edited by June Hinckley. Reston, Va.: MENC–The National Association for Music Education, 1994.

Nash, Grace C. *Creative Approaches to Child Development with Music, Language, and Movement: Incorporating the Philosophies and Techniques of Orff, Kodály, and Laban.* Van Nuys, Calif.: Alfred Publishing Company, Inc., 1974.

The New Grove Dictionary of Music and Musicians (Second edition). Edited by Stanley Sadie and John Tyrrell. New York: Groves Dictionaries, Inc., 2001.

The New Handbook of Research on Music Teaching and Learning: A Project of the Music Educators National Conference. Edited by Richard Colwell and Carol P. Richardson. New York: Oxford University Press, 2002.

Opportunity-to-Learn Standards for Music Instruction: Grades PreK–12. Reston, Va.: MENC–The National Association for Music Education, 1994.

Phillips, Kenneth H. *Teaching Kids to Sing.* Belmont, Calif.: Wadsworth Publishing Company, 1996.

Reimer, Bennett. *A Philosophy of Music Education: Advancing the Vision* (Third edition). Old Tappan, N.J.: Prentice-Hall, 2002.

The School Music Program: A New Vision. Reston, Va.: MENC–The National Association for Music Education, 1994.

Spotlight on Assessment in Music Education. Reston, Va.: MENC–The National Association for Music Education, 2001.

Stauffer, Sandra L., and Phyllis R. Kaplan. *Cooperative Learning in Music.* Reston, Va.: MENC–The National Association for Music Education, 1994.

Strategies for Teaching Beginning and Intermediate Band. Edited by Edward J. Kvet and Janet M. Tweed. Reston, Va.: MENC–The National Association for Music Education, 1996.

Strategies for Teaching Elementary- and Middle-Level Chorus. Edited by Ann R. Small and Judy K. Bowers. Reston, Va.: MENC–The National Association for Music Education. 1997.

Strategies for Teaching High School Band. Compiled and edited by Edward J. Kvet and John E. Williamson. Reston, Va.: MENC–The National Association for Music Education, 1998.

Strategies for Teaching High School Chorus. Compiled and edited by Randal Swiggum. Reston, Va.: MENC–The National Association for Music Education, 1998.

Strategies for Teaching High School General Music. Edited by Gloria J. Kiester and Keith P. Thompson. Reston, Va.: MENC–The National Association for Music Education, 1997.

Strategies for Teaching K–4 General Music. Edited by Sandra Stauffer and Jennifer Davidson. Reston, Va.: MENC–The National Association for Music Education, 1995.

Strategies for Teaching Middle-Level and High School Guitar. Edited by Bill Purse, James L. Jordan, and Nancy L. Marsters. Reston, Va.: MENC–The National Association for Music Education, 1998.

Strategies for Teaching Middle-Level and High School Keyboard. Edited by Martha Hilley and Tommie Pardue. Reston, Va.: MENC–The National Association for Music Education, 1996.

Strategies for Teaching Middle-Level General Music. Edited by June Hinckley and Suzanne M. Shull. Reston, Va.: MENC–The National Association for Music Education, 1996.

Strategies for Teaching Strings and Orchestra. Edited by Louis Bergonzi, Anne Cleino Witt, and Dorothy Straub. Reston, Va.: MENC–The National Association for Music Education, 1996.

Strategies for Teaching Technology. Edited by Sam Reese, Kimberly McCord, and Kimberly Walls. Reston, Va.: MENC–The National Association for Music Education, 2002.

Teaching Examples: Ideas for Music Educators. Edited by Paul Lehman. Reston, Va.: MENC–The National Association for Music Education, 1994.

TIPS: Teaching Music to Special Learners. Compiled by Gail Schaberg. Reston, Va.: MENC–The National Association for Music Education, 1988.

Volk, Terese M. *Music, Education, and Multiculturalism: Foundations and Principles.* New York: Oxford University Press, 1997.

Walker, Darwin E. *Teaching Music: Managing the Successful Music Program* (Second edition). Belmont, Calif.: Wadsworth Publishing Company, 1997.

What Works: Instructional Strategies for Music Education. Edited by Margaret Merrion. Reston, Va.: MENC–The National Association for Music Education, 1989.

Wiggins, Jackie. *Teaching for Musical Understanding.* Burr Ridge, Ill.: McGraw-Hill Higher Education, 2000.

Theatre References and Resources

Alessi, Stephen M., and Stanley R. Trollip. *Multimedia for Learning: Methods and Development* (Third edition). Needham Heights, Mass.: Allyn & Bacon, 2000.

Barranger, Milly S. *Theatre: A Way of Seeing* (Fifth edition). Belmont, Calif.: Wadsworth Publishing Company, 2001.

Benedetti, Robert L. *The Actor at Work* (Eighth edition). Needham Heights, Mass.: Allyn & Bacon, 2000.

Bordwell, David, and Kristin Thompson. *Film Art: An Introduction and Film Viewers Guide* (Seventh edition). Burr Ridge, Ill.: McGraw-Hill Higher Education, 2003.

Bray, Errol. *Playbuilding: A Guide for Group Creation of Plays with Young People.* Sydney: Currency Press, 1994.

Brockett, Oscar G. *History of the Theatre* (Ninth edition). Needham Heights, Mass.: Allyn & Bacon, 2002.

Bruder, Melissa. *A Practical Handbook for the Actor.* Westminster, Md.: Vintage Books, 1986.

Cantine, John, and Brady Lewis. *Shot by Shot: A Practical Guide to Filmmaking* (Third edition). Pittsburgh: Pittsburgh Filmmakers, 2000.

Carlisle, Barbara, and Don Drapeau. *Hi Concept–Lo Tech Theatre for Everyone in Any Place.* Portsmouth, N.H.: Heinemann, 1996.

Cook, Wayne. *Centerstage: A Curriculum for the Performing Arts, K–3, 4–6.* Palo Alto, Calif.: Dale Seymour Publications, 1993.

Cooper, Gary. *The Art of Digital Filmmaking.* New York: Allworth Press, 2002.

Corson, Richard. *Stage Makeup* (Ninth edition). Needham Heights, Mass.: Allyn & Bacon, 2000.

Dean, Alexander, and Lawrence Carra. *Fundamentals of Play Directing* (Fifth edition). Fort Worth, Tex.: Harcourt College Publishers, 1989.

Engelsman, Alan and Penny. *Theatre Arts I* (Third edition). Colorado Springs, Colo.: Meriwether Publishing, Ltd., 1997.

Gerke, Pamela. *Multicultural Plays for Children, Grades 4–6.* The Young Actors Series. Lyme, N.H.: Smith & Kraus Publishers, 1996.

Giannetti, Louis. *Understanding Movies* (Ninth edition). Englewood Cliffs, N.J.: Prentice-Hall, 2001.

Hagen, Uta, and Haskel Frankel. *Respect for Acting.* Somerset, N.J.: John Wiley & Sons, Inc., 1973.

Laybourne, Kit. *The Animation Book: A Complete Guide to Animated Film-making—From Flip-Books to Sound Cartoons to 3-D Animation.* New York: Crown Publishing Group, 1998.

McCaslin, Nellie. *Creative Drama in the Classroom and Beyond* (Seventh edition). White Plains, N.Y.: Longman Publishing Group, 1999.

Meserve, Walter J. *An Outline History of American Drama* (Second edition). New York: Feedback Theatrebooks and Prospero Press, 1994.

Monaco, James. *How to Read a Film: The World of Movies, Media, and Multimedia—Language, History, Theory* (Third edition). New York: Oxford University Press, 2000.

Motter, Charlotte Kay. *Theatre in High School: Planning, Teaching, Directing.* Lanham, Md.: University Press of America, 1984.

O'Neill, Cecily. *Drama Worlds: A Framework for Process Drama.* Portsmouth, N.H.: Heinemann, 1995.

Parker, W. Oren; Harvey K. Smith; and R. Craig Wolf. *Scene Design and Stage Lighting* (Eighth edition). Belmont, Calif.: Wadsworth Publishing Company, 2003.

Rabiger, Michael. *Developing Story Ideas.* Boston: Focal Press, 2000.

Rabiger, Michael. *Directing the Documentary* (Third edition). Boston: Focal Press, 1997.

Salisbury-Wills, Barbara. *Theatre Arts in the Elementary Classroom, Grade Four Through Grade Six* (Second edition). New Orleans: Anchorage Press, 1996.

Salisbury-Wills, Barbara. *Theatre Arts in the Elementary Classroom, Kindergarten Through Grade Three* (Second edition). New Orleans: Anchorage Press, 1996.

Shurtleff, Michael. *Audition: Everything an Actor Needs to Know to Get the Part.* New York: Walker and Company, 1984.

Spolin, Viola. *Theatre Games for Rehearsal: A Director's Handbook.* Evanston, Ill.: Northwestern University Press, 1985.

Stern, Lawrence. *Stage Management* (Seventh edition). Needham Heights, Mass.: Allyn & Bacon, Inc., 2001.

Sweet, Harvey. *Handbook of Scenery, Properties, and Lighting: Scenery and Properties.* (Second edition). Old Tappan, N.J.: Allyn & Bacon, Inc., 1994.

Theodosakis, Nikos. *The Director in the Classroom: How Filmmaking Inspires Learning.* San Diego: TechFourLearning, Inc., 2001.

Thistle, Louise. *Dramatizing Aesop's Fables, Grades K–6.* White Plains, N.Y.: Dale Seymour Publications, 1997.

Thompson, Kristin, and David Bordwell. *Film History: An Introduction* (Second edition). Boston: McGraw-Hill, 2002.

Zettl, Herbert. *Television Production Handbook* (Eighth edition). Belmont, Calif.: Wadsworth Publishing Company, 2002.

Zettl, Herbert. *Video Basics* (Third edition). Belmont, Calif.: Wadsworth Publishing Company, 2001.

Web Resources

Society for Cinema and Media Studies, an organization of film educators. *http://www.cmstudies.org*

University Film and Video Association, an organization of film and video educators. *http://www.ufva.org*

Visual Arts References and Resources

Addiss, Stephen, and Mary Erickson. *Art History and Education.* Disciplines in Art Education: Contexts of Understanding. Champaign: University of Illinois Press, 1993.

Addiss, Stephen; Marilyn Stokstad; and David Cateforis. *Art History* (Second edition). Upper Saddle River, N.J.: Prentice-Hall, 2001.

Anderson, Richard L. *Calliope's Sisters: A Comparative Study of Philosophies of Art.* Englewood Cliffs, N.J.: Prentice-Hall, 1989.

Art Education in Practice Series. Edited by Marilyn G. Stewart. Worcester, Mass.: Davis Publications, Inc., 1997.

Barrett, Terry. *Criticizing Art: Understanding the Contemporary* (Second edition). Burr Ridge, Ill.: McGraw-Hill Higher Education, 1999.

Barrett, Terry. *Talking About Student Art.* Art Education in Practice Series. Worcester, Mass.: Davis Publications, 1997.

Battin, Margaret P., and others. *Puzzles About Art: An Aesthetics Casebook.* New York: Bedford/St. Martin's Press, 1990.

Beattie, Donna Kay. *Assessment in Art Education.* Worcester, Mass.: Davis Publications, 1997.

Berger, John. *Ways of Seeing.* New York: Viking Press, 1995.

Block, Jacqueline, and Benjamin Martinez. *Visual Forces: An Introduction to Design* (Second edition). Upper Saddle River, N.J.: Prentice-Hall, 1994.

Brown, Maurice, and Diana Korzenik. *Art Making and Education.* Disciplines in Art Education: Contexts of Understanding. Champaign: University of Illinois Press, 1993.

Carter, Rita. *Mapping the Mind.* Berkeley: University of California Press, 2000.

Cohen, Kathleen, and others. *Gardner's Art Through the Ages* (Eleventh edition). Fort Worth, Tex.: Harcourt College Publishers, 2001.

Csikszentmihalyi, Mihaly, and Rick E. Robinson. *The Art of Seeing: An Interpretation of the Aesthetic Encounter.* Los Angeles: Getty Publications, 1991.

Eisner, W. Elliot. *Enlightened Eye: Qualitative Inquiry and the Enhancement of Educational Practice* (Second edition). Upper Saddle River, N.J.: Prentice-Hall, 1997.

Gilbert, Rita. *Living with Art* (Fifth edition). New York: McGraw-Hill, 1997.

Hurwitz, Al, and Michael Day. *Children and Their Art: Methods for the Elementary School* (Seventh edition). Belmont, Calif.: Wadsworth Publishing Company, 2000.

Janson, Anthony F., and H. W. Hanson. *History of Art for Young People* (Sixth edition). New York: Harry N. Abrams, 2001.

Kent, Corita, and Jan Steward. *Learning by Heart: Teachings to Free the Creative Spirit.* Westminster, Md.: Bantam Books, 1992.

Lewis, Samella S. *Art: African American* (Second revised edition). Los Angeles: Hancraft Studios, 1990.

Lippard, Lucy. *Mixed Blessings: New Art in Multicultural America.* New York: New Press, 2000.

Mittler, Gene. *Art in Focus* (Third edition). Westerville, Ohio: Glencoe, 1994.

Moore, Ronald. *Aesthetics for Young People.* Reston, Va.: National Art Education Association, 1995.

Ocvirk, Otto G. *Art Fundamentals: Theory and Practice* (Ninth edition). Burr Ridge, Ill.: McGraw-Hill Higher Education, 2001.

Parsons, Michael J., and H. Gene Blocker. *Aesthetics and Education.* Disciplines in Art Education: Contexts of Understanding. Champaign: University of Illinois Press, 1993.

Perkins, David N. *The Intelligent Eye: Learning to Think by Looking at Art.* Los Angeles: Getty Publications, 1994.

Preble, Duane; Sarah Preble; and Patrick Frank. *Artforms: An Introduction to the Visual Arts* (Seventh edition). Old Tappan, N.J.: Prentice-Hall, 2001.

Schuman, Jo Miles. *Art from Many Hands.* Worcester, Mass.: Davis Publications, Inc., 1984.

Smith, Ralph A. *Discipline-Based Art Education: Origins, Meaning, and Development.* Champaign: University of Illinois Press, 1989.

Stankowicz, Mary Ann. *Roots of Art Education Practice.* Worcester, Mass.: Davis Publications, Inc., 2001.

Stewart, Marilyn G. *Thinking Through Aesthetics.* Worcester, Mass.: Davis Publications, Inc., 1997.

Stone, Denise L. *Using the Art Museum.* Worcester, Mass.: Davis Publications, Inc., 2001.

Wachowiak, Frank, and Robert D. Clements. *Emphasis Art: A Qualitative Art Program for Elementary and Middle Schools* (Seventh edition). Boston: Allyn & Bacon, Inc., 2000.

Walter, Sydney A. *Teaching Meaning in Art Making.* Worcester, Mass.: Davis Publications, 2001.

Web Resources

Artcyclopedia. This site features a search engine for exploring 125,000 works of art and contains links to museums housing those works. *http://www.artcyclopedia.com*

California History–Social Science Course Models. This site contains history–social science course models for use by California teachers. *http://www.history.ctaponline.org*

Carol Gerten's Fine Art (CGFA). This site offers an A-to-Z list of fine arts resources. *http://sunsite.dk/cgfa/index.html*

Professional Development Resources

The following entities offer professional development resources in the visual and performing arts:

American Alliance for Theatre and Education
Arizona State University, Theatre Department
P.O. Box 873411
Tempe, AZ 85287-3411
(602) 965-6064

California Arts Council
1300 I Street, Suite 930
Sacramento, CA 95814
(800) 201-6201; (916) 322-6555.

The California Arts Project
P.O. Box 4925
San Rafael, CA 94913
(415) 499-5893

Educational Theatre Association
2343 Auburn Avenue
Cincinnati, OH 45219
(513) 421-3900

The Getty Center for Education in the Arts
401 Wilshire Boulevard, Suite 950
Santa Monica, CA 90401-1455
(310) 395-6657

The John F. Kennedy Center for the Performing Arts
2700 F Street, NW
Washington, DC 20566-0001
(800) 444-1324

Music Educators National Conference
1806 Robert Fulton Drive
Reston, VA 20191
(800) 336-3768; (703) 860-4000

National Art Education Association
1916 Association Drive
Reston, VA 20191-1590
(703) 860-8000

National Dance Association
1900 Association Drive
Reston, VA 20191-1598
(800) 213-7193

National Endowment for the Arts
Nancy Hanks Center
1100 Pennsylvania Avenue, NW
Washington, DC 20506-0001
(202) 682-5400

National Endowment for the Humanities
1100 Pennsylvania Avenue, NW
Washington, DC 20506
(800) 634-1121; (202) 606-8400

The following professional arts education associations change officers periodically. For the names and telephone numbers of current contact persons, call the California Department of Education, Curriculum Frameworks and Instructional Resources Office, at (916) 319-0881.

California Alliance for Arts Education
California Art Education Association
California Dance Education Association
California Education Theatre Association
California Humanities Association
California Music Educators Association

Copyright Resources

The following organizations provide information on copyright and guidance on fair use:

American Library Association, Office for Information Technology Policy: Copyright Page. This site includes sections on copyright basics, fair use, copyright and the library, copyright and learning, copyright and research, and copyright and the Internet. *http://www.ala.org/ala/washoff/WOissues/copyrightb/copyright.htm*

California Lawyers for the Arts. *http://www.calawyersforthearts.org*

The Copyright Society of the USA. This site contains information about the protection and use of rights in literature, music, art, theatre, motion pictures, and so forth. *http://www.csusa.org*

Fullerton School District: Copyright Guidelines for Teachers. This site includes copyright guidelines for print, music, audiovisual, and computer materials. *http://www.fsd.k12.ca.us/menus/Copyright/Guidelines.html*

Music Library Association: Guidelines for Educational Uses of Music. The guidelines at this site were developed and approved in April 1976 by the Music Publishers' Association of the United States, Inc.; the National Music Publishers' Association, Inc.; the Music Teachers National Association; the Music Educators National Conference; the National Association of Schools of Music; and the Ad Hoc Committee on Copyright Law Revision. *http://www.musiclibraryassoc.org/Copyright/guidemus.htm*

Siskiyou County Office of Education. This site, developed by Kathy Graves, Director of Instructional Media Services, Siskiyou County Office of Education, offers links to a wide variety of copyright resources available on the Web. *http://sisnet.ssku.k12.ca.us/~imcftp/copyright.html*

Stanford University Libraries: Copyright and Fair Use. This site provides links to primary materials, current legislation, cases and issues, Web resources, and an overview of copyright law. *http://fairuse.stanford.edu*

United States Copyright Office. This official source provides useful copyright information. *www.copyright.gov*

Contemporary Media References and Resources

Allen, Bryan. *Digital Wizardry: Creative Photoshop Techniques.* New York: Amphoto Books, 1998.

Bartlett, Larry, and Jon Tarrant. *Black and White Printing Workshop.* Hauppauge, N.Y.: Silver Pixel Press, 1996.

Frost, Lee. *The A–Z of Creative Photography: Over 70 Techniques Explained in Full.* New York: Watson-Guptill Publications, 2003.

Hedgecoe, John. *John Hedgeco's New Introductory Photography Course.* Stoneham, Mass.: Focal Press, 1998.

Klasey, Jack. *Photo & Digital Imaging*. Tinley Park, Ill.: Goodheart-Wilcox Company, 2002.

London, Barbara, and others. *Photography* (Seventh edition). Old Tappan, N.J.: Prentice-Hall, 2001.

Luciana, James, and Judith Watts. *The Art of Enhanced Photography: Beyond the Photographic Image*. Gloucester, Mass.: Rockport Publishers, 1999.

O'Brien, Michael, and Norman Sibley. *Photographic Eye: Learning to See with a Camera*. Worcester, Mass.: Davis Publications, Inc., 1995.

Smith, Bill. *Designing a Photograph: Visual Techniques for Making Your Photographs Work*. New York: Watson-Guptill Publications, 2003.

Stone, Jim. *Darkroom Dynamics: A Guide to Creative Darkroom Techniques*. Stoneham, Mass.: Focal Press, 1985.

Suess, Bernhard. *Mastering Black and White Photography: From Camera to Darkroom*. New York: Allworth Press, 1995.

Vineyard, Jeremy. *Setting Up Your Shots: Great Camera Moves Every Film Maker Should Know*. Studio City, Calif.: Michael Wiese Productions, 2000.

Web Resources

The Film Foundation. This educational site is sponsored by the Artists Rights Foundation and the Directors Guild of America. *http://admitone.org*

International Visual Literacy Organization. This site offers information, contacts, links, and definitions of terms related to visual literacy. *http://www.ivla.org*

Media Literacy Clearinghouse. Several organizations share this site, which is dedicated to media literacy concepts, issues, and education. *http://medialit.med.sc.edu/*

Media Literacy Review. This site contains recent articles, information, and a comprehensive A–Z index of all media literacy organizations, noting the particular focus of each organization. *http://interact.uoregon.edu/medialit/mlr/home/index.html*

Publications Available from the California Department of Education

This publication is one of approximately 600 that are available from the California Department of Education. Some of the more recent publications or those most widely used are the following:

Item no.	Title (Date of publication)	Price
001559	Aiming High: High Schools for the Twenty-first Century (2002)	$13.25
001537	Arts Education Program Toolkit: A Visual and Performing Arts Program Assessment Process (2001)	13.25
001372	Arts Work: A Call for Arts Education for All California Students: The Report of the Superintendent's Task Force on the Visual and Performing Arts (1997)	11.25
001591	California Public School Directory 2004	22.50
001509	Elementary Makes the Grade! (2000)	10.25
001570	Foreign Language Framework for California Public Schools, Kindergarten Through Grade Twelve (2003)	15.50
001574	Health Framework for California Public Schools, Kindergarten Through Grade Twelve (2003)	17.50
001531	History–Social Science Framework for California Public Schools, Kindergarten Through Grade Twelve, 2001 Updated Edition with Content Standards (2001)	15.50
001266	Literature for the Visual and Performing Arts, Kindergarten Through Grade Twelve (1996)	10.25
001508	Mathematics Framework for California Public Schools, Kindergarten Through Grade Twelve (2000 Revised Edition)	17.50
001462	Reading/Language Arts Framework for California Public Schools, Kindergarten Through Grade Twelve (1999)	17.50
001553	Recommended Literature: Kindergarten Through Grade Twelve (2002)	38.00
001526	The Results of the Arts Work Survey of California Public Schools (2001)	10.50
001572	Science Framework for California Public Schools, Kindergarten Through Grade Twelve (2003)	17.50
001532	Standards for Evaluating Instructional Materials for Social Content (2000 Edition) (2001)	8.00
001503	Taking Center Stage: A Commitment to Standards-Based Education for California's Middle Grades Students (2001)	13.50
001592	Visual and Performing Arts Framework for California Public Schools, Kindergarten Through Grade Twelve (2004)	19.95

Orders should be directed to:

California Department of Education
CDE Press, Sales Office
1430 N Street, Suite 3207
Sacramento, CA 95814-5901

Please include the item number and desired quantity for each title ordered. Shipping and handling charges are additional, and purchasers in California also add county sales tax.

Mail orders must be accompanied by a check, a purchase order, or a credit card number, including expiration date (VISA or MasterCard only). Purchase orders without checks are accepted from educational institutions, businesses, and governmental agencies. Telephone orders will be accepted toll-free (1-800-995-4099) for credit card purchases. *All sales are final after 30 days.*

The *Educational Resources Catalog* contains illustrated, annotated listings of departmental publications, videos, and other instructional materials. Free copies of the catalog may be obtained by writing to the address given above or by calling (916) 445-1260.

Visit the Web site *http:/www.cde.ca.gov.*

Prices and availability are subject to change without notice.
Please call 1-800-995-4099 for current prices and shipping charges.

Visual Arts Resources in California CD-ROM
A Supplement to the *Visual and Performing Arts Framework*

The images of artwork contained in this CD-ROM have been contributed by museums throughout California. Included are works by California artists, portrayals of California and its history, classical works, and pieces that highlight new trends in the visual arts. The intent of this CD is to provide teachers and students examples of visual resources that will supplement the *Visual and Performing Arts Framework* and encourage teachers and students to visit nearby museums to see the original works of art.

The CD includes the following resources:

- Artwork from Museums
- Italian Street Painting
- Cover Art for the Framework
- Additional California Art Museum Resources
- Index of Artists
- Index of Titles

Instructions for Viewing the CD

Insert the CD in the CD-ROM drive. Open your Netscape or Internet Explorer browser, then open the file "START.HTM," on the CD, from within your browser application.

You will need Adobe® Acrobat® Reader to view the contents of the CD. You can access readers free of charge at the Department's Web site. Go to *http://www.cde.ca.gov/re/di/fd/*.
